HONDA K-SERIES ENGINE SWAPS

Upgrade to More Horsepower & Advanced Technology

Aaron Bonk

CarTech®

CarTech®

CarTech®, Inc.
838 Lake Street S.
Forest Lake, MN 55025
Phone: 651-277-1200 or 800-551-4754
Fax: 651-277-1203
www.cartechbooks.com

© 2014 by Aaron Bonk

All rights reserved. No part of this publication may be reproduced or utilized in any form or by any means, electronic or mechanical, including photocopying, recording, or by any information storage and retrieval system, without prior permission from the Publisher. All text, photographs, and artwork are the property of the Author unless otherwise noted or credited.

The information in this work is true and complete to the best of our knowledge. However, all information is presented without any guarantee on the part of the Author or Publisher, who also disclaim any liability incurred in connection with the use of the information and any implied warranties of merchantability or fitness for a particular purpose. Readers are responsible for taking suitable and appropriate safety measures when performing any of the operations or activities described in this work.

All trademarks, trade names, model names and numbers, and other product designations referred to herein are the property of their respective owners and are used solely for identification purposes. This work is a publication of CarTech, Inc., and has not been licensed, approved, sponsored, or endorsed by any other person or entity. The Publisher is not associated with any product, service, or vendor mentioned in this book, and does not endorse the products or services of any vendor mentioned in this book.

Edit by Bob Wilson and Wes Eisenschenk
Layout by Monica Seiberlich

ISBN 978-1-61325-464-6
Item No. SA276P

Library of Congress Cataloging-in-Publication Data

Bonk, Aaron.
  Honda K-series engine swaps / by Aaron Bonk.
    pages cm
  ISBN 978-1-61325-103-4 (alk. paper)
  1. Honda automobile–Motors. I. Title.
  TL215.H58B665 2014
  629.25'040288–dc23
                           2014010516

Printed, written, edited, and designed in the U.S.A.

Title Page: *The first-generation TSX K24A2 engine remains one of the most desirable K-series power plants primarily because it's the only North America-bound, 2.4L K-series engine to feature VTEC on both camshafts, much like the performance-oriented K20A2, K20Z1, and K20Z3. Like the K20Z3, the TSX's electronic drive-by-wire throttle body and ECU are not compatible with most chassis.*

Back Cover:

Top Left: *Mounting the Accord-style shifter box into any of these Accord or Prelude chassis isn't terribly difficult. Simply place it on top of the unmodified exhaust tunnel, drill the appropriate mounting holes, and bolt it into place using a series of nuts, bolts, and washers. The shifter cables may even pass through the original opening in the exhaust tunnel. (Photo Courtesy Hasport Performance Products)*

Top Right: *An aftermarket fuel pressure regulator must be integrated with every K-series engine swap into any non-native chassis. There are two reasons for this. First, K-series engines don't feature fuel pressure regulators; the system is regulated from within the fuel tank on native K-series chassis. Second, the fuel pressure regulator serves as a bypass tee that allows fuel to travel toward the fuel rail but to also return to the fuel tank.*

Middle Left: *Choosing the right K-series engine can be challenging. Beyond cost, you have to consider horsepower, potential upgrades, ECU, engine wiring harness compatibility, and any clearance considerations. Beyond that, selecting the right transmission is just as crucial. Not every aftermarket engine mount kit is compatible with every K-series transmission, so be sure to confirm whether or not a particular transmission may be used before moving forward.*

Middle Right: *Hasport supplies a billet aluminum engine mount that connects the already-installed right-side framerail bracket to the timing-chain-side engine mount. Be sure that the correct timing-chain-side engine mount has been installed. An incorrect bracket can lead to an engine that sits too high or two low, depending upon bracket type and engine deck height. (Photo Courtesy Hasport Performance Products)*

Bottom Left: *Aftermarket sub-harnesses such as this one from Hybrid Racing significantly simplify the wiring process. Each harness features labeled connectors that terminate at the ECU, engine harness, and chassis harness. Instructions are also included for hooking up the few remaining wires that differ slightly depending on the manufacturer. (Photo Courtesy Hybrid Racing)*

Bottom Right: *Intake manifold selection is crucial if unnecessary cutting is to be avoided. Notice how much shorter the RSX Type-S intake manifold on the right is than the Accord Euro R version on the left. The Accord Euro R's shape and volume has proven to result in more power, but in the case of the 2001–2005 Civic, it comes at a cost. (Photo Courtesy Hasport Performance Products)*

OVERSEAS DISTRIBUTION BY:

PGUK
63 Hatton Garden
London EC1N 8LE, England
Phone: 020 7061 1980 • Fax: 020 7242 3725
www.pguk.co.uk

Renniks Publications Ltd.
3/37-39 Green Street
Banksmeadow, NSW 2109, Australia
Phone: 2 9695 7055 • Fax: 2 9695 7355
www.renniks.com

CONTENTS

About the Author 4
Acknowledgments 4
Preface 5
Introduction 6

Chapter 1: Engine Identification 7
K-Series Development 7
Choosing the Right K-Series 8
Performance i-VTEC 9
Economy i-VTEC 16
The Other Economy i-VTEC 21
A Word About Transmissions 26

Chapter 2: Engine Swap Safety 28
Workspace 28
Tools 28
Equipment 29
Fluid Control 32
Planning 32
Legalities 32

Chapter 3: Electrical Essentials 36
Electrical Toolbox 36
Non-Native versus Native Chassis 38
On-Board Diagnostics 38
ECU Selection 38
Wiring 40

Chapter 4: 1992-2000 Civic and 1994-2001 Integra 43
1992-1995 Civic 44
1993-1997 del Sol 45
1996-2000 Civic 46
1994-2001 Integra 46
Engine and Transmission 47
Mounts 48
Car Preparation 49
Engine Preparation 54
Engine Installation 56
Axles 57
Throttle Cable 58
Clutch Hydraulics 58

Brake Booster 59
Shifter Assembly 59
Fuel System 63
Cooling System 65
A/C and Power Steering 70
Intake and Exhaust Systems 73
ECU Selection 75
Wiring 77
Suspension and Braking 79

Chapter 5: 1988-1991 Civic and 1990-1993 Integra 80
1988-1991 Civic 81
1988-1991 CRX 82
1990-1993 Integra 83
Engine and Transmission 83
Mounts 84
Car Preparation 84
Engine Preparation 89
Engine Installation 90
Axles 91
Throttle Cable 92
Speedometer Cable 92
Clutch Hydraulics 93
Brake Booster 93
Shifter Assembly 93
Fuel System 97
Cooling System 100
A/C and Power Steering 102
Intake and Exhaust Systems 104
ECU Selection 105
Wiring 107
Suspension and Braking 108

Chapter 6: 2001-2005 Civic 110
2001-2005 Civic 111
Engine and Transmission 112
Mounts 112
Car Preparation 112
Engine Preparation 115
Engine Installation 115
Axles 116

Throttle Cable 116
Clutch Hydraulics 117
Brake Booster 117
Shifter Assembly 117
Fuel System 118
Cooling System 118
A/C and Power Steering 119
Intake and Exhaust Systems 121
ECU Selection 121
Wiring 122
Suspension and Braking 122

Chapter 7: 1990-1997 Accord and 1992-1996 Prelude 124
1990-1993 Accord 124
1994-1997 Accord 125
1992-1996 Prelude 126
Engine and Transmission 126
Mounts 126
Car Preparation 127
Engine Preparation 129
Engine Installation 129
Axles 130
Throttle Cable 130
Clutch Hydraulics 130
Brake Booster 131
Shifter Assembly 131
Fuel System 133
Cooling System 134
A/C and Power Steering 137
Intake and Exhaust Systems 138
ECU Selection 139
Wiring 140
Suspension and Braking 141

Appendix
Diagnostic Trouble Code Reference .. 142
Post-Swap Checklist 143
Swap Difficulty 144

Source Guide 144

About the Author

Aaron Bonk first took an interest in Honda performance in the early 1990s. After studying mechanical engineering, he established Holeshot Racing, one of the first tuning shops to specialize in Honda engine swaps. There he developed many Honda-specific engine transplants, long before engine mount kits and aftermarket wiring harnesses were realities.

After more than a decade of development and professionally swapping Honda engines, he transitioned into a career as an automotive journalist, authoring two Honda technical books. He has since held staff positions and contributed regularly to landmark Honda performance magazines, including *Sport Compact Car, Turbo & High-Tech Performance, Super Street, Import Tuner,* and many other print and online publications. There's perhaps no other author who's written more articles or penned more words about the Honda brand.

Bonk recently served as *Honda Tuning* magazine Editor-in-Chief

where he continues to contribute regularly and, today, resides in Southern California with his wife, daughter, son, and Acura NSX.

Acknowledgments

Nobody understands K-series engine swaps better than Hasport Performance's Brian Gillespie. He's a true pioneer of nearly every imaginable Honda engine transplant and a book like this simply couldn't have been possible without his knowledge, support, and savant-like nature when it comes to obscure Honda information.

Other great companies with truly innovative products, such as Hybrid Racing and K-Tuned, also make writing such a book and, incidentally, the K-series engine swap process, easier. I've been driving, modifying, and racing Hondas for more than 20 years and have watched countless companies come and go. Hasport, K-Tuned, and Hybrid Racing are among the few that I'm proud to associate myself with and include in the following pages.

Top-shelf manufacturers aren't the only ones who've lent themselves to this book. Installation and tuning facilities, such as Sportcar Motion, Makspeed Motorworks, Laskey Racing, and Whitfield Manufacturing also offered up their facilities, their knowledge, and their time to help complete all of this.

A special thanks goes out to all these individuals and companies for their support.

Preface

A lot has changed since I wrote *Honda Engine Swaps,* which was first published in 2004. It was only a couple of years before that that I'd laid eyes on my first K-series engine at which time I quietly surmised that Honda's new 4-cylinder marked the end of high-performance Honda tuning. I don't have to tell you that I was wrong.

I first started transplanting Honda engines between chassis in the early 1990s. After 10 years, the B-series engine swap became obligatory and arguably lost its excitement. The K-series changed all of that and breathed new life into what was once an otherwise predictable set of circumstances. Its more sophisticated version of variable valve timing, roller-driven camshafts, higher-displacement configurations, and available 6-speed transmissions made sure of that.

Unlike the early days of swapping various Honda engines between chassis, today, such information is far more prevalent. That's mostly because of the Internet, which, when the first B-series engine swaps were being done, simply wasn't accessible to most households. Today, the Internet hosts an abundance of K-series-related information, a substantial amount of which is simply incorrect, incomplete, or just plain confusing. *K-Series Engine Swaps* wasn't written under the guise of uncovering engine swap secrets that have yet to be discovered but rather to serve as an information repository that doesn't require second-guessing or lead to mistakes. It was written to result in the most complete, turnkey engine swap you could hope for.

Introduction

Since the engine's introduction for the 2002 model year, the K-series has transcended into the almighty of all Honda engine transplants. No other Honda engine offers as much power in stock form with as much potential as the K-series. It's no surprise then that thousands of Honda performance enthusiasts agree, as do some of the world's fastest race car teams and drivers.

Unlike B-series or H-series engine transplants from decades past, K-series engine swaps are more complex and, as a result, must be approached differently. Here, installation and wiring procedures are more complicated in comparison but differ minimally between chassis, instead sharing many of the same characteristics and processes from one to another. Unlike earlier Honda engines, K-series power plants are oriented within the engine bay in 180-degree opposition and feature a clockwise rotation, which means all sorts of ancillaries that wouldn't have been addressed with past Honda engine swaps must be addressed now. For example, K-series exhaust manifolds, intake manifolds, and transmissions are all located on opposite sides of the engine bay compared to older Civic, Integra, Accord, and Prelude layouts.

As you read on, bear in mind that there are likely multiple methods and a variety of parts that can be used to complete almost every transplant in this book. The methods, components, and specific procedures are those used by some of the most renowned and respected names in the Honda tuning world. As such, you can be assured that following them can lead to your own successful K-series engine swap.

Finally, a few words about how this book has been structured. For obvious reasons, the 1992–1995 Civic, 1996–2000 Civic, and 1994–2001 Integra remain the most popular K-series engine swap candidates. As such, Chapter 4, which deals specifically with those chassis, provides the basis of all K-series engine transplant information and should be read regardless of which chassis you plan to use. If you plan on swapping a K-series engine into any other chassis, be sure to also read whichever chapter deals with your specific vehicle. Or simply read the entire book and be sure that you don't miss out on any important details. Happy swapping.

CHAPTER 1

ENGINE IDENTIFICATION

It's no surprise that over the past decade countless Hondas and Acuras have been stripped of their factory-issued engines in favor of Honda's more powerful and technologically advanced K-series. With little exception, Honda's K-series engine family possesses a rare combination of impressive power output, cutting-edge technology, and widespread aftermarket support. Combination is key. Two years before the introduction of the K-series, Honda's S2000 debuted with an impressive 240 hp, yet its aftermarket support pales in comparison to the K-series. More than a decade earlier, Honda released the ubiquitous B-series: this is an engine family that benefits from tremendous aftermarket support yet began life with mediocre power output. In terms of combination, Honda's K-series leads the way.

K-series engine swaps are slightly more complex and significantly more costly than B-series or even H-series engine swaps. As such, understanding what makes the K-series such a worthwhile donor candidate, and making sure the proper engine is selected, makes good sense before embarking on the engine swap process.

K-Series Development

The K-series was first introduced to the North American market under the guise of the 2002 RSX, Civic Si, and CR-V. Following a 12-year reign among enthusiasts and tuners, the automaker's B-series was finally laid to rest and, in late 2001, replaced with the then-unfamiliar K20A2, K20A3, and K24A1. Hondaphiles, who'd grown accustomed to the intricacies, modular nature, and enormous potential of Honda's B-series engine family, first met the all-new 4-cylinder engines with an air of uneasiness. That uneasiness didn't last long though. Once early adopters began experimenting with and proving the merits of Honda's B-series replacement, any hesitations were soon put to

Those seasoned in the Honda engine swap process didn't immediately embrace K-series engines following their debut for the 2002 model year. Their clockwise orientation, 180-degree opposed layout, and more complex electronics meant many weren't willing to abandon Honda's proven B-series for something new.

CHAPTER 1

Not since the B-series has Honda made such a capable four-cylinder engine available. Few engines offer the same sort of potential, durability, and aftermarket support as the K-series, which is partially what has made it such a popular engine swap candidate.

rest. Honda's K-series was initially offered to North American consumers in three variations: entry-level K20A3, larger-displacement K24A1, and slightly more powerful K20A2. The Civic Si, which reemerged after a one-year hiatus, and RSX base model both feature the K20A3 as standard equipment while the CR-V benefits from what is essentially a larger-displacement version of that engine, the K24A1. Only the higher-end RSX Type-S features the 200-hp K20A2. The all-new platform's most notable difference compared to previous 4-cylinder Honda engines is its direct-fire ignition system, reverse layout, and clockwise rotation. In an effort to improve catalytic converter light-off by positioning the engine's exhaust side toward the rear of the vehicle, Honda was forced to develop a clockwise-rotating architecture, which is in sharp contrast to the decades' worth of counter-clockwise-rotating engines the company has become famous for.

The K-series has numerous engine designations. Fortunately, almost all of them can be traced back to Honda's initial K20A2 and K20A3. Although similar in many respects and both featuring Intelligent Variable Valve Timing and Lift Electronic Control (i-VTEC), the engines' valvetrains and VTEC implementation are where they differ most.

Choosing the Right K-Series

In terms of performance in stock configuration, few engines beat the K-series. It's true that Honda's B-series remains the engine of choice for the world's most powerful, record-setting turbocharged drag cars, but the K-series wins on almost every other front, including the street. The hardest part is choosing the right one.

As you'd expect, selecting the right K-series engine is a compromise between performance, price, and availability. For example, although

Although all K-series engines feature Honda's Intelligent Variable Valve Timing and Lift Electronic Control (i-VTEC), two very different versions have been implemented. Factors such as performance, cost, and horsepower potential are affected by how Honda's engineers allow each engine's valvetrain to be orchestrated.

Few engines are more capable than the Integra Type R or Civic Type R K20A. However, they'll cost you. It isn't uncommon for Type R engines to be valued at three to four times more than entry-level K-series power plants. Once the accompanying transmission and ECU have been selected, such swaps can easily exceed the value of the chassis they're being swapped into.

ENGINE IDENTIFICATION

it's not the least expensive, the Japanese-spec K20A Type R yields the most power in stock form, which makes it an ideal choice if you want to avoid aftermarket modifications. The K24A1, on the other hand, makes for a good donor candidate if you're looking for a reasonable balance between performance and cost. When considering which K-series engine is right for you, look beyond an engine's ancillaries, transmission, and emissions components (such as its throttle body, intake manifold, or ECU), and instead consider its architecture, internals, and performance potential. Engine and transmission weight must also be considered (see the K-Series Weight Comparison sidebar on page 23 for more information).

A few points are important to keep in mind before selecting an engine: Unlike B-series engine swaps, engine wiring harness and ECU selection is limited and components, such as factory exhaust manifolds, are generally not transferable. Arguably, all of this makes selecting the right engine even easier since bolt-ons and accessories can't easily cloud the decision.

For most K-series engine swaps, a 2002–2004 RSX or Japanese-spec Type R ECU is preferred as is the RSX engine wiring harness (more on why later on). As such, using either a North American-based K20A2 or Japanese-spec K20A Type R can often simplify the parts-sourcing process. In almost all cases, an aftermarket header is required, so choosing an engine based on exhaust manifold type is irrelevant. Honda's drive-by-wire electronic throttle bodies also aren't compatible with most engine transplants at this time. Keep that in mind when selecting an engine that may or may not be equipped with one.

Finally, refer to the two transmission charts on page 27 for specific information on all available gearboxes. Depending on chassis, engine mount type, and ECU selection, transmission options may vary.

Further details as to which engines and transmissions might work best with specific chassis are covered throughout the book.

Performance i-VTEC

Generally referred to as performance i-VTEC engines, these engines feature Honda's most technologically impressive valvetrain to date. At the heart of performance i-VTEC engines is something familiar: VTEC. Like its predecessors, inside the cylinder head lies Honda's renowned, hydraulically operated variable valve timing system. Simple and elegant, VTEC allows the engine to alternate between two different camshaft profiles, depending on various conditions.

In twin-cam configurations, each camshaft features three lobes per cylinder (its two primary lobes and its larger, longer-duration secondary lobe), which correspond to three respective rocker arms. Under normal conditions, the center rocker arm, which is paired to the camshaft's larger center VTEC lobe, does little more than ride on what Honda calls its Lost Motion Assembly. On the intake side, valve timing remains staggered within each cylinder, resulting in asymmetrical valve lift,

Engine Identification Codes

All sorts of design characteristics and ancillaries distinguish various K-series engines from one another but only the engine identification code, which is stamped directly onto its engine block, definitively identifies an engine.

Even with engine identification codes, though, confusion persists. For example, Japanese engine identification codes aren't concluded by numbers, as are Northern American and European cars. In other words, while there's no doubt exactly what a K20A2 engine is, the K20A can take on many forms, ranging from Honda's top-of-the-line 222-hp 2007–2011 Civic Type R engine to its most basic series of 2.0L engines found throughout the remainder of its lineup. The key to differentiating all of these often lies in being able to recognize each engine's ancillaries, such as the intake manifold, throttle body, alternator, and exhaust manifold. ∎

Every K-series engine can be distinguished by the four- or five-digit series of letters and numbers located on the front of its engine block, which in this case reads K20A3.

which creates a swirl effect within the combustion chamber to help promote an optimal burn.

All of that changes once VTEC engages. At a predetermined engine speed based on the ECU, a 12V signal is sent to the engine's VTEC solenoid, which activates the process. Oil pressure forces a series of pins into place, engaging the center rocker arm, which reacts against the camshafts' larger center lobes, forcing both valves to operate under the VTEC lobe's higher-lift longer-duration profile. The results allow more air and fuel into the combustion chambers, which means more power. Once engine speed is reduced and the VTEC signal is terminated, the pins retract, disengaging the middle rocker arm, allowing the engine to operate normally.

Developed in the late 1980s and first released in the Japanese-only 1989 Integra XSi and RSi, VTEC was one of the most important solutions to balancing low emissions and high performance since the internal combustion engine was created nearly 100 years earlier.

These i-VTEC engines also have Variable Timing Control (VTC). A specialized camshaft gear allows for continuously variable intake camshaft phasing throughout the RPM range. Based on all sorts of things that the driver doesn't have to worry about, such as camshaft position, ignition timing, exhaust oxygen content, and throttle position, a 50-degree range of camshaft phasing is possible (25-degree range on K24A2 and select K24A engines). Much like VTEC, the camshaft gear is electronically controlled and hydraulically driven, resulting in reduced timing at idle and advanced timing at higher engine speeds, which increases valve overlap and power. Fittingly, the "i" in i-VTEC stands for "intelligent" and, together, VTEC and VTC offer an unprecedented balance between performance and emissions. All of this is very good news for everyone except aftermarket cam gear makers.

Honda's performance i-VTEC cylinder heads are nothing short of remarkable. In terms of airflow and potential, they put even the best B-series Type R heads to shame. This is, in part, due to oversized valves 2 mm larger than on B-series VTEC engines. Performance i-VTEC K-series engines also feature more optimally shaped intake and exhaust ports compared to the B-series and larger ports of other K-series engines. On the intake side, their ports form a nearly straight path into their combustion chambers. On the exhaust side, the humps that are expected of B-series heads are non-existent; it's another straight shot, this time into the exhaust manifold.

Unlike older B-series engines, only K-series engines feature VTC. An electronically controlled and hydraulically driven intake camshaft gear allows for dynamically adjustable valve timing at any engine speed. Imagine the adjustable camshaft gear on older D-, B-, or H-series engines. Now imagine being able to make adjustments to that camshaft gear while the engine is in motion. That's exactly what VTC does.

Honda's twin-camshaft VTEC implementation hasn't changed much since it was introduced in 1989; however, K-series engines feature a number of other advancements. Although their valvetrains may appear similar to older Honda engines, K-series engines feature roller rocker arms, billet camshaft cores, and more sophisticated cylinder heads.

ENGINE IDENTIFICATION

Aside from port characteristics, all K-series engines benefit from highly sophisticated roller rocker arms, which reduce valvetrain friction and allow for all manner of billet camshafts. This is in stark contrast to older Honda engines that exclusively feature standard pad-style rocker arms.

The K-series also makes use of an entirely new engine block, which, like the B-series, is highly modular, resulting in exceptional parts interchangeability between engines, as Honda enthusiasts have come to expect. Of course, it's made of aluminum and features cast-in iron liners but it's stronger than anyone has come to expect from Honda, featuring significant exterior gusseting and ribbing.

All K-series engines also feature an open-deck design with exposed water jackets, as on earlier Honda engines. Inside, the K-series features a one-piece aluminum crankshaft carrier that increases overall block strength. This split-case design is significantly stronger than Honda's previous internal bearing girdle architecture that features individual crankshaft main caps. What's more, inside the block there's plenty of room for boring, stroking, or both.

Each of Honda's 2.0L K-series engines features an 86-mm bore and 86-mm stroke. Also known as a square design, such engine architectures are generally a good compromise between adequate low-end torque and sufficient top-end power.

The 2.4L engine's over-square design, which features a longer stroke, results in more torque but at

All K-series engine blocks are manufactured from cast aluminum and feature an open-deck design with cast-in iron cylinder liners. Compared to previous Honda platforms, K-series engines are noticeably more durable, and feature extensive gusseting and ribbing throughout. A split-case design adds to the engines' overall rigidity and reduces the risk of crankshaft movement under extreme conditions.

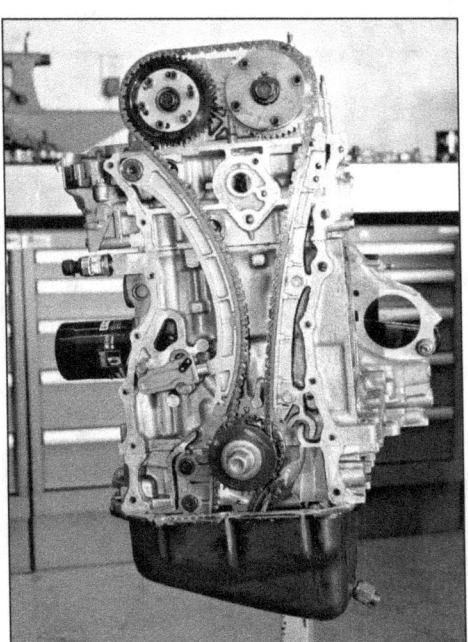

Apart from the clockwise rotation and 180-degree opposed orientation, one of the biggest changes implemented among K-series engines is the timing chain. Unlike a conventional timing belt that can stretch over time, this valvetrain and rotating assembly are able to better sync with each other. The entire system is also virtually maintenance-free.

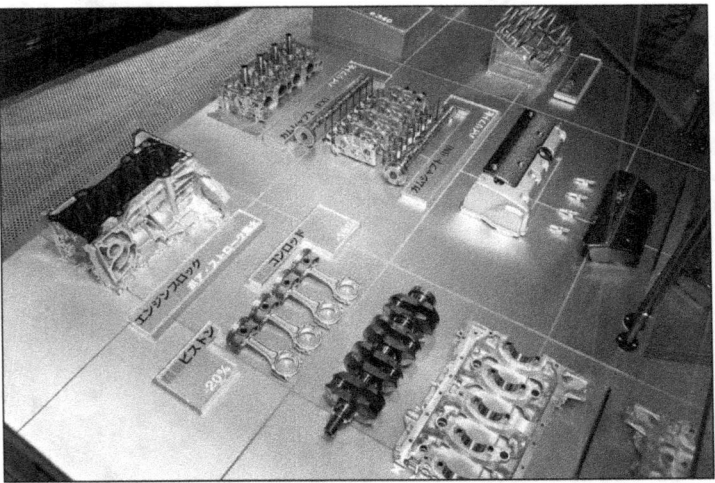

Much of what's made B- and H-series engines so popular among enthusiasts has been implemented into performance i-VTEC K-series engines. Under-piston oil squirters that reduce rotating assembly temperatures, high-strength connecting rods, and forged crankshafts that have been proven to handle as much as 1,000 hp without failure are standard issue.

CHAPTER 1

the expense of any additional top-end power. For reference, under-square engines such as the B16A typically produce impressive horsepower but lack torque.

K-series crankshafts are also similar to those in the B-series. Each is forged from high-quality steel but only performance i-VTEC versions feature a fully counter-weighted design.

Performance i-VTEC engines also feature under-piston oil squirters for increased cooling, stronger connecting rods, and, generally, higher-compression pistons.

Finally, in an effort to meet new federal regulations that now require automakers to produce engines that surpass 100,000 miles before an initial tune-up, Honda replaced its belt-driven valvetrain with its silent chain-driven system that's virtually maintenance-free.

In terms of North American–spec and Japanese-spec K-series engines, the K20A2, K20Z1, K20Z3, K24A2, K20A, and K24A all share a similar i-VTEC architecture. Although engine geometry and ancillaries (such as intake manifolds, throttle bodies, wiring harnesses, ECUs, and exhaust manifolds) may differ between them, all of these have more in common than not and make up some of the most desirable engine swap donor engines.

K20A2

The most established of Honda's performance i-VTEC engines, the K20A2 can be found in the 2002–2004 RSX Type-S. In stock form it yields 200 hp at 7,400 rpm and 142 ft-lbs of torque at 6,000 rpm. Indeed, Honda is familiar with 200-hp 4-cylinder engines; its Japanese-spec Integra Type R engine produced roughly as much six years before the K-series appeared. What's unprecedented is the K20A2's broad power range and mid-range torque supply. The K20A2's 1,998 cc of displacement and 11.0:1 compression ratio are partially what makes all of this possible. Like all K-series engines, the K20A2 is based on an all-aluminum block and DOHC 16-valve cylinder head configuration.

Compared to economy-minded K-series engines, the K20A2 features larger intake and exhaust

Chassis Codes

Sometime during the late 1990s someone thought it would be a good idea to start calling Hondas and Acuras not by their given names but by a series of letters and numbers associated with their 17-digit vehicle identification numbers (VIN). Since then EF, EG, EK, DA, and DC could have been given to all manner of Civics and Integras.

Understanding a vehicle's VIN is the first step toward understanding chassis codes. Every Honda's VIN is a unique combination of numbers and letters assigned by the manufacturer. The VIN can be found stamped on the firewall, riveted on top of the dash, and applied to a sticker on nearly every body panel on most of the 1996-and-newer vehicles. Since its implementation, a vehicle's 17-digit VIN has been used for everything from registration to identification to aiding in theft recovery.

When properly interpreted, each character of any given VIN identifies specific information about the vehicle. The VIN must also be located during emissions testing procedures and compared with the information found underneath the hood. This provides the necessary information, such as whether or not the vehicle is OBD-II-equipped or if it's supposed to have a DOHC engine with a manual transmission in it, so the technician can run the appropriate tests and procedures.

One of the many pieces of additional information the VIN divulges is the vehicle's chassis code. Three digits located in positions four, five, and six within the VIN indicate exactly what the chassis is. For example, a 2001 Integra GS-R VIN may be JH4DC23981S000394 where DC2 indicates all sorts of important information and immediately clues us in to chassis specifics.

Here's what the seemingly complex series of numbers and letters actually means for 1981-and-newer U.S.-spec vehicles:

JH4 DC2 3 9 8 1 S 000394

JH4	Origin and make (Japan, Honda Motor Co., Acura passenger vehicle)
DC2	Body and engine type (Integra hatchback, B18C, B18C1, or B18C5)
3	Body and transmission type (hatchback, 5-speed manual)
9	Trim (GS-R with leather interior)
8	Check digit
1	Model year (2001)
S	Origin (Suzuka, Japan)
999999	Production number ■

ENGINE IDENTIFICATION

The K20A2 found underneath the hood of the 2002–2004 RSX Type-S was North America's first taste of Honda's new K-series engine that featured VTEC on both camshafts. Even today, the 2.0L i-VTEC engine, transmission, and ECU remain among the most popular series of donor components for nearly every chassis in the following pages.

The 2006–2011 Civic Si K20Z3 built upon the already impressive RSX Type-S engine and made it even better. A higher-flowing intake manifold and revised camshafts lead to even more potential. The engine's electronics, like its drive-by-wire throttle body and ECU, are not compatible with every chassis.

ports, a higher compression ratio, and a single-stage aluminum intake manifold designed for top-end performance. As is the case with all performance i-VTEC engines, a stiffer, cast-aluminum oil pan is also incorporated to increase the block's overall rigidity.

K20Z1

As Acura performed its mid-model refresh on its RSX, a revised K20Z1 was placed underneath its hood for the model's final two years of production, which concluded in 2006. Generally speaking, there isn't much difference between the two other than the K20Z1's slightly more aggressive camshafts, a higher-flowing catalytic converter, and a larger intake duct and exhaust that altogether net an additional 10 horsepower compared to the K20A2. ECUs and engine wiring harnesses also differ between the two.

Of course, when considering engine swaps, the K20Z1's intake duct, catalytic converter, and exhaust are irrelevant, making the K20Z1 and K20A2 all the more indistinguishable from each other. When matched with its corresponding intake and exhaust systems, the K20Z1 measures 210 hp at 7,800 rpm and 143 ft-lbs of torque at 7,000 rpm.

K20Z3

Honda introduced the K20Z3 with the 2006 Civic Si where it remained exclusively through 2011. The most powerful Civic Si engine to date, it yields 197 hp at 7,800 rpm and 139 ft-lbs of torque at 6,200 rpm. The Si's powertrain is, not surprisingly, similar to the K20A2 with the exception of its electronics and ancillaries, the most notable of which are its free-flowing intake manifold, drive-by-wire, electronic throttle body, and corresponding ECU.

The K20Z3's intake manifold, also known as the RBC manifold (PN RRB on the Si), which is indicative of Honda's parts naming system, has gone on to serve as one of the most popular bolt-ons for non-Z3 K-series engines because of its exceptionally short runners, straight-through design, and high-flowing capabilities. Even high-performance aftermarket intake manifolds fail to better the performance capabilities of the RBC.

K20Z3 engines also feature revised camshaft profiles compared to the K20A2 as well as internal balance shafts and electric power steering. Naturally, in an effort to minimize engine vibrations, the balance shafts rob the K20Z3 of power but the slightly more aggressive camshafts and intake manifold ensure that its power level remains consistent with the K20A2.

Like the K20A2, the K20Z3 also benefits from Honda's high-performance version of i-VTEC, which transitions to the camshafts' larger lobes at 5,800 rpm. The results are respectable low-end torque and the most top-end power any Civic Si previously saw. When matched with VTC, the K20Z3 produces one of the broadest, smoothest powerbands the company has ever created.

Finally, the K20Z3 features a deeper, larger-sumped aluminum oil pan compared to other K-series engines.

K24A2

Honda began producing 2.4L K-series engines for the 2002 model year but didn't release a proper performance i-VTEC version to the United States until the 2004 TSX was unveiled. Similar to the K20A2, the K24A2 measures 200 hp at 6,800 rpm but produces an impressive 166 ft-lbs of torque at 4,500 rpm.

The 13-mm stroke increase and 1-mm bore increase yield the additional displacement and, as a result, the additional torque. Unlike the K20A's square-bore configuration, 2.4L K-series engines feature a significantly longer 99-mm stroke and, in the case of the K24A2, a lower, 10.5:1 compression ratio. What's more, Honda's 2.4L K-series engines are the largest 4-cylinders that the company has ever produced. Still, the K24 engine family shares many of its design characteristics with its 2.0L counterparts save for the slightly larger bores, longer strokes, and taller deck heights.

Compared to other North American–spec 2.4L K-series engines, the K24A2's internals were made stronger to cope with its higher redline, and like many 2.4L K-series engines, the K24A2's crankshaft girdle is slightly thicker than those found in 2.0L engines.

Unfortunately, as with all 2.4L K-series engines, the K24A2's oil pump is also counter-balanced, making it less effective at higher engine speeds. Fortunately, the K20A2 oil pump of the RSX transfers over relatively easily, with slight modifications, to clear the K24A2's slightly thicker crankshaft girdle. This is an important modification to keep in mind for anyone considering a 2.4L K-series.

Up top, all K24A2s feature cylinder heads similar to other performance i-VTEC engines but with slightly narrower ports that yield increased air velocity. All K24A2 engines also feature a single-stage aluminum intake manifold with long, narrow runners, and a drive-by-wire, electronic throttle body.

Several changes for the 2006 model year, such as 1-mm-larger intake valves and a higher-lift longer-duration intake camshaft that's arguably better than some Type R camshafts result in an additional 5 hp. Other mid-model changes include even stronger connecting rods, a more thoroughly counterweighted crankshaft, and additional oil passages within the block, which help reduce windage. A larger throttle body and freer-flowing exhaust components were also added, both of which don't matter much because neither may be used once the engine is transplanted.

On paper, the K24A2 is just about the most desirable K-series engine to date but keep in mind that they aren't inexpensive and their corresponding ECUs and throttle bodies are not compatible with most of the transplants covered in this book. To

The first-generation TSX's K24A2 engine remains one of the most desirable K-series power plants. That's primarily because it's the only North America-bound, 2.4L K-series engine to feature VTEC on both camshafts, much like the performance-oriented K20A2, K20Z1, and K20Z3. Like the K20Z3, the TSX's electronic drive-by-wire throttle body and ECU are not compatible with most chassis.

For the 2006 model year, Honda performed a mid-model refresh on its first-generation TSX, which included a moderately updated engine. Later-model K24A2 engines, including these from 2006–2008 chassis, feature higher-lift, longer-duration camshafts and a more durable rotating assembly with improved oiling characteristics.

ENGINE IDENTIFICATION

K-series engines sourced from Type R–badged Civics and Integras are among the most powerful and durable of all. Aggressive camshafts, higher-flowing intake and exhaust manifolds, and higher compression ratios all lend themselves to such engines' increased power, which measures as high as 222 hp on select overseas-only K20A engines.

make the K24A2 more compatible, its drive-by-wire electronic throttle body must be swapped out for the K20A2's and the appropriate ECU must be sourced.

K20A

As with its B-series lineup, Honda didn't disappoint when it came to developing its top-of-the line K-series: the K20A Type R. Honda produced several versions of its Japanese-spec K20A, of which only some were designated for Type R–badged chassis. It's important to mention that because Japanese-spec Honda engines use slightly different nomenclature compared to the rest of the world (note the absence of any number following the K20A) there are several variations of what, at first, might appear to be the same engine.

For example, Honda fitted its top-of-the-line 2007–2011 Civic Type R with the K20A, which yields 222 hp at 8,000 rpm and 159 ft-lbs of torque at 6,100 rpm. Honda also placed a similarly named K20A inside of its Integra Type-S, which isn't much different power-wise than the North American RSX Type-S.

Other Type R engines to be aware of include the 2001–2006 Integra Type R, the 2001–2005 Civic Type R, and the 2006–2008 Accord Euro R, which, despite its name, remains a Japanese-exclusive model.

The K20A Type R engine family features the same square-bore architecture as other K20A engines and compression ratios ranging from 11.5:1 to 11.7:1. Power varies slightly among the mix (222 hp is the maximum) but compared to their North American counterparts, they remain among the most sought K-series engines to date.

Type R engines also have even more aggressive camshafts and a performance-tuned, short-tract, aluminum intake manifold. As with previous Type R engines, in stock form they're difficult to beat, but if

The Wrong K-Series: Acura's K23A1

On paper, the 2007–2012 RDX's K23A1 engine sounds like just about the best K-series engine Honda's engineers could've hoped to develop. That's mostly because of its factory turbocharged and intercooled design, a path seldom taken with Honda engines. The results are 240 hp, 260 ft-lbs of torque, and, unfortunately, an architecture that's in no way compatible with any of the chassis in this book.

For starters, the K23A1's engine block is an entirely different casting. As a result, it's compatible with no aftermarket engine mount kit or any K-series manual transmission. To make matters worse, its cylinder head and block also can't be matched with other K-series engines and its turbocharger system is just as unique, resulting in incompatibility with every other 2.0L and 2.4L engine.

In other words, adapting an aftermarket turbocharger system to any approved K-series engine will be a whole lot easier. ∎

In 2007, Honda fans could hardly contain themselves at the introduction of the RDX factory turbocharged K-series engine. Unfortunately, the now-discontinued K23A1 is less like every other K-series engine than you'd believe. Perhaps worst of all, it's compatible with no manual transmission, which makes it a poor choice for any engine swap.

Performance i-VTEC Engines

Engine	Vehicle	Chassis Code	HP	Torque	Origin*	Throttle Body	Compression Ratio
K20A2	2002–2004 RSX Type-S	DC5	200 hp @ 7,400 rpm	142 ft-lbs @ 6,000 rpm	USDM	cable	11:01
K20Z1	2005–2006 RSX Type-S	DC5	210 hp @ 7,800 rpm	143 ft-lbs @ 7,000 rpm	USDM	cable	11:01
K20Z3	2006–2011 Civic Si	FG2, FA5	197 hp @ 7,800 rpm	139 ft-lbs @ 6,200 rpm	USDM	drive-by-wire	11:01
K20A	2001–2005 Civic Type R	EP3	212 hp @ 8,000 rpm	150 ft-lbs @ 7,000 rpm	JDM	cable	11.5:1
K20A	2001–2006 Integra Type R	DC5	217 hp @ 8,000 rpm	152 ft-lbs @ 7,000 rpm	JDM	cable	11.5:1
K20A	2007–2011 Civic Type R	FD2	222 hp @ 8,000 rpm	159 ft-lbs @ 6,100 rpm	JDM	drive-by-wire	11.7:1
K20A	2009–2012 Civic Type R Euro	FN2	198 hp @ 7,800 rpm	142 ft-lbs @ 5,600 rpm	JDM	drive-by-wire	11:01
K20A	2006–2008 Accord Euro R	CL7	217 hp @ 8,000 rpm	152 ft-lbs @ 7,000 rpm	JDM	cable	11.5:1
K24A2	2004–2005 2006–2008 TSX	CL9	200 hp @ 6,800 rpm 205 hp @ 7,000 rpm	166 ft-lbs @ 4,500 rpm 164 ft-lbs @ 4,500 rpm	USDM	drive-by-wire	10.5:1
K24A	2004–2006 Accord 24S, 24T, 24TL	CL9	197 hp @ 6,800 rpm	171 ft-lbs @ 4,500 rpm	JDM	drive-by-wire	10.5:1
K24A	2006–2008 Accord 24TL, Type S	CL9	197 hp @ 6,800 rpm	171 ft-lbs @ 4,500 rpm	JDM	drive-by-wire	10.5:1
K24A	2008–2013 Accord Type-S	CU2	206 hp @ 7,000 rpm	171 ft-lbs @ 4,300 rpm	JDM	drive-by-wire	11:01

* USDM = U.S. domestic market; JDM = Japanese domestic market

significant modifications are planned, starting with a less-expensive North American-spec engine isn't a bad idea.

K24A

Similar to the Japanese-spec K20A, Honda also made a variety of 2.4L performance i-VTEC engines available to its homeland. The K24A, which can be found in the 2004–2006 Accord 24S, 24T, 24TL, and 2006–2008 Accord 24TL and Type S, is of particular interest. Like the North American-spec K24A2, the K24A shares a similar design yet produces slightly less power and slightly more torque, measuring 197 hp at 6,800 rpm and 171 ft-lbs of torque at 4,500 rpm. Like the K24A2, the K24A features a drive-by-wire, electronic throttle body, and a modest, 10.5:1 compression ratio.

Economy i-VTEC

Although similar in some respects, the economy i-VTEC version of Honda's variable valve timing is different enough to command its own nickname. Much like Honda's emissions-conscious VTEC-E of the mid–1990s, impressive power figures were not the primary concern when developing these engines. Most notably, their exhaust camshafts are stripped of VTEC and their intake camshafts feature only two lobes and two rocker arms per cylinder instead of three.

Before VTEC engagement, economy i-VTEC engines make use of only

ENGINE IDENTIFICATION

Economy i-VTEC engines also feature VTEC and VTC, but for very different reasons than the performance-minded K-series engines. VTEC is only present on the intake camshaft and features a unique, two-lobe system that was designed primarily for reduced emissions and improved fuel consumption.

a single intake valve per cylinder, even though they feature 16-valve cylinder heads. The remaining intake valve cracks open slightly, just enough to prevent unburned fuel from puddling up behind the valve. Also known as valve idling, the process allows the engine to operate using a conservative amount of fuel at low engine speeds with improved power at higher engine speeds when both valves open and close normally.

VTC is tuned differently, with low emissions in mind. As a result, a unique swirl develops inside the combustion chambers along with an extremely lean air/fuel mixture, resulting in impressive combustion and fuel efficiency but not a whole lot of power. At 2,200 rpm, the secondary intake valve opens, at which time the valvetrain operates, as you'd expect. Unfortunately, overall lift and duration don't increase as with traditional VTEC engines.

Unlike performance i-VTEC cylinder heads, economy i-VTEC top ends also exhibit an awkward groove cut into the walls between each intake valve, which plays a role in their single-valve VTEC operation but costs in terms of airflow and performance. To the disappointment of Honda fans everywhere, as of the 2012 model year, only economy i-VTEC engines are offered.

Underneath, economy i-VTEC engines share some of the same characteristics as the performance-oriented K-series. The blocks are essentially the same, the crankshafts are similar but not as thoroughly counter-weighted, and their connecting rods share similar geometry albeit a generally thinner and weaker design. Their pistons are where most of the differences lie. To help with emissions, many economy i-VTEC pistons feature a rounded dish on top that, together with their curious intake valve operation, help further promote the swirling effect. Economy i-VTEC engines are also missing under-piston oil squirters (although provisions for them are still there), which help promote lower temperatures but aren't necessarily needed when upgrading to forged pistons. Underneath, a more conventional stamped-steel oil pan can be found on most economy i-VTEC engines, which is in stark contrast to performance i-VTEC engines' more rigid aluminum versions.

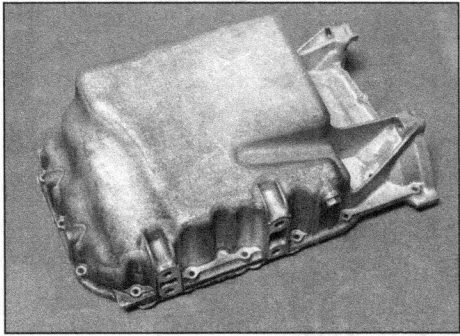

Higher-end performance i-VTEC engines and a select number of economy i-VTEC engines were manufactured with cast-aluminum oil pans that further increase engine block rigidity. Some later-model engines, including the 2006–2011 Civic Si K20Z3, feature engine mount provisions built into their oil pans, which link them directly to their chassis.

On their exhaust sides, economy i-VTEC engines don't feature any sort of variable valve timing. However, even the least powerful economy i-VTEC engines yield 160 hp and can be sourced inexpensively, making them K-series engine swap candidates worth considering for those on a budget.

The easiest way to identify any K-series engine is by its four- or five-digit code, which can be found stamped onto the front of the engine block. A number of attributes further distinguish economy i-VTEC engines from performance-oriented models such as stamped-steel oil pans, which are unique to such less expensive engines that feature VTEC only on their intake sides.

CHAPTER 1

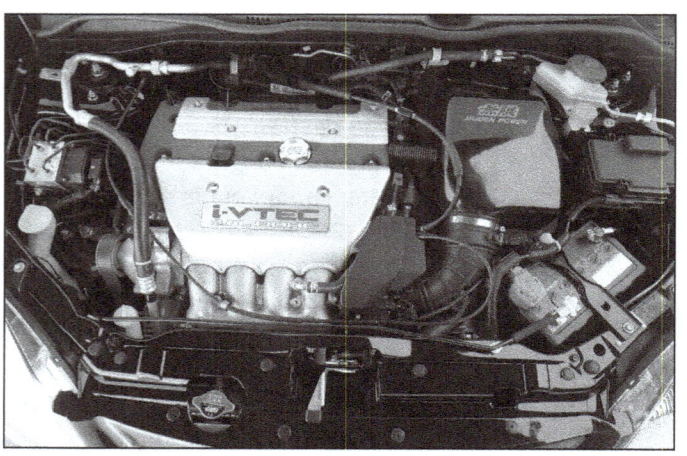

The 2002–2006 RSX base model and seventh-generation Civic Si K20A3 was among North America's first exposure to the K-series engine family. Although the engines are fundamentally the same between the two chassis, only Civic Si versions feature the same cast-aluminum intake manifold that's found on K20A2 and K20Z1 engines as well as electric power steering.

The RSX version of the K20A3 features a dual-stage, composite intake manifold. The two-stage system features short and long air tracts; air may be bypassed toward or away from these tracts. Depending on the circumstances, this results in increased mid-range response or high-RPM power. Composite intake manifolds such as these fall short in terms of maximum airflow potential and should be avoided or replaced whenever possible.

K20A3

Perhaps the most famous of Honda's economy i-VTEC engines, the K20A3 can be found in both the 2002–2006 RSX base model and the 2002–2005 Civic Si. The fact that the entry-level RSX was fitted with Honda's entry-level K-series was understandable but why the company did the same with its performance-based flagship Civic remains a mystery today.

The K20A3 doesn't immediately look all that different from the K20A2. As it turns out, the important differences between the two are mostly internal. Because of the K20A3's conservative implementation of VTEC and lower 9.8:1 compression ratio, only 160 hp at 6,500 rpm and 141 ft-lbs of torque at 4,000 rpm are registered. Worse yet, the Civic Si version yields an even more conservative 132 ft-lbs of torque at 5,000 rpm. Despite all of this, considering their entry-level cost, there are far worse engine swap candidates than the K20A3.

Although internally the same, the RSX's and Civic Si's K20A3 engines share different intake manifolds, which results in the Si's torque loss. The RSX version features a composite two-stage intake manifold, not unlike the second-generation Integra GS-R's or NSX's aluminum versions, which increases low-end torque by essentially adjusting its plenum volume with a series of throttle plates depending on engine speed.

The dual-stage design incorporates a short runner and a long runner for each cylinder. Below 4,600 rpm, the long runners deliver air exclusively. Above 4,600 rpm, a rotary valve placed inside of each short runner opens, allowing additional air into the cylinders. The results, much like VTEC, are better mid-range torque as well as sufficient top-end power.

The Si's K20A3 features a standard single-stage aluminum intake manifold, much like what's found on the RSX's higher-end K20A2. As it turns out, the Si's compact intake manifold design is partially what allows the K20A3 to fit within the confines of the Civic's tight engine bay.

K24A1/K24Z1

Released alongside the K20A2 and K20A3 for the 2002 model year, the CR-V's K24A1, at least in theory, is very much like its predecessor's 2.0L B-series engine. For example, both engines were designed with low-end torque production in mind, and neither seem to feel all that comfortable at higher engine speeds as the more nimble B16A, B18C, or K20A engines do.

The 2.4L engine's additional torque is provided by means of a slightly larger bore and significantly longer stroke, similar to the K24A2, geometrically speaking but with entirely different components. The results of its over-square architecture are an impressive 162 ft-lbs of torque

ENGINE IDENTIFICATION

The 2002–2006 CR-V K24A1 is a favorite among those seeking exceptional, but inexpensive, mid-range torque. Other 2.4L economy i-VTEC options are available, but only the K24A1 shares design characteristics with performance i-VTEC engines such as the K20A2, which means parts interchanging between the two is relatively easy. K24A1 engines also feature some of the most impressive-flowing cylinder heads of any economy i-VTEC engine.

Although the K24A1's replacement—the K24Z1—may seem like the better engine because of its cast-aluminum oil pan and intake manifold, it isn't necessarily. That's primarily because of the electronic, drive-by-wire throttle body, which must typically be replaced with a cable-operated version as well as the higher cost when compared to older 2.4L engines.

at only 3,600 rpm. Surprisingly, its compression ratio is a modest 9.6:1 yet the 2,394-cc K24A1 still achieves impressive performance.

Like all 2.4L K-series engines, the K24A1's connecting rods are stronger than 2.0L economy i-VTEC versions and their crankshafts are better counter-weighted. A composite two-stage intake manifold is present on the K24A1, which, along with its larger displacement, ensures respectable power and impressive torque: 160 hp at 6,000 rpm and 162 ft-lbs at 3,600 rpm.

Although the K24A1 doesn't feature VTEC on both camshafts, its cylinder head port configuration and flow characteristics are very much like the RSX's K20A2 and K20Z1, which make it an ideal candidate for cost-effective 2.4L engine swaps. The K24A1 also shares much of the K20A2's casting underneath, allowing for the popular RSX Type-S oil pump to bolt on without modification, unlike with other 2.4L K-series engines, including the TSX's K24A2. Finally, much like the B-series' popular LS-VTEC configuration, the K24A1 makes for the perfect candidate for such conversions, allowing for easy adaptation with performance i-VTEC cylinder heads like the K20A2 thanks to its nearly flat pistons.

In 2007, Honda updated its economy i-VTEC K-series for the new CR-V. Regarding horsepower, the K24Z1 marginally beats out the K24A1; it produces 166 hp at 5,800 rpm, although its bottom-end internals remain the same. Surprisingly, the K24Z1, which can be found in the 2007–2009 CR-V, features a cast-aluminum oil pan that's proven to increase the block's overall rigidity and a cast-aluminum single-stage intake manifold. All K24Z1 engines are also equipped with drive-by-wire, electronic throttle bodies. The K24Z1's oil filter housing has also been relocated and interferes with any of the manual transmission intermediate shafts that are required of every K-series engine swap. The oil filter and its housing may be repositioned elsewhere; however, it's an additional expense that must be considered.

Because of design similarities between the 2002–2006 CR-V K24A1 and performance i-VTEC engines, it's easy to transfer over the popular K20A2 oil pump from the RSX Type-S. Oil pump swaps such as these are an important modification once significant upgrades have been made or any time a performance i-VTEC cylinder head is swapped into place.

Honda manufactured more K24A4 Accord and Element engines than just about any other K-series engine, which means they're easy to source and inexpensive to buy. When matched with the appropriate engine mount kit, ECU, and transmission, such engines have the makings for some of the least expensive K-series engine swaps.

K24A4/K24A8

The 2003–2005 Accord and 2003–2006 Element's K24A4 and the 2006–2007 Accord and 2007–2008 Element's K24A8, structurally, aren't much different than the K24A1 except for the fact that K24A8 Accord engines feature a drive-by-wire, electronic throttle body, single-stage aluminum intake manifold, and smaller, more restrictive cylinder head port configurations that don't flow as well. Later-model engines also feature the same relocated oil filter housing as the K24Z1. The presence of an exhaust gas recirculation valve as well as a single-stage intake manifold, unlike the CR-V's dual-stage system, also separate the Accord and Element engines from the K24A1.

Economy i-VTEC Engines

Engine	Vehicle	Chassis Code	HP	Torque	Origin*	Throttle Body	Compression Ratio
K20A3	2002–2005 Civic Si 2002–2006 RSX base model	EP3 DC5	160 hp @ 6,500 rpm	132 ft-lbs @ 5,000 rpm 141 ft-lbs @ 4,000 rpm	USDM	cable	9.8:1
K24A1	2002–2006 CR-V	RD7	160 hp @ 6,000 rpm	162 ft-lbs @ 3,600 rpm	USDM	cable	9.6:1
K24A4	2003–2005 Accord 2003–2006 Element	CM5, CM7 YH1, YH2	160 hp @ 5,500 rpm	161 ft-lbs @ 4,500 rpm	USDM	cable	9.7:1
K24A8	2006–2007 Accord 2007–2008 Element	CM5, CM7 YH1, YH2	166 hp @ 5,800 rpm	160 ft-lbs @ 4,000 rpm 161 ft-lbs @ 4,000 rpm	USDM	drive-by-wire	9.7:1
K24Z1	2007–2009 CR-V	RE3, RE4	166 hp @ 5,800 rpm	161 ft-lbs @ 4,200 rpm	USDM	drive-by-wire	9.7:1

* USDM = U.S. domestic market

Marginally different from the K24A1, the K24A4 yields similar power (160 hp at 5,500 rpm and 161 ft-lbs of torque at 4,500 rpm) while the power of the K24A8 betters both slightly, measuring 166 hp at 5,800 rpm. The K24A4, in particular, was designed to meet stringent low-emissions standards, which is an impressive feat considering power wasn't sacrificed during the process.

The K24A4's VTC mechanism is emissions conscious. Here, VTC allows for a lower idle and reduced pumping losses and significant valve overlap in the upper RPM range through an exhaust gas recirculation effect, similar to the way older Honda engines' exhaust gas recirculation valves worked, only now internally. As redline is approached with the throttle fully opened, timing is continually retarded to allow for better cylinder scavenging and pumping efficiency. The K24A4 also features internal balance shafts located within the oil pan, which help minimize second-order harmonic vibrations for a smoother ride.

Neither engine shares many similarities with K20A2 engines (as the K24A1 does) but such Accord and Element engines are among the least expensive Honda has to offer.

The Other Economy i-VTEC

With integrated exhaust manifolds and non-existent performance-oriented VTEC, the case for choosing any of the following engines instead of Honda's performance i-VTEC or more conventional economy i-VTEC engines isn't good. In an effort to further improve catalytic converter efficiency, Honda eliminated its standard exhaust manifold and instead integrated it into the cylinder head.

With the abundance of more conventional economy i-VTEC engines, there's really no reason to look to Honda's more recent K-series engines when considering an engine swap. Their integrated exhaust manifolds prohibit airflow potential beyond what Honda's engineers determined necessary, making them much more challenging to modify.

The results are reduced emissions but a severely limited platform in terms of exhaust system modifications. Honda also went on to eliminate all 2.0L configurations from its lineup, now exclusively relying on the larger, 2.4L platform, which isn't necessarily a bad thing.

K24Z2/K24Z6

The K24Z engine family (excluding the 2007–2009 CR-V's K24Z1), which can be found in the 2010–2011 CR-V and select 2008–2012 Accords, builds upon the already successful tenants of its predecessor, the K24A, yet now places even more emphasis on low emissions. These 2.4L i-VTEC engines produce more power and torque than earlier engines but the K24Z engine family makes for a much more challenging engine to build upon thanks to their integrated exhaust manifolds. No longer is adapting a true header or exhaust manifold possible with these types of cylinders heads, which, arguably, over time may prove to be a blessing, considering the potential simplification of turbocharger and exhaust systems.

Still, the K24Z engine family can make for a solid foundation. Aside from the same downward-facing oil filter placement as the K24Z1, the bottom end of the new 2.4L family of K-series engines isn't much different than those that preceded it.

K24Z3/K24Z7

Honda once again updated its K-series engine platform for the

Later-model K24Z engines may seem like a worthwhile alternative to older 2.4L K-series engines because of their increased horsepower ratings; however, their electronic, drive-by-wire throttle bodies, composite intake manifolds, and integrated exhaust manifolds should all be considered before settling on any one of them. K24Z2 and K24Z6 short blocks are very much like older 2.4L engines, though, which means interchanging cylinder heads for an earlier style one is entirely possible.

Other Economy i-VTEC Engines

Engine	Vehicle	Chassis Code	HP	Torque	Origin*	Throttle Body	Compression Ratio
K24Y2	2012–2014 Crosstour	TF3	192 hp @ 7,000 rpm	162 ft-lbs @ 4,400 rpm	USDM	drive-by-wire	10:01
K24Z2	2008–2012 Accord	CS1, CP2	177 hp @ 6,500 rpm	161 ft-lbs @ 4,300 rpm	USDM	drive-by-wire	10.5:1
K24Z3	2008–2012 Accord	CS1, CP2	190 hp @ 7,000 rpm	162 ft-lbs @ 4,400 rpm	USDM	drive-by-wire	10.5:1
	2009–2014 TSX	CU2	201 hp @ 7,000 rpm	172 ft-lbs @ 4,500 rpm			11.0:1
K24Z6	2010–2011 CR-V	RE3, RE4	180 hp @ 6,800 rpm	161 ft-lbs @ 4,100 rpm	USDM	drive-by-wire	10.5:1
K24Z7	2012–2014 Civic Si	FG4, FB6	201 hp @ 7,000 rpm	170 ft-lbs @ 4,400 rpm	USDM	drive-by-wire	11.0:1
	2012–2014 CR-V	RM3, RM4	185 hp @ 7,000 rpm	163 ft-lbs @ 4,400 rpm			10.0:1

* USDM = U.S. domestic market

completely redesigned 2009 TSX and 2012 Civic Si. To better suit the second-generation TSXs and ninth-generation Civics slightly larger size and heavier (about 3,000 pounds for the Civic) chassis, the all-new larger-displacement K24Z3 and K24Z7 were selected. Similar to the older TSX's K24A2, both feature 2,354 cc of displacement by means of Honda's standard 87-mm bore and 99-mm stroke yet benefit from a higher 11.0:1 compression ratio. The results are 201 hp at 7,000 rpm and 170 ft-lbs of torque at 4,400 rpm (172 ft-lbs at 4,500 on the TSX).

In a seeming effort to confuse everyone, Honda went on to develop

The second-generation TSX's 2.4L power plant may seem like another worthwhile engine swap candidate, mostly because of its 172 ft-lbs torque rating, but it isn't. Like every other modern K-series engine, it features an integrated exhaust manifold, a composite intake manifold, and electronics that can't easily be adapted to older, more popular chassis.

The ninth-generation Civic Si abandoned the previous generation's 2.0L performance i-VTEC engine for a more emissions-minded 2.4L version. VTEC is stripped from the exhaust camshaft and, like every other K-series engine of its generation, features an integrated exhaust manifold and more complex electronics. Despite all of that, its K24Z7 produces 201 hp and 170 ft-lbs of torque, more than any Si throughout Honda's history.

ENGINE IDENTIFICATION

K-Series Weight Comparison

Engine and transmission weight should be considered carefully before performing any engine swap. Excessive weight can result in poor handling and decreased ride quality. Fortunately, because of their modern designs and updated materials, K-series engines weigh less than you might think.

All of the following weights include engine and transmission, intake and exhaust manifolds, axles, and major accessories. All weights are approximate and measured without fluids. All weights include manual transmissions only.

2.0L K-series: 405 Pounds

K-series engines weigh in a bit sporadically, depending on whether or not they feature counter-balance shafts, such as the 2006–2011 Civic Si's K20Z3, which carries an additional 9 pounds of baggage. The lightest of the 2.0L K-series bunch is the 2002–2005 Civic Si's K20A3 engine.

2.4L K-series: 413 Pounds

Honda's 2.4L K-series engines vary. For example, the TSX's K24A2 that features VTEC on both camshafts weighs in at the top, followed by 2.4L Accord engines, and, finally, the CR-V's K24Z1.

D-series: 309 Pounds

The unofficial baseline for all Honda engines, 1.5L and 1.6L single-cam D-series engines, all weigh about the same, whether or not they feature VTEC or cable-actuated or hydraulic-actuated gearboxes.

B-series non-VTEC: 395 Pounds

For the most part, all B-series non-VTEC engines weigh the same. Although newer OBD-I B18B1 engines feature updated and more comprehensive emissions components and hydraulic-style transmissions, the additional weight from those bits is negligible and is measured in ounces.

B-series VTEC: 405 Pounds

The obvious differences between Honda's two 1.8L VTEC engines (the GS-R's B18C1 and the Type R's

Despite what Honda fans have been led to believe, the average K-series engine and drivetrain isn't any heavier than many of the B-series engine swaps that have been taking place for nearly two decades. As a matter of fact, a K-series engine transplant is significantly lighter than the popular H22A powertrain, which has routinely made its way into Civics, Integras, and Accords for nearly two decades. (Photo Courtesy Hasport Performance Products)

B18C5) are their cylinder heads and intake manifolds, both of which tip the scales at roughly the same weight. The Japanese-spec B16B, because of its 1.8L-like deck height and Type R top end, also weighs about the same. Although smaller in displacement, Honda's B16A family weighs about 5 pounds less than its 1.8L VTEC counterparts, mostly due to a shorter deck height. Like non-VTEC B-series engines, all B-series VTEC transmissions weigh approximately the same.

H-series VTEC: 485 Pounds

Honda's heaviest 4-cylinder engine isn't its most powerful but that doesn't mean it hasn't served as a worthwhile swap for years.

J-series: 550 Pounds

Different intake manifold configurations result in small variances in weight but most 3.2L J-series engines measure relatively the same. Larger 3.5L and 3.7L engines feature longer-stroke, heavier crankshafts and larger-diameter sleeves, which result in roughly 25 pounds of additional weight. ■

Intake Manifold Spotter's Guide

Intake Manifold	Engine Origin	Chassis Origin	Notes
PRB	K20A2	2002–2004 RSX Type-S	Exceptional clearance, ideal for mid-range power
PRB	K20Z1	2005–2006 RSX Type-S	
PRB	K20A3	2002–2005 Civic Si	
PRC	K20A	2001–2005 Civic Type R	Similar to PRB but with more effective runners
PRC	K20A	2001–2006 Integra Type R	
RBC	K20A	2006–2008 Accord Euro R	Ideal for top-end power or high displacement
RRB	K20Z3	2006–2011 Civic Si	Identical to RBC manifold
RRC	K20A	2007–2011 Civic Type R	Similar to RBC manifold with even better performance gains
RSP	K20A	2009–2012 Civic Type R Euro	Significantly more costly with minimal benefits
RBB	K24A2	2004–2008 TSX	Ideal for mid-range torque
RBB	K24A	2004–2006 Accord 24S, 24T, 24TL	
RBB	K24A	2006–2008 Accord 24TL, Type S	
RAA	K24A4	2003–2005 Accord	Smaller version of RBB manifold
RAA	K24A4	2003–2006 Element	
RTB	K24A8	2006–2007 Accord	Similar to RAA manifold
RTB	K24A8	2007–2008 Element	
RTB	K24Z1	2007–2009 CR-V	
PPA	K20A3	2002–2006 RSX base model	Composite, not advised
PPA	K24A1	2002–2006 CR-V	
R40	K24A	2008–2013 Accord Type-S	Composite, not advised
R40	K24Y2	2012–2014 Crosstour	
R40	K24Z2	2008–2012 Accord	
R40	K24Z3	2008–2012 Accord	
R40	K24Z3	2009–2014 TSX	
R40	K24Z6	2010–2011 CR-V	
R40	K24Z7	2012-2014 Civic Si	
R40	K24Z7	2012–2014 CR-V	

During the early development years of Honda's K-series, a number of intake manifolds were made available, some of which have become highly desirable among those looking for added power. The most obvious intake manifold upgrade is the RBC, which can be sourced from the 2002–2008 Accord Euro R. Incidentally, a nearly identical (and easier to obtain) manifold is available from the 2006–2011 Civic Si: the RRB. Such manifolds lend themselves especially well to 2.4L performance i-VTEC engines or K20/K24 conversions. The short-runner large-plenum design leads to more top-end power compared to other manifolds but can exhibit some mild low-end losses.

Honda's K-series Type R manifold, the PRC, is almost identical to the North American-based PRB manifold, which can be found on the 2002–2006 RSX Type-S. About the only difference between the two are marginally different

Perhaps the most infamous K-series intake manifold, the 2002–2008 Accord Euro R's RBC version is one of the most popular K-series engine upgrades. An easier-to-source and nearly identical intake manifold can be found on the 2006–2011 Civic Si's K20Z3 engine.

The Integra Type R's PRC intake manifold may look like the same one from the 2002-2006 RSX Type-S, but it isn't. The PRC version features slightly reshaped runners that can result in marginally more power provided ECU tuning is addressed.

Any of the 2.4L Accord or TSX intake manifolds, such as the RAA, can be used but typically aren't sought after as replacements for anything else. Their long runners and small plenums result in respectable mid-range torque but weren't designed to perform well at higher engine speeds.

Composite intake manifolds, such as these, should be avoided. Under no circumstances are they the only option. For example, if using the RSX version of the K20A3, simply swap the cast-aluminum intake manifold from the 2002–2005 Civic Si version into place for a direct fit.

runners. The manifold's short design must also be considered, especially when engine bay space is at a premium.

The RBB manifold, which can be sourced from the 2004–2008 TSX as well as a number of Japanese-spec 2.4L engines, features a cast-aluminum two-piece design and is among the best for yielding additional mid-range torque.

Another two-piece manifold, the RAA, can be found on the Accord and Element K24A4. It's nearly identical to the TSX RBB manifold but features a smaller plenum and smaller throttle-body opening.

Throttle body bolt patterns aren't the same for every K-series intake manifold. For example, the K20A2's cable-style throttle body is not directly compatible with the RBC intake manifold, which typically accepts an electronic drive-by-wire version. Fortunately, a number of aftermarket adapter flanges are available that make it possible to transition almost any K-series throttle body onto almost any K-series intake manifold.

Not every intake manifold is directly compatible with every K-series engine. Coolant passages that either don't line up or aren't present are typically to blame. A number of adapters are available from the aftermarket to help address all of this; however, be aware of what's required of a particular intake manifold swap before settling on a particular one. (Courtesy Hasport Performance Products)

CHAPTER 1

Intake Manifold Spotter's Guide CONTINUED

A moderately popular manifold upgrade, the RRC from the 2007–2011 Civic Type R, appears similar to RBC manifolds but is among the most expensive. It features longer and wider runners and a slightly reshaped plenum. When tuned properly with an appropriately matched throttle body, RRC manifolds have demonstrated being one of the best-performing manifolds of all K-series engines.

Another multi-piece yet marginally more expensive manifold, the RSP from the 2009–2012 Civic Type R Euro, is a worthy upgrade but hasn't been proven to outshine the others in terms of mid-range torque or top-end power.

The other manifolds are multi-stage or composite-constructed designs that are typically avoided for reasons of clearance or performance potential.

Also, be mindful that although any K-series intake manifold may be swapped onto any K-series engine, oftentimes modifications must be made to the cooling system, throttle body, and more to properly work. ■

---

another K24Z3, this time for the 2008–2012 Accord, and another K24Z7, now for the fourth-generation 2012–2014 CR-V. Although a K24Z3 and K24Z7 in name, their compression ratios, horsepower, and torque figures all pale to the TSX's and Civic Si's. What's even more curious is that none of these engines benefit from performance i-VTEC or performance-oriented aluminum intake manifolds, which TSX and Si enthusiasts have thus far come to expect.

It isn't just the TSX and Civic Si that were being singled out, though; by the time the eighth-generation Si's final production run was completed, so was performance i-VTEC.

K24Y2

For the 2012 model year Honda released its K24Y2 engine for the 2012–2014 Accord Crosstour, now offering consumers a 4-cylinder option. In most respects, the K24Y2 isn't all that different than the K24Z lineup. Although it produces an impressive 192 hp at 7,000 rpm and 162 ft-lbs of torque at 4,400 rpm, the K24Y2 also features an exhaust manifold that's integrated directly into its cylinder head and Honda's limited version of i-VTEC.

A Word About Transmissions

In addition to the number of gears, gear ratios, and cost, before choosing a transmission you have to consider which chassis you'll be swapping into and whether or not an engine mount kit with the appropriate transmission brackets or mounts is available. (For transmission specifics such as gear ratios, see the chart on page 27.)

In terms of mounting orientation, two types of K-series-compatible manual transmissions are available: those from 2002–2006 RSX, 2002–2005 Civic Si, 2001–2005 Civic Type R, 2001–2006 Integra Type R, 2006–2011 Civic Si, and 2007–2011 Civic Type R chassis and those from the 2003–2007 Accord, 2006–2008 Accord Euro R, and 2004–2008 TSX. This list is by no means all-inclusive; there are a number of other less-popular overseas transmissions that can also be used. Other later-model transmissions can also be adapted but considering the number of readily available and directly compatible transmissions, the scope of this book is limited to the most popular gearboxes.

RSX- and Civic-style transmissions can be differentiated from Accord- and TSX-style gearboxes by their mounting orientation. Entirely different cases and mounting points between the two mean that different brackets or mounts are required when bolting them into the chassis. The two styles can also be distinguished by their gear selectors, which operate in opposing directions. This means that the appropriate shifter assembly and cables must be used to properly function.

Finally, it's important to mention the 2006–2011 Civic Si and 2007–2011 Civic Type R transmissions, which are a cross between the two styles. Both transmissions share mounting orientations similar to RSX- and Civic-style gearboxes but feature gear selectors more like the Accord and TSX transmissions. For vehicles that are compatible with either of these later-model Civic transmissions, details on how to properly adapt them to those chassis are covered in the pertinent chapters.

6-Speed Transmissions

Vehicle Type	Code	1st	2nd	3rd	4th	5th	6th	Reverse	Final Drive	LSD	Shifter Box	Mount
2002–2004 RSX Type-S	X2M5	3.267	2.13	1.517	1.147	0.921	0.738	3.583	4.389	No	RSX-style *	RSX-style †
2005–2006 RSX Type-S	NSN4	3.267	2.13	1.517	1.147	0.921	0.738	3.583	4.764	No	RSX-style *	RSX-style †
2006–2011 Civic Si	PNN4	3.267	2.13	1.517	1.147	0.921	0.659	3.583	4.764	Yes	Accord-style **	RSX-style †
2004–2008 TSX	ASU5	3.267	1.88	1.355	1.028	0.825	0.659	3.583	4.764	No	Accord-style **	Accord-style ††
2001–2005 Civic Type R	NPR3	3.266	2.13	1.517	1.212	0.972	0.78	3.583	4.764	Yes	RSX-style *	RSX-style †
2001–2006 Integra Type R	Y2M3	3.266	2.13	1.517	1.212	0.972	0.78	3.583	4.764	Yes	RSX-style *	RSX-style †
2007–2011 Civic Type R	NTS3	3.266	2.13	1.517	1.147	0.921	0.738	3.583	5.062	Yes	Accord-style **	RSX-style †
2006–2008 Accord Euro R	RBC3	3.266	2.13	1.517	1.147	0.921	0.738	3.583	4.764	Yes	Accord-style **	Accord-style ††

* RSX-style shifter boxes include: 2002–2006 RSX, 2001–2005 Civic (non-Si)
** Accord-style shifter boxes include: 2003–2007 Accord, 2004–2008 TSX
† RSX-style mounts include those designed for the following transmissions: 2002–2006 RSX, 2002–2005 Civic Si, 2001–2005 Civic Type R, 2001–2006 Integra Type R, 2006–2011 Civic Si, 2007–2011 Civic Type R
†† Accord-style mounts include those designed for the following transmissions: 2003–2007 Accord, 2006–2008 Accord Euro R, 2004–2008 TSX

5-Speed Transmissions

Vehicle	Code	1st	2nd	3rd	4th	5th	Reverse	Final Drive	LSD	Shifter Box	Mount Type
2002–2005 Civic Si	NRH3	3.062	1.769	1.212	0.921	0.738	3.583	4.764	No	RSX-style *	RSX-style †
2002–2006 RSX base model	W2M5	3.267	1.88	1.212	0.921	0.738	3.583	4.389	No	RSX-style *	RSX-style †
2003–2007 Accord	APG6	3.267	1.769	1.147	0.872	0.659	3.583	4.389	No	Accord-style **	Accord-style ††

* RSX-style shifter boxes include: 2002–2006 RSX, 2001–2005 Civic (non-Si)
** Accord-style shifter boxes include: 2003–2007 Accord, 2004–2008 TSX
† RSX-style mounts include those designed for the following transmissions: 2002–2006 RSX, 2002–2005 Civic Si, 2001–2005 Civic Type R, 2001–2006 Integra Type R, 2006–2011 Civic Si, 2007–2011 Civic Type R
†† Accord-style mounts include those designed for the following transmissions: 2003–2007 Accord, 2006–2008 Accord Euro R, 2004–2008 TSX

CHAPTER 2

ENGINE SWAP SAFETY

Disregarding safety and proper planning is never a good idea, especially when 400 pounds of engine and transmission are being yanked out of and stuffed back into an engine bay. The appropriate tools, equipment, and planning can mean the difference between you finishing your engine swap or ending up in a hospital.

Workspace

Start by preparing your work area. A clean workspace free of obstacles and other hazards can prevent tripping, slipping, or fumbling around; it also ensures organization, which can lead to a successful engine swap.

Adequate lighting and ventilation are also important. Some K-series engine swaps require drilling, cutting, grinding, and welding, all of which an appropriate amount of light helps make easier, not just for the sake of accurate fabrication but also for safety.

A well-ventilated workspace (especially when depressurizing the fuel system, draining fluids, and applying touch-up paint) helps prevent inhalation of all sorts of harmful fumes and can help keep the floor dry in colder climates.

Tools

Once the workspace has been prepared, it's time to assemble the engine swap toolbox. There's no replacement for high-quality tools, and investing in them if you plan on maintaining your own vehicle following the engine swap is always a good idea. Although less-expensive tools may suffice, safety can often be compromised. High-quality forged tools from Snap-on, Matco, and others remain undisputed among professional mechanics but less-expensive quality tools can also be sourced from other manufacturers.

For example, Kobalt and Bahco tools, both higher quality but

A torque wrench can be helpful to ensure that engine and transmission mounts and brackets have been properly tightened. However, if you're experienced with removing and replacing engines and transmissions, chances are good that you've got a grasp on how much leverage to apply to a specific fastener and a more conventional ratchet or air tool can be used when fastening everything into place.

ENGINE SWAP SAFETY

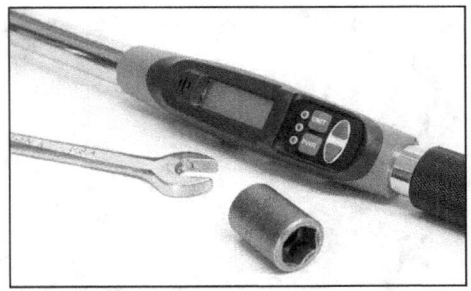

High-quality forged tools and an accurate torque wrench can lead to a successful engine swap. Lower-quality tools can break and even lead to injury. Be sure to use the right tool for the job. When using air tools, be sure to use the appropriate impact sockets that are designed to withstand additional abuse.

Recommended Torque Values

Applicable to plated, grade 10.9 bolts only, the following are recommended torque values for dry unlubricated fasteners. All values are approximate; consult the factory service manual or manufacturer instructions for specific values. Values may vary depending upon purpose and fastener length; these values are limited to external engine and transmission components only, such as mounts, brackets, manifolds, and ancillaries.

Bolt Diameter (mm)	Wrench Size (mm)	Torque Value (ft-lbs)
6	10	7 to 10
8	12	17 to 23
10	14	33 to 43
12	17	42 to 61
14	19	86

affordable brands, are manufactured by Snap-on but are designed for home mechanics and do-it-yourselfers. Craftsman, another long-standing, respected brand, remains affordable and shares the same parent manufacturer as Matco. These tools are made of forged steel, manufactured to precise tolerances, and designed for doing things such as engine swaps. The same can't be said of inexpensive, low-quality tools that can quickly wear, break, or damage whatever

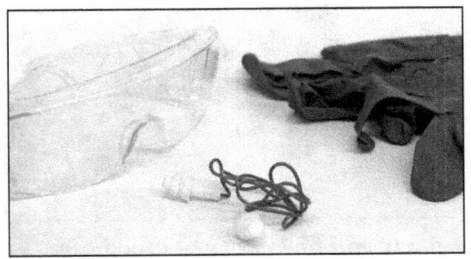

Proper safety gear is crucial to any successful engine swap, especially when fabrication including cutting, grinding, and welding must be done. Safety glasses and hearing protection are especially useful. Gloves (whether disposable or reusable) should also be worn to help prevent injuries, such as cuts, or worse.

nut, bolt, or fastener you're trying to loosen or fasten; not to mention injure yourself in the process.

Regardless of the tools chosen, using them properly is just as important as the tools themselves. Keep in mind these important points before beginning any engine swap: When removing stubborn nuts and bolts during the engine removal process, always rotate the wrench or ratchet toward you for better control and, when possible, use six-point sockets for removing hardware, which provide better stability compared to those with 12 points. Tools should also be kept clean and free of grease and if signs of damage are obvious should be replaced immediately.

If your experiences removing and replacing engines are minimal, consider investing in a torque wrench. Experienced mechanics rarely torque things such as engine mounts and transmission housing bolts to factory specifications because, over time, they've come to feel and know how much leverage to apply but if you lack that sort of experience, a torque wrench can give you the peace of mind of knowing that everything's been fastened properly.

Air tools also aren't required but can mean the difference between a one-day engine swap and a weekend-long project. If you don't have access to them, be sure that a 1/2-inch-drive breaker bar is accessible for removing and installing larger engine and transmission mounting bolts as well as the axle retaining nuts located on each of the front knuckles. See "Engine Swap Toolbox" on page 30 for a complete list of recommended tools.

Before starting the engine swap process, be sure you have a supply of towels on hand. They are especially useful when removing the original engine and draining its fluids.

Disposable gloves, safety glasses, a face shield, and hearing protection are important additions to the engine swap toolbox for the fabrication stage. Snug-fitting clothes that can withstand abuse and steel-toed shoes are also worth considering.

Equipment

Having the appropriate shop equipment is just as important as using the right tools. A proper floor jack and jack stands (the only things

CHAPTER 2

Engine Swap Toolbox

- 10-, 12-, 14-, 17-, and 19-mm sockets
- 32- or 36-mm socket
- 10-, 12-, 14-, 17-, and 22-mm open-end wrenches
- 8-, 10-, and 14-mm line wrenches
- 1/2- and 3/8-inch-drive ratchet and extensions
- Phillips-head screwdriver
- 8-mm nut-driver
- Needle-nose pliers
- Wire cutters and strippers
- Soldering iron, solder, and electrical tape
- Funnel
- Cut-off grinder, angle grinder, or reciprocating saw
- Drill and 1/8- to 1/2-inch drill bit set
- Spot-weld-removing drill bit
- Center punch
- 8-mm roll-pin punch
- Felt-tip pen
- Hammer
- Pry bar
- Floor jack and jack stands or vehicle lift
- MIG welder (depending on chassis)
- Service manuals (for vehicle and engine)

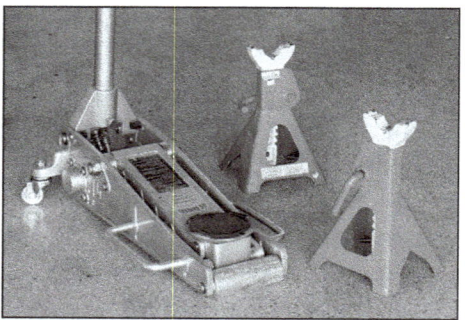

If you don't have access to a lift, you need some sort of floor jack and at least two jack stands. Before lifting the vehicle, be sure that the floor jack is in good working order and free of any hydraulic fluid leaks. Raise the vehicle, secure it on jack stands, and gently rock the chassis from above to ensure that it's positioned steadily.

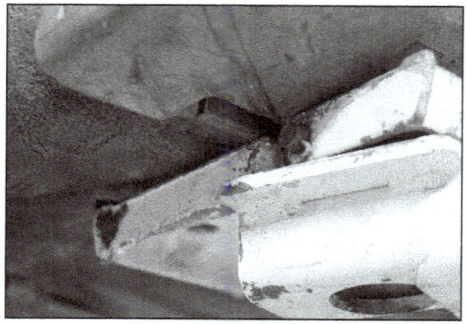

Every vehicle has specific jack points underneath its chassis recommended by the manufacturer. The jack points on most Hondas are located along the pinch welds on each side of the chassis, just below the side mirrors. Be sure to raise the vehicle at its front crossmember using a floor jack and position the jack stands underneath both jack points. Do not rely on the floor jack alone to support the vehicle.

Unless you have access to a lift, an engine hoist is vital to the engine swap process. Be sure that the hoist is free of any hydraulic fluid leaks and that all its hardware and casters have been appropriately fastened. Adjust the hoist's arm according to the weight of the engine and transmission assembly and be sure to clear a path for it to slide underneath the vehicle.

keeping your 2,600-pound Integra safely above you) are critical.

Verify the vehicle weight and be sure that the floor jack and jack stands you select are capable of supporting the car and K-series engine and transmission you are swapping into it. Inspect the floor jack for hydraulic fluid leaks and the jack stands for proper engagement before using them. Consult the vehicle's service manual to locate its appropriate jack points; most earlier Hondas and Acuras can be raised by positioning the floor jack underneath the center of the front crossmember and supported with jack stands at specified locations at the chassis' pinch welds below the front doors. Many newer models may not be raised by means of their front crossmembers and instead must be lifted at their pinch welds located below their front doors.

Avoid raising the car completely off the ground using four jack stands; leaving the rear wheels on the ground increases stability. Before raising the vehicle, place blocks behind the rear wheels and engage the emergency brake; all of this prevents the car from rolling backward when jostling the engine and transmission around during the removal and installation processes.

A quality engine hoist is important; it must be used to lower the engine and transmission assembly into the engine bay or to raise the vehicle so that the assembly may be slid in from underneath. If using an

ENGINE SWAP SAFETY

An adjustable load leveler can be attached to almost any engine hoist; it allows the angle or pitch of the engine and transmission assembly to be altered as it's being removed or lowered into place. This can be especially useful since most Honda engine and transmission assemblies are most easily installed at a downward angle with the transmission entering the engine bay first.

engine hoist to raise the vehicle, be sure to securely connect it to the car's front crossmember using a series of heavy-duty straps, spreading its load across the entire beam. If you don't have access to an engine hoist, check with your local equipment rental company. Many of them rent engine hoists by the hour. Whichever engine hoist is chosen, like the floor jack, be sure that there are no hydraulic fluid leaks, that its casters move freely, and that whatever hardware holds it together is properly fastened.

Before starting, adjust the engine hoist's extension arm so that it's

Honda Hardware Basics

Contrary to the general Honda enthusiast's vernacular, an individual fastener's size is classified by the dimensions of its thread diameter and thread pitch, not by what size of wrench or socket it may require. All of this makes the topic of Honda hardware confusing. For example, what many consider to be a 12-mm bolt is, in fact, according to Honda, an 8-mm one. That's because, despite the size of the bolt's head, the diameter of its threads measures exactly 8 mm across.

Metric hardware can be further classified by tensile strength, which is designated by grade; 8.8 or 10.9, for example, may appear on top of a bolt's head. If anything smaller or neither are present, the bolt is most likely low grade, which means the amount of tension it can bear before failing is minimal. (Factory Honda hardware is comparable to grade 10.9 or higher but does not feature such markings.) A bolt's tensile strength is something anybody who's swapping a K-series engine into place should be concerned with because, oftentimes, non-factory hardware must be used.

When determining bolt sizes, look at the numbers. With an M6-1.0 x 10 bolt, for example, the M means that the bolt is metric and the 6 tells you that its threads have an outside diameter of 6 mm. The second number (1.0 in this case) represents the distance between threads. Also known as thread pitch, this can be measured from peak to peak or from valley to valley. The final number represents the length of the bolt, measured from the bottom of the bolt's head to the end of its threads (10 mm in this case). To determine an unknown bolt's diameter and thread pitch, you can use a thread gauge. If no such tool can be found, try threading the bolt into a nut of known dimensions. ∎

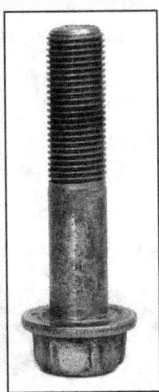

A fastener's size is never indicative of the tool it may require. For example, although many consider the series of bolts that fasten the transmission's bell housing to the engine block to be 17 mm, they are in fact 12 mm, the exact diameter of the bolts' threads. Since each thread is positioned 1.25 mm apart from another, such bolts are classified as M12-1.25.

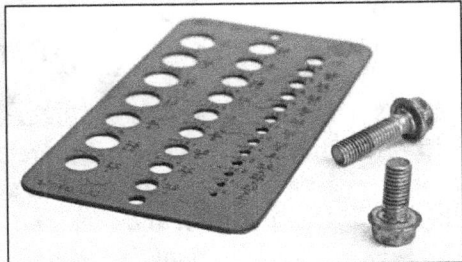

A thread gauge can be used to determine any unknown bolt or stud's dimensions. Simply thread the fastener into its corresponding hole to verify its size. Any nut of known size can also be used, but be sure that the bolt or stud threads in and out relatively effortlessly before concluding its size.

applicable to the weight of the engine and transmission and so that it can be moved toward the vehicle and positioned onto the engine without hitting the front bumper. In some cases, the vehicle's hood may also need to be removed to allow for proper clearance when removing and installing the engine.

Connect the engine hoist to the engine and transmission assembly using a minimum of 10-mm hardware (14-mm wrench). When attaching the engine hoist's chains to the engine, choose locations that don't interfere with engine mount placement and that position the engine relatively level, both laterally and longitudinally, once raised. Typical mounting locations include any of the transmission's upper mounting bolts, for example, and the timing-chain-side engine bracket.

Many engine hoists are equipped with adjustable load levelers that allow the engine and transmission assembly to be tilted side to side when lowering it into place. Such levelers can reduce installation time and the chances of any damage to the vehicle or engine during the removal and installation processes.

Finally, protect the engine's valve cover with a large shop towel before connecting the engine hoist. Once pre-loaded, the engine hoist's chains are firmly positioned against the engine, which can scratch or gouge smooth surfaces such as the valve cover. However, avoid removing the valve cover altogether; dropping hardware into the depths of the cylinder head isn't hard to do.

Fluid Control

Several harmful fluids must be dealt with when removing the original engine. The A/C system's contents (if applicable), power steering fluid (if applicable), transmission fluid, engine oil, coolant, fuel, and hydraulic clutch fluid (if applicable) can all come into contact with eyes or skin. Be sure that running water and towels are nearby and accessible and always protect your eyes with safety glasses and your hands with gloves.

Every chassis' A/C system must also be drained and partially removed whether or not A/C will be retained. Depending on your location, chances are good that draining your own A/C refrigerant is illegal. Before beginning the engine swap take the car to a suitable facility to have the system's contents properly evacuated.

All other fluids can be drained at home and discarded or recycled according to the appropriate regulations.

Finally, wait for the engine to be fully cooled, relieve the system's fuel pressure, and avoid smoking anywhere near the vehicle if fluids are exposed. Have a fire extinguisher nearby that's suitable for gasoline, oil, and electrical fires.

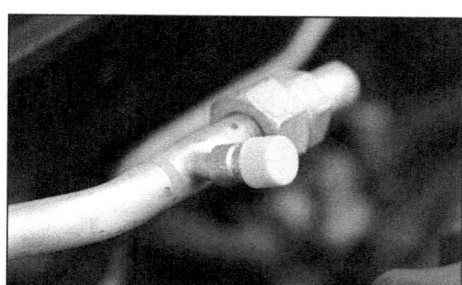

Unlike with older B- or H-series engine swaps, the A/C system's contents must be drained. Be sure to have a qualified technician evacuate and contain the system's contents before beginning the engine removal process. Although you may drain and recycle all other fluids, in most cases, it's illegal to drain an A/C system's contents.

Planning

Winging any sort of engine swap rarely ends in success and, when it does, can add days, even weeks, to the process. Thoughtful planning and a thorough understanding of the entire engine swap process help ensure a quick, safe, and complete engine swap. Be sure you understand each of the car's systems and how they must be converted to be compatible with the K-series engine, transmission, and ECU before beginning. Also avoid removing the original engine until all necessary parts have arrived. When applicable, have the appropriate service manuals near the work area along with whatever instructions may be needed for any aftermarket components, such as engine mounts and wiring harnesses.

Legalities

Before beginning any engine swap, it's a good idea to consult with your region's appropriate authorities and determine whether or not the engine you're considering is legal for use in your chassis. Depending on location, this may include your state's department of motor vehicles or equivalent organization or, in some areas, a state-certified emissions referee may have to be contacted. Some municipalities require little more than the engine be of the same year or newer than the vehicle it's transplanted into. Others may require all sorts of emissions modifications be made to the chassis, which may include the donor engine's evaporative emissions control system and fuel tank. Such requirements can add hours of labor and thousands of dollars to a once-affordable engine swap.

ENGINE SWAP SAFETY

In terms of emissions, however, almost every K-series engine has the ability to pass any state's tailpipe emissions test, especially when a modifiable ECU is used that allows fuel and ignition adjustments to be made.

Whichever route is chosen, be sure to thoroughly consider all of this before settling on an engine or investing in any components or with your time.

AN Plumbing

Almost any K-series engine swap exposes you to specialty fluid components, such as steel-braided hose and anodized-aluminum fittings, and they might lead you to the home improvement warehouse's plumbing aisle in search of enlightenment. At first, it all seems simple: Like plumbing underneath a bathroom sink, your car's fuel, cooling, and oiling systems simply displace fluid from one place to the next. Any differences between the two seem inconsequential but, as it turns out, they really aren't.

For one thing, home improvement hardware isn't exposed to corrosive, 200-degree-Fahrenheit fluids and doesn't undergo the sort of movement that, for example, a radiator cooling hose might. Neither can be said of whatever's flowing through your engine right now. Caustic fluids, high temperatures, and moving parts all make its fluid transfer systems exponentially more complex than anything in your home. Thread sizes, thread pitches, and sealing surfaces only add to the complexity.

AN (Army/Navy) plumbing, as it's commonly known, is exactly the sort of stuff you should be considering for your car and is exactly the sort of stuff that you won't find at a hardware store. AN plumbing was developed just before World War II by the aerospace industry as a military standard but has moved into the high-performance realm; its usefulness in a K-series engine swap is significant. Understanding the good and the bad of all of this as well as what is and isn't compatible with one another is important if you really want to separate what's appropriate for the home as opposed to your engine bay.

Braided Hose

The poster-child of competition plumbing is the stainless steel braided hose. A closer look reveals that it's more than just a shiny cover over any old rubber hose. Internally, it's made of synthetic rubber or Teflon.

Rubber-based versions consist of a steel-braided sheath that's embedded into the hose itself and a second that wraps about its exterior. Hoses such as these are best suited for oil, fuel, or coolant and can handle temperatures as high as 300 degrees Fahrenheit at relatively moderate pressures.

Teflon-based steel-braided hose is able to withstand pressures as high as 4,000 psi, making it ideal for custom hydraulic clutch lines, which are required of almost every K-series engine swap.

When assembling hoses and hose ends, be sure to pressure test them appropriately before installation and subjecting them to use.

Teflon-based hose is made of extruded Teflon tubing that's also covered with a protective steel braiding. Such hoses are capable of withstanding pressures as high as 4,000 psi, which makes them the obvious choice for hydraulic systems, such as those for brake and clutch assemblies as well as for various exotic fuels that typically don't play nicely with rubber.

Steel-braided hose isn't always the best choice, though, and isn't always better than whatever was in your car originally. Surprisingly, the synthetic rubber typically found in steel-braided applications isn't always as versatile as automakers' modern hose compounds. Depending on whatever's flowing through it, it can crack over time and without warning because of its protective covering. Steel-braided hose can also be difficult to route because of its large radiuses and when rubbed against softer materials can damage them from abrasion. Steel-braided hose also isn't compatible with slip-over barb fittings or hose clamps (regardless of how often you see it done), which means the appropriate and equally expensive AN hose ends and adapters must always be used, of which several different types are available, depending on the hose.

Hose selection doesn't end with the steel-braided variety. A number of Kevlar- and nylon-covered rubber-based

AN Plumbing CONTINUED

hoses are available as well as rubber-based hoses that don't feature any sort of protective sheathing at all. Applications vary and there's a material that's compatible with just about any fluid, temperature, or pressure.

Not all rubber hoses are created equal. When choosing a hose (steel-braided or not) be sure that it features a woven-fabric core, which increases its strength and durability, and that it's suitable for whatever fluid you're expecting it to carry.

Hose Ends

Figuring out what hose ends you need isn't any less complicated. The fact that they're available in configurations specific to each type of hose in a variety of shapes and radiuses make the process even more muddled. Each serves a purpose. For example, the most common single- and double-nipple tube-style hose ends are generally less expensive but are susceptible to damage from vibration or leverage.

Forged hose ends are typically stronger and feature a lower profile but can lead to fluid cavitation because of their harsh bends. Some hose ends can swivel, which allows them to be reoriented even after assembly for precise fitment. Stationary hose ends are less expensive. Choosing the proper shape and type of hose end can typically reduce the need to bend the hose itself and provide for an overall tidier appearance.

All hose ends designed for use with steel-braided hose are based on the same principles. Here, a threaded socket slips over the hose. The hose's male-threaded end screws into the socket, wedging the hose into the small space between the socket and the nipple; it creates an interference fit that's exponentially stronger than any clamp.

In some cases, a crushable brass, aluminum, or stainless steel olive is also used, such as with a Teflon-based hose. Most other hoses that don't feature protective sheathings, such as steel-braided ones, can be used with barb adapters that can be pushed into place with a small amount of lubricant and retained using a hose clamp.

Adapters

All hose ends hook up to the appropriate hose but don't expect its other end to magically connect to anything on your car. The appropriate adapter(s) must be used to transition from the male- or female-threaded connection or nipple on, for example, your engine to the hose end's AN threads. Scores of adapters with the appropriate AN threads are available for transitioning from NPT (National Pipe Thread), BSPT (British Standard Pipe Thread), banjo, barb, metric, or just about anything else you can imagine to whatever hose end you use. Simply figure out what exactly it is you're trying to adapt to, what size hose end you'd like to adapt, and source the appropriate adapter(s) to make it all work. In some cases, more than one adapter may be needed depending on location, angle, and thread orientation.

AN components, such as steel-braided hose, use a unique measurement system that's based off of 1/16-inch increments, preceded by a dash. For example, -8 hose features an internal diameter of approximately 8/16 inch. Common AN sizes include -3, -4, -6, -8, -10, -12, and -16 although larger sizes and oddballs, such as -2 and -5, are available but are also more expensive because of their rarity. The complexities don't end there, though.

You would think that whatever size hose you're considering is a measurement based on the hose's internal diameter but you'd be wrong. Instead, an individual AN size is a measurement of the hypothetical tube's outer diameter that would presumably flow the same. As you'd expect, hypothetical tubes that presumably flow a certain amount can vary in size, which means one manufacturer's -8 hose is almost always just a little bit smaller or larger than another manufacturer's.

Hose ends may be connected to their respective hoses by crimping, swaging (a form of crimping that compresses a ferrule), or by hand, depending on the style used. Swaging and crimping require expensive hydraulic tooling, which makes assembling them by hand the method you'll likely choose.

First, the hose must be cut to size before doing anything. Most hose can be cut with hose cutters or a blade; however,

AN hose and fitting sizes are typically represented as a number preceded by a dash. To determine a particular AN size, multiply the advertised number by 1/16 inch. For example, -4, -6, and -8 can be interpreted as 1/4, 3/8, and 1/2 inch, respectively.

ENGINE SWAP SAFETY

A rubber-based steel-braided hose assembly typically includes the hose itself, a hose end, and a threaded socket that interfaces the two components. When assembled properly, the AN connection can be removed from its corresponding adapter and reused almost forever; it requires no form of sealing compound.

Frequently, AN fittings must be adapted to a dissimilar NPT component. A number of adapters are available that make this easy; however, the first step is recognizing the difference between the two. NPT threads (left) are tapered, and when threaded together with another NPT fitting or adapter, they create an interference fit. AN threads (right) are straight and seal by means of flared ends that compress against each other when tightened. NPT threads require some sort of sealant; AN threads do not.

steel-braided hose must be cut using a toothless-blade chop saw. A fine-tooth hacksaw may also be used but the chances of a poor cut and possible leaking increase.

Regardless of the method chosen, wrap the area to be cut with masking tape to avoid fraying and cut perpendicular to the hose; a square cut is critical to the seal.

Once cut, trim any frayed edges and thread the hose end's socket onto the end of the hose.

Apply anti-seize compound to the hose end's threads and nipple before assembly and thread it into the socket. AN components should never be assembled dry; stripping may occur or, over time, their threads can seize.

Although most of the hoses mentioned feature tremendous pressure ratings, the truth is that they're only as capable as their hose ends and their assembly method. A poor connection or inappropriate adapter is generally the cause of failure, not the actual hose.

Improper sealing surfaces and incorrect thread compatibility are two other common causes of failure. Before selecting a hose end, adapter, or fitting, you've got to understand the difference between the two most popular threads: AN and NPT. First, they aren't compatible with each other, which is why there's an abundance of AN-to-NPT adapters. AN threads feature a straight design and seal by means of a 37-degree-flared seat or O-ring. NPT threads are tapered for an interference-fit and require some sort of sealant, such as Teflon paste or tape. It's important to know that applying any such sealant to AN threads only increases the likelihood of leaking.

Adapters such as these and any other AN components aren't typically available from the local hardware store. Instead, look to manufacturers including Earl's, XRP, or Aeroquip.

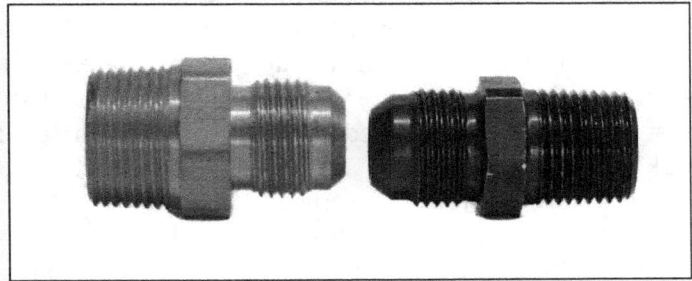

Not all flared fittings that seal by compression are the same. Typical hardware store fittings designed for home improvement projects feature a 45-degree flare. AN fittings are based on a 37-degree design. It's important to never mix and match the two. Combining the two may seem as if it'll work at first; however, their incompatibility with each other almost always results in failure.

Fittings

Not all flared fittings are the same, either, which is what makes your trip to the home improvement store either a waste of time or an experience that ends with something underneath your hood catching on fire. For example, although the plumbing aisle's flared fittings may look like what you need, they aren't.

Home improvement plumbing is based on a 45-degree flare that, when matched with a 37-degree AN fitting, seals only along a razor-thin surface. This may work for a short time but soon fails; it either makes a mess of a home improvement project or all sorts of trouble underneath your hood. ■

CHAPTER 3

ELECTRICAL ESSENTIALS

The electrical system is typically the most complex part of any engine swap. Because of engine orientation, OBD differences, and production periods (unlike with older B-series or H-series engine swaps), most of the vehicles covered in this book do not retain their original engine wiring harnesses. A separate charge harness that distributes current from the battery to the starter, alternator, fuse box, and engine wiring harness must also be fashioned to account for K-series engines' unique layout compared to older Honda engines. The good news is that, like older Honda engine transplants, pre-made wiring harnesses can be sourced from a number of aftermarket manufacturers, such as Hasport, Hybrid Racing, K-Tuned, and Rywire, in which case only a minimal amount of electrical modifications must be made.

Of course, pre-made wiring harnesses can greatly simplify the installation process but they come at a cost. Whether or not you plan to modify your wiring harness yourself or purchase a pre-made harness, you must understand several key points in terms of Honda electrical systems as they relate to K-series engine swaps before moving on.

Electrical Toolbox

Before beginning, be sure that you have access to the appropriate electrical tools and supplies. Your electrical toolbox should include the necessary equipment for making wiring harness modifications as well as for performing any electrical system diagnostics should trouble occur once the engine swap is complete. Keep in mind that, depending on the chassis, engine, and whether or not a pre-made wiring harness is used, some of the following equipment may or may not be necessary.

Soldering Equipment

Every engine swap outlined in this book requires some form of wiring modification. When joining two or more wires together, soldering is

The electrical system is arguably the most challenging part of any K-series engine swap. It all starts with the engine wiring harness, a sub-harness, or a combination of both. A number of manufacturers offer pre-made wiring harnesses that can simplify any engine swap significantly; however, a small amount of electrical work is almost always required.

ELECTRICAL ESSENTIALS

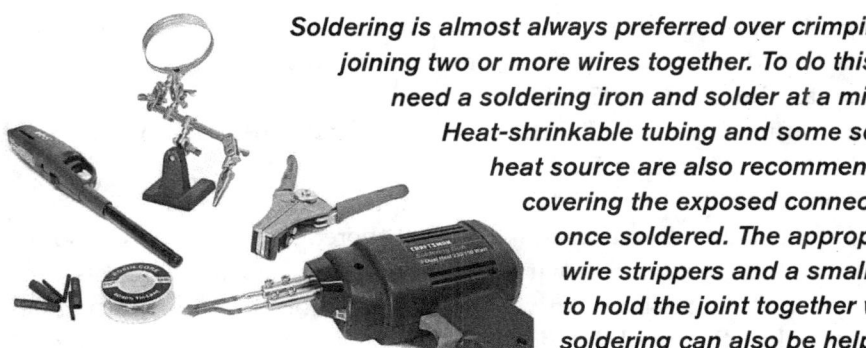

Soldering is almost always preferred over crimping when joining two or more wires together. To do this, you need a soldering iron and solder at a minimum. Heat-shrinkable tubing and some sort of heat source are also recommended for covering the exposed connection once soldered. The appropriate wire strippers and a small clamp to hold the joint together while soldering can also be helpful.

almost always preferred to crimp connectors. A soldering iron or butane torch, solder, heat-shrinkable tubing to cover the exposed connections, and some sort of heat source must be used. If using crimp connectors, wire-crimping pliers can be used along with either heat-shrinkable tubing or electrical tape to cover and secure the exposed connector once finished.

Before soldering, slip a short section of heat-shrinkable tubing over one of the wires. Once soldered together, slide the tubing over the connection and apply heat using a small lighter or other heat source. Be careful to not burn the wire. When soldering, apply the soldering iron's tip directly against the wires, not the solder. Once hot, dab the solder onto the wire, allowing it to melt and spread on its own. Only a small amount is needed to secure the wires together.

Pick Set

If an electrical connector must be swapped, de-pin its terminal(s) from the connector using a pick whenever possible. Although the connector may be cut off its original wiring harness, preserving some of its wiring and soldering it onto another wiring harness, de-pinning and re-pinning a terminal from its connector eliminates the need to cut and solder any wiring, preserving the harness' integrity.

Wire Strippers

When soldering or crimping wires, their protective sheathing

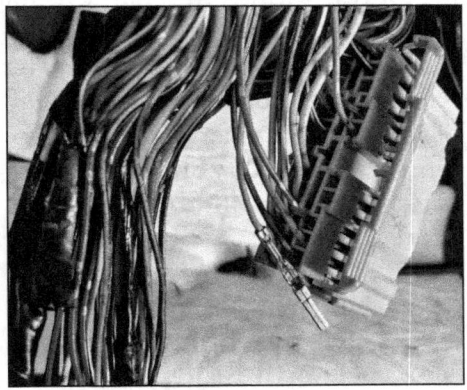

A number of wires must connect to various connectors throughout the chassis and at the ECU. Instead of cutting the wire near the connector and soldering on a new section that leads to its new source, de-pin the wire directly at its connector. Once de-pinned, the original wire can be discarded and the new one (that leads to the new source) can be pinned in its place. Most pins can be undone by inserting a small pick in the connector's opposite end, and then pushing the wire and pin out from the rear. Some connectors feature plastic locking clips along their top or bottom sides that must be released first. (Photo Courtesy Hasport Performance Products)

TECH TIP: Soldering Basics

Soldering is the preferred method for joining two or more wires together. Heat is applied to a joint, allowing a tin-and-lead-based alloy to melt and ultimately harden within and around the individual strands of wire, resulting in a highly secure connection. Soldering isn't difficult but creating a joint that can withstand the vibrations and general wear and tear to which a wiring harness can be subjected takes practice. Begin by removing about an inch of protective sheathing from each wire that will be joined together.

Generally, the sheathing must be removed at the wire's end, although in some cases a splice may be made someplace midstream. With the bare wire exposed, wrap the wires' bare sections together in a pigtail fashion, forming a relatively secure joint.

Next, apply the tip of the soldering iron or torch flame to the newly formed joint. Once hot, unroll a section of solder and dab it onto the joint. Do not allow the soldering iron tip and solder to directly contact one another. Continue dabbing solder along the joint, allowing the heated surface to draw the solder into itself. The entire process should take mere seconds, depending on the gauge of the wire.

Once applied, allow the joint to cool and protect it with electrical tape or heat-shrinkable tubing. If using the latter, be sure to slip a section over one of the wires before initially joining them together. ■

must be pulled back, exposing a short section of bare wire. Wire strippers work best here and eliminate the risk of cutting the wire in two as often happens with wire cutters. Many wire-crimping pliers perform several functions besides crimping, such as stripping as well as cutting, allowing the job to be completed with a single tool.

Digital Multimeter

A digital multimeter, although not always necessary, may come in handy not just for diagnosing any potential electrical issues once the swap is completed but for tracing wires within the harness for easy access when making modifications. Be sure that the multimeter is configured for DC voltage when diagnosing the charging system or sensor functionality and ohms when determining continuity or tracing a wire's source.

Non-Native versus Native Chassis

Dozens of chassis may accommodate a K-series engine swap but in terms of electrical systems, there are really only two: non-native and native. Non-native vehicles are those that were not originally sold with nor are directly compatible with any K-series engine, such as any pre-2001 Honda or Acura chassis. Non-native chassis covered in this book include any 1988–2000 Civic, CRX, or del Sol; 1990–2001 Integra; 1990–1997 Accord; and 1992–1996 Prelude.

Native vehicles include those that weren't necessarily equipped with a K-series engine but share many of the same underpinnings as those that do. For example, although the K-series was not offered for the 2001–2005 Civic coupe or sedan, their chassis and electrical systems are similar to the 2002–2005 Civic Si, which features the K20A3. The CR-Z and second-generation Fit may also be considered native because their engine bays and electrical systems share much in common with K-series-equipped chassis. Native chassis covered in this book include the 2001–2005 Civic.

On-Board Diagnostics

Every car manufactured since 1981 has some sort of diagnostic control system that monitors engine parameters through sensors and makes the appropriate adjustments for proper performance and emissions control through its engine control unit (ECU) or powertrain control module (PCM). Simply known as OBD, the first mass-produced version of on-board diagnostics was developed by General Motors before being implemented by every other major automaker.

Early Honda versions were referred to as pre-OBD but were OBD in every sense, were implemented with the company's first fuel-injected vehicles, and were prevalent until the introduction of OBD-I for the 1992 model year. (The NSX and select Accords received OBD-I and, later, OBD-II a year early.)

For the 1996 model year Honda introduced OBD-II diagnostics for its entire lineup, which offered additional and more precise engine monitoring for better performance and more regulated emissions control. State emissions testing procedures are also more complex for later OBD systems. Because the K-series engine was released after OBD-II had been fully implemented, all K-series engine swaps are based on Honda's most recent diagnostics system.

ECU Selection

Unlike older Honda engine swaps, there are only two ECU solutions when transplanting a K-series engine: a factory K-series-compatible OBD-II ECU or some sort of stand-alone engine management system that behaves more like OBD-I. Because all stand-alone engine management systems, such as those from AEM or MoTeC, feature their own specific setup and operating procedures (and aren't exactly necessary for the typical K-series engine transplant), this book only covers factory-issued K-series ECUs.

Before choosing a factory Honda computer, several criteria must be addressed. First and most obvious, the ECU must be sourced from a vehicle that was originally equipped with a K-series engine. Second, because

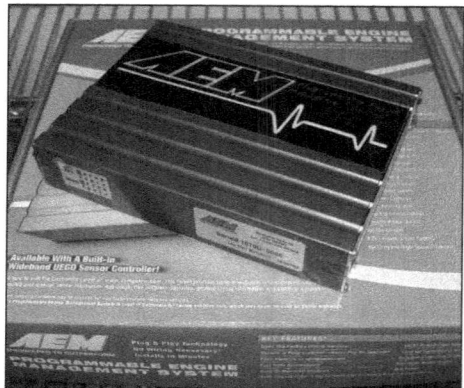

A stand-alone engine management system, such as those from AEM, can be used on any K-series engine swap. However, such systems' installation and setup procedures are unique to each manufacturer, and are often far more complex than those involved when using a factory K-series ECU. (Photo Courtesy Hasport Performance Products)

you'll likely be using a manual transmission, be sure that the appropriate ECU that was acquired from a manual transmission-equipped vehicle is used. Third, be sure to select an ECU that is compatible with your type of i-VTEC K-series engine (unless the ECU will be modified with Hondata's K-Pro).

For example, when using an economy i-VTEC engine, the appropriate ECU sourced from an economy i-VTEC engine should be used. If doing a performance i-VTEC engine swap, the appropriate performance i-VTEC ECU should be used. Other features, such as dual-stage intake manifolds, rely on the appropriate ECU to properly function. (Vehicle-specific ECU information and ECU upgrades are addressed in forthcoming chapters.)

In most cases, the ECU can be sourced from the same salvage yard as the engine and transmission. Like engines and transmissions, though, pricing can vary significantly depending on supply and ECU type.

Immobilizer Considerations

Unfortunately, not every K-series ECU is directly compatible. Many are equipped with theft-deterrent immobilizers that, when left unmatched with the appropriate transponder key and receiver, are virtually useless. To work properly, the appropriate immobilizer system indicator, ECU, and immobilizer control unit (located at the ignition switch) must all be present. Later-model, native K-series chassis feature all of this but older, non-native vehicles do not, which makes choosing an ECU equipped with an immobilizer a concern.

Fortunately, you have a number of solutions for swapping into non-native chassis, the simplest of which is to source the appropriate Japanese-spec ECU, many of which feature immobilizers that can be bypassed quite easily. Immobilizer-bypass devices that tap into the wiring harness and eliminate the system can also be wired into place.

Finally, the ECU may be modified, by Hondata, for example, which also has the capability to disable the immobilizer. (Immobilizers and how they relate to particular chassis are discussed in coming chapters.)

Transmission Considerations

Unlike with older B-series or H-series engine transplants, transmission selection must be considered carefully when settling on an ECU. First, each of the ECUs listed in the "ECU Locator" chart on page 40 may be accompanied by either a 5-speed or a 6-speed transmission. However, when using an ECU that was originally matched with a 5-speed gearbox with a 6-speed transmission, the reverse-gear lockout must be modified to operate properly. The challenges don't end there, though.

Unlike older Honda and Acura transmissions that all feature similar vehicle speed sensors, two versions are available for K-series transmissions: low frequency and high frequency. The differences between them go beyond whether or not, mechanically, the two may be interchanged. It's the speed sensor's job to communicate with the ECU and, ultimately, the instrument cluster. The two types of sensors go about all of this in entirely different ways.

Low-frequency vehicle speed sensors communicate with the ECU and the instrument cluster through a low-frequency signal that initiates at the transmission's final-drive gear. High-frequency vehicle speed sensors only communicate with the ECU and

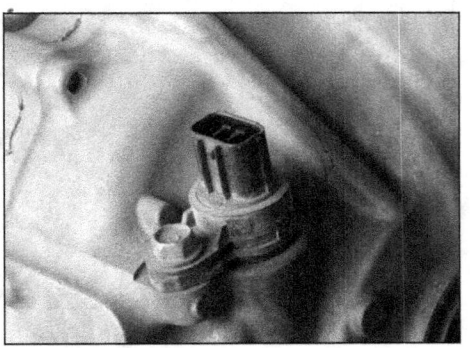

Transmission selection must be considered carefully when settling on an ECU. K-series transmissions feature two different vehicle speed sensors, both of which are only compatible with their designated ECUs. If mismatched, the ECU and instrument cluster can't interpret vehicle speed correctly, which can lead to inoperable VTEC and a malfunctioning speedometer, among other problems.

do so by means of a high-frequency signal that initiates at the transmission's third gear.

If the ECU and vehicle speed sensor are not appropriately matched, a number of problems occur, including inoperable VTEC and the inability to interpret vehicle speed at the instrument cluster.

As you'd expect, there are at least two solutions to this mismatch, the easiest of which is to select an ECU, transmission, and vehicle speed sensor that are all compatible with one another. If an otherwise incompatible transmission is selected, depending on the chassis, the aftermarket presents its own solutions.

Oxygen Sensor Considerations

Using the appropriate primary oxygen sensor is important. Because Honda implemented both narrowband and wideband sensors in its K-series lineup, some are transferable between other ECUs but many

CHAPTER 3

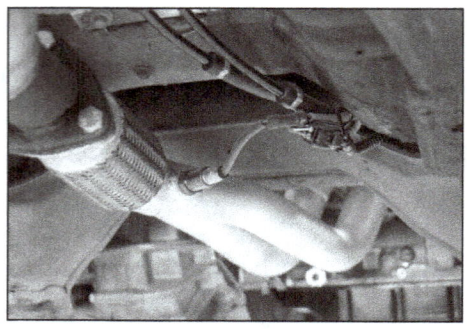

Unlike with older Honda engines, a number of different oxygen sensors are used throughout the K-series lineup. As such, selecting the right one is important. Generally, using the oxygen sensor that's normally sourced from the engine of your ECU is preferred. For example, if you plan to use an engine from an Accord but an ECU from an RSX, be sure to source an RSX oxygen sensor.

ECU Locator

Chassis	ECU Part Number	Features
2002–2004 RSX Type-S	PRB	Performance i-VTEC, reverse-gear lockout
2002–2004 RSX base model	PND	Economy i-VTEC
2002–2005 Civic Si	PNF	Economy i-VTEC
2002–2006 CR-V	PPA	Economy i-VTEC, dual-stage intake manifold
2001–2006 Integra Type R	PRC	Performance i-VTEC, reverse-gear lockout, no immobilizer
2001–2005 Civic Type R	PRD	Performance i-VTEC, reverse-gear lockout, no immobilizer

Dozens of K-series ECUs are available, which can make sourcing the appropriate one confusing. Look at the serial number on the side of the ECU's case for clarification. Locate the 12-digit serial number, specifically referencing its center three digits that are preceded and concluded by dashes. Such three-digit codes, such as PRB, are unique identifiers for each ECU.

are not. For example, oxygen sensors normally paired with the TSX K24A2 engine and ECU are not compatible with RSX computers. Generally, it's best to source the primary oxygen sensor from the ECU's original engine.

Wiring

Every Honda vehicle features separate engine and under-dash wiring harnesses that connect to one another at or near the firewall or at the ECU. Depending on the vehicle, the number of connections and locations at or near the firewall or at the ECU may be different. In addition, the process can vary significantly depending on whether or not the car was offered with any sort of K-series engine as an option.

Non-Native K-Series Wiring

The non-native K-series engine swap wiring process has three major components: engine har-

Swapping K-series engines into older chassis requires a relatively intact K-series engine wiring harness as well as a custom-made sub-harness that interfaces between the K-series ECU, engine wiring harness, and chassis. Sub-harnesses can be made from scratch or sourced from a number of manufacturers. If you make your own, you need electrical schematics for your vehicle as well as for the vehicle from which the K-series ECU was sourced. You also need to source the appropriate connectors from any 2002–2004 RSX or 2002–2005 Civic Si to complete the conversion. (Photo Courtesy Hasport Performance Products)

ness, sub-harness, and charge harness. Every K-series engine swap starts with a K-series engine wiring harness. In terms of wiring, each of these chassis, which were introduced before Honda released the K-series, must be approached differently than with past B-series or H-series engine swaps where the original engine wiring harness could be modified and retained. The car's original engine wiring harness can be discarded with a K-series-compatible version taking its place.

ELECTRICAL ESSENTIALS

Once the appropriate engine wiring harness has been selected, its two large connectors simply plug directly into the ECU's A and B slots. The sub-harness connector then plugs into the ECU's remaining E slot. Not all K-series ECUs share the same pinouts. Be sure to use only one of the recommended ECUs to ensure that its pinouts are compatible with the engine wiring harness and sub-harness.

The 20-pin connector joins the sub-harness to the engine wiring harness. If you make your own sub-harness, you need to source the appropriate connector from any 2002–2004 RSX or 2002–2005 Civic Si and manually wire it into place.

Non-native K-series vehicles must use an engine wiring harness sourced from any left-hand-drive manual transmission–equipped 2002–2004 RSX, 2002–2005 Civic Si, or 2002–2006 CR-V. Harnesses sourced from automatic transmission models as well as the later-model 2005–2006 RSX may also be used but extensive modifications must be made; as such, look to the previously mentioned harnesses whenever possible.

Generally speaking, the 2002–2004 RSX Type-S harness is preferred, mostly because of its compatibility with both 5- or 6-speed transmissions and its overall flexibility. Any of the previously mentioned harnesses, however, can plug directly into compatible K-series ECU A and B connectors, resulting in an E connector and 20-pin engine wiring harness connector that must be manually wired into place.

The sub-harness is the intermediary between the K-series engine wiring harness, ECU, and the car, including the instrument cluster. It's responsible for allowing everything to communicate with one another. Sub-harnesses can be made from scratch, which requires a significant amount of experience working with Honda electrical systems as well as service manuals and electrical schematics for both your chassis and whatever ECU you plan on using. The sub-harness must connect to the ECU's E connector plug and engine wiring harness' 20-pin connector. The appropriate connectors can be sourced from a number of vehicles; the easiest is the 2002–2004 RSX or 2002–2005 Civic Si.

Aftermarket sub-harnesses can be purchased from a number of sources, which can greatly simplify the process. Aftermarket sub-harnesses offer a simple, plug-and-play solution that can allow you to get up and running in no time.

Typical sub-harnesses have six major components that plug into the ECU, the engine wiring harness, and the chassis wiring harness: an E connector that plugs directly into the ECU's remaining slot; a connector that plugs directly into the engine wiring harness' open 20-pin connector; a connector that plugs directly into the chassis wiring harness; an oxygen sensor connector; an oxygen sensor relay; and either a data link connector for monitoring error codes or another chassis wiring harness connector, depending on the chassis.

If you plan to assemble your own sub-harness, start by sourcing the appropriate connectors from any 2002–2004 RSX or 2002–2005 Civic

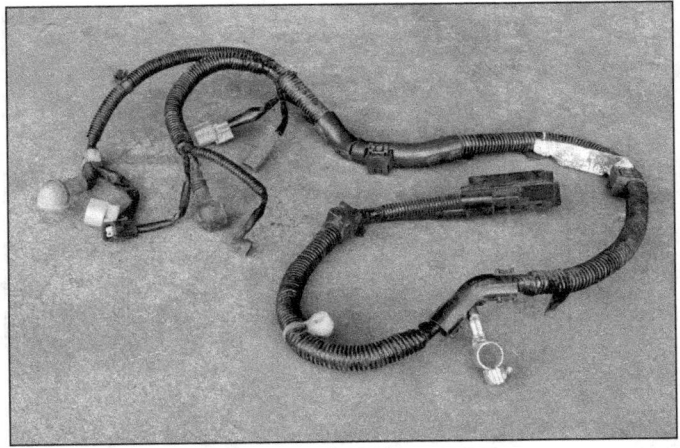

A charge harness that distributes power from the battery to the alternator, starter, and fuse box is required for every K-series engine swap. K-series charge harnesses are too short and aren't compatible with older chassis' fuse box terminals. The K-series charge harness must be modified using the vehicle's original charge harness; its length must be increased and its connections must be switched at the fuse box for compatibility.

CHAPTER 3

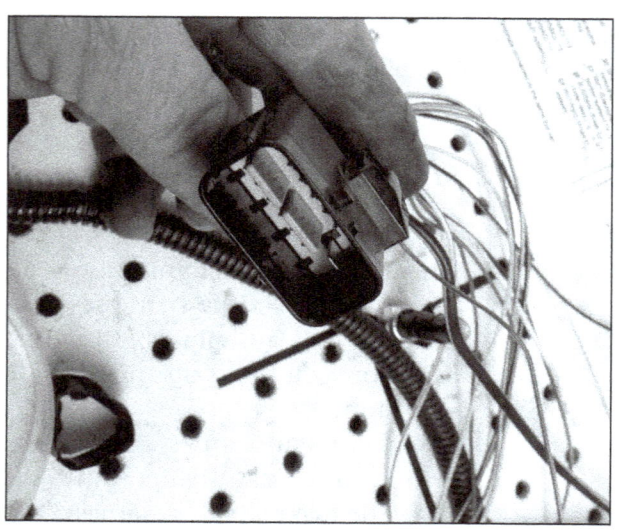

Later-model native chassis don't require any sort of sub-harness. The appropriate K-series engine wiring harness must be modified for compatibility with the chassis. When using the appropriate engine wiring harness, it simply plugs directly into the ECU as well as all of the engine and transmission sensors. (Photo Courtesy Hasport Performance Products)

Si chassis wiring harness. Be sure to retain the harness relays or source the appropriate universal relays to complete the conversion. (For wiring harness specifics, see the diagram on page 42.)

Finally, a charge harness must be prepared that sends current from the positive battery terminal to the alternator, starter, and fuse box. Native K-series vehicles feature fuse boxes that are located near the front of the vehicle, as opposed to older chassis where the fuse box and battery are positioned near the firewall. As such, K-series charge harnesses are too short. A combination of the car's original charge harness and the new engine's charge harness can be used, which eliminates significant modifications. A properly designed charge harness should span from the positive battery terminal to the starter, from the positive battery terminal to the fuse box, and from the fuse box to the alternator.

Native K-Series Wiring

Chassis that were originally offered with K-series engines or were built during the same model years are much easier to wire. An even later-model engine wiring harness must be sourced and modified to fit whether the car was originally equipped with a K-series or not. The process is very much like how older B-series or H-series engine swaps were performed. Any necessary wiring takes place at the ECU, under the hood, which is also much like you'd encounter with older B-series or H-series engine swaps, the specifics of which are addressed in the following chapters.

Non-Native K-Series Wiring Diagram

ECU E Connector (wire side)

Pin	Function	Connect To
1	Drives Fuel Pump Relay	Fuel Pump Relay (position 86)
7	Drives PGM-FI Main Relay	Main Relay (position 86)
8	Drives Oxygen Sensor Heater Control Relay	Oxygen Sensor Heater Control Relay (position 86)
9	Detects Ignition Signal	12V Ignition Switch Power; Oxygen Sensor Heater Control Relay (position 30)
15	Detects Electrical Load Detector Signal	Electrical Load Detector signal wire at chassis harness' unused ECU connector
18	Drives A/C Clutch Relay (optional)	A/C Switch signal wire at chassis harness' unused ECU connector
22	Detects Brake Pedal Position Switch Signal	Brake Pedal Position Switch Signal wire on chassis harness' unused ECU connector
26	Engine Speed Pulse Output	Tachometer signal wire at instrument cluster
31	Malfunction Indicator Lamp	Malfunction Indicator Lamp Warning Light at chassis harness' unused ECU connector

Engine Wiring Harness 20-Pin Connector (wire side)

Pin	Function	Connect To
1, 2	Reverse Lights	Corresponding wires on chassis harness
3	Vehicle Speed Sensor Signal Input	Speedometer signal wire at instrument cluster
7	Radiator Fan Control	Radiator Fan Control wire on chassis harness' unused ECU connector
9	Ignition Switch Power for Multiple Devices	Main Relay (position 87); Fuel Pump Relay (position 85); Oxygen Sensor Heater Control Relay (position 85)
10	Oxygen Sensor Heater Control	Primary Oxygen Sensor Pin 4
13	Oxygen Sensor Ground	Primary Oxygen Sensor Pin 2
14	Ignition Switch Power for ECU, fuel injectors, other sensors	Main Relay (position 87); Fuel Pump Relay (position 85); Oxygen Sensor Heater Control Relay (position 85)
15	Oxygen Sensor Reference Voltage	Primary Oxygen Sensor Pin 3; Oxygen Sensor Heater Control Relay (position 87)
16	Starter	Starter signal wire on chassis harness
18	Oil Pressure Switch	Oil pressure warning light wire on chassis harness
19	Oxygen Sensor Input	Primary Oxygen Sensor Pin 1
20	Ignition Switch Power for coils	Main Relay (position 87); Fuel Pump Relay (position 85); Oxygen Sensor Heater Control Relay (position 85)

Primary Oxygen Sensor Connector (wire side; see above Engine Wiring Harness 20-Pin Connector for associated connections)

Notes:
- Required: 2002-2004 RSX or 2002-2005 Civic Si chassis wiring harness ECU E connector, 20-pin engine wiring harness connector, and three associated relays.
- Main Relay positions 30 and 85 connect to 12V constant power.
- Fuel Pump Relay position 87 connects to fuel pump signal wire.
- Connect Alternator Signal wire at ECU connector B, pin 10, to Alternator Control wire on chassis harness' unused ECU connector
- Chassis harness pinouts vary by vehicle; consult vehicle's service manual for specific connector locations and pin designations.

CHAPTER 4

1992–2000 CIVIC AND 1994–2001 INTEGRA

Exactly 20 years after Long Beach, California, longshoremen took delivery of the first North America–bound Honda Civics, with little fanfare, the once dedicated-motorcycle company released what is arguably the most iconic of the subcompact's nearly 40-year lifespan. Its fifth-generation adaptation, manufactured and sold during the brand's 1992–1995 model years, Honda's hatchback, coupe, and sedan trio helped peak and later carry Honda performance on its shoulders. The then-revolutionary all-new unibody with its rounded egg-shaped lines and timeless looks remains beloved by true Hondaphiles, even today. Two years later, the second-generation Integra played its part and, along with the del Sol and the following generation's Civic, a lineage of destined-to-be-classic Hondas had begun.

With a heritage and fan base that runs as deep as Ford's Model T, Volkswagen's Beetle, even Porsche's 911, the Civic nameplate has stood time's test; longer, in fact, than nearly any other Japanese subcompact, second only to the Toyota Corolla, which, for all intents and purposes, has no such following. Such staying power and model recognition has made both the Civic and the Integra go-to chassis for a number of sport-compact-specific aftermarket parts manufacturers and engine swaps. The fifth-generation Civic historically lending its simplistic self as the first to receive support and various performance upgrades, such as K-series engine swaps.

To be sure, manufacturers looked to Honda's fifth-generation coupes, hatchbacks, and sedans as well as the second-generation Integra when developing the industry's first

Fifth- and sixth-generation Civics are among the most popular chassis for a K-series engine swap. That's mostly because they are among the most popular chassis to modify. Their lightweight, double-wishbone suspensions, and ability to accept parts from so many other chassis are a partial reason.

CHAPTER 4

adjustable coil-over suspensions, bolt-on turbocharger and supercharger kits, and cat-back exhaust systems before all else. Indeed, the list of companies that exist today because of Honda's golden-child generation of Civics and Integras is large.

Nevertheless, the success of Honda's mid–1990s renditions lies beyond production quantities and universal mass appeal. The fifth-generation Civic unibodies were the first to lend themselves to bolt-in engine swaps courtesy of the more-expensive Acura B-series engines and transmissions. Like many manufacturers, Honda began cross-pollinating parts among its lineup in an effort to reduce production costs as well as to simplify manufacturing. Although earlier Civics and Integras shared much, 1992 marked the year that later Integra drivetrains, suspension and electrical components, interiors, and more could be transferred with little effort. Engine mounts and brackets, electrical connectors, instrument clusters, throttle cables, braking systems, and more were all compatible.

By the time Honda's 1992 Civic was launched, engine swapping experimentation had already begun on earlier chassis but the compatibility between the 1992–1995 Civic and later 1994–2001 Integra proved to be the catalyst that launched an engine swap phenomenon. When the 170-hp Integra GS-R engine was first swapped into the sub-2,100-pound CX hatchback, well, the performance world was all but forced to take the Honda name seriously. The 1992–1995 Civic later even went on to be the first bearer of H-series and K-series engine swaps.

Whether Honda knew it or not (and they likely didn't), the fifth-generation Civic's mechanical simplicity and no-nonsense parts interchangeability with other chassis was enough to spark a new generation of otherwise timid tuners and enthusiasts.

Honda didn't just revolutionize the auto industry with the most recognizable subcompact of all time; it revolutionized the world. Its two-decade-old technology continues to rattle modern-day performance Goliaths such as Mitsubishi's and Subaru's AWD turbocharged Evo and WRX (even the newest Mustangs and Camaros with their exponentially more powerful engines). Its 20-plus-year-old CX and VX hatchbacks continue to reap better mileage than most any of today's mass-produced hybrids, including Honda's own.

Honda's 1990s lineage of Civics and Integras remains among the most tunable platforms in automotive history. With their double-wishbone suspensions, lightweight structures, and capable braking, they're the makings for record-setting race cars or even durable, all-around daily drivers. All of this makes them the most likely candidates for K-series engine swaps and a good place to start in terms of analyzing the process as it pertains to just about any Honda.

No other Honda is as popular to modify as the 1992–1995 Civic. The chassis shares the same engine bay as the 1994–2001 Integra, which led to its initial popularity. You can choose among hatchback, coupe, and sedan body styles in a variety of trims that range from the stripped-down CX hatchback to the feature-loaded EX four-door.

The remaining chapters that cover other vehicles are somewhat shorter and less detailed; that's simply because much of the engine swap process that applies to each of the chassis in this chapter remain universal to almost everything else.

1992–1995 Civic

Honda's fifth-generation Civic was offered in three body configurations (hatchback, coupe, and sedan) with a variety of trim levels that include the Si, EX, EX-S, LX, DX, CX, and VX. All three body styles share a similar chassis with the 1994–2001 Integra, which helped ensure their compatibility with twin-cam B-series engine swaps, suspension and braking components, as well as their popularity among enthusiasts. Their Integra-like engine bays don't necessarily make them any better candidates for an engine transplant than any other generation Civic because the K-series remains native to none of them.

Honda introduced its fifth-generation Civic hatchback for the 1992 model year in four trim levels: Si (EH3), DX, CX, and VX (EH2). The Civic Si features the 125-hp SOHC VTEC D16Z6 while the DX and CX were sold with the less-powerful D15B7 and D15B8, respectively. The Civic VX was offered with an interesting combination of the two: the 92-hp D15Z1. Known as a VTEC-E engine, the D15Z1 makes use of an emissions-conscious version of Honda's famed variable valve timing that achieves nearly 50 mpg. The CX and VX remain popular engine swap candidates because of their stripped-down chassis and extremely light weight, less than 2,100 pounds for 1992–1993 versions. Si models are equally as popular but for altogether different reasons, such as their power sunroofs and rear disc brakes.

The Civic coupe, which wasn't offered until 1993, is available in EX, EX-S (EJ1), and DX (EJ2) configurations. The EX and EX-S are very much like the Si hatchback, featuring the same SOHC VTEC engine and rear disc brakes. The DX was sold with the less-powerful D15B7 and remains the lightest-weight Civic coupe of the period.

Honda also reintroduced the Civic sedan for the 1992 model year, which is available in EX (EH9), LX, and DX (EG8) trims. Like the coupe, the EX sedan is similar to the Si (powertrain-wise) while the remaining trims were sold with the same non-VTEC engines used throughout the rest of the Civic line.

Chassis Pros and Cons

Honda's fifth-generation Civic is considered the pinnacle of small-car performance for many enthusiasts. It's slightly larger than the previous generation (but not too large) has a longer, more manageable wheelbase, and a much more aerodynamic shape. The body style's front end also allows for a suspension that features more shock travel than previous Civics could accommodate. Even the heaviest of fifth-generation Civics (the EX sedan) is diminutive compared to today's entry-level Hondas. Perhaps best of all, many of the Integra's suspension and braking components are easily transferable across the Civic line thanks to similar chassis.

In terms of K-series engine swaps, it's difficult to do much better than the 1992–1995 Civic. The chassis requires only minimal fabrication, which includes removing the right-side framerail bracket from the chassis. Minor trimming of the hood's underside webbing is also required with some engine and aftermarket engine mount kit combinations or if power steering is retained. With most engine mount kits, models equipped with ABS must either convert to non-ABS braking systems or relocate the system's pump because it may interfere with the K-series exhaust manifold. Finally, A/C is not compatible with right-hand-drive models due to interference issues.

1993–1997 del Sol

Honda's del Sol is very much like its sibling Civic hatchback, coupe, and sedan trio. They're all built on the same platform, share similar electronics, and accept K-series engine transplants in the same manner. Considered the successor to the CRX, the only generation of del Sols released in the United States is available in three trims: S, Si, and VTEC. Despite its wide range of more powerful engines, the del Sol was not nearly as popular as Honda's first two-seater front-wheel-drive sports car.

In late 1992 Honda introduced the del Sol S (EG1 and later EH6), which shares the same D15B7 non-VTEC engine as the rest of the Civic line. In 1996 the D15B7 was replaced with the similar D16Y7. Higher-end Si (EH6) models were sold with the same D16Z6 VTEC engine that can be found in the Civic until 1996 when they too were updated with an OBD-II version of the same engine: the D16Y8. The top-of-the-line del Sol VTEC (EG2) was introduced during the model's second production year and, like the rest of the car's lineage, received two engines with its mid-model refresh that coincided with the implementation of OBD-II electronics. The del Sol's B16A3 and later B16A2 are nearly identical to each other and, at 160 hp, are the model's most powerful engines.

Chassis Pros and Cons

The del Sol's curb weight is as attractive as any other Civic of this era but because of lower manufacturing

1992–1995 Civic Chassis Codes

1992–1995 Civic CX, DX, VX Hatchback	EH2
1992–1995 Civic Si Hatchback	EH3
1993–1995 Civic EX Coupe	EJ1
1993 Civic EX-S Coupe	EJ1
1993–1995 Civic DX Coupe	EJ2
1992–1995 Civic DX, LX Sedan	EG8
1992–1995 Civic EX Sedan	EH9

1993–1997 del Sol Chassis Codes

1993–1995 del Sol S	EG1
1994–1997 del Sol VTEC	EG2
1996–1997 del Sol S	EH6
1993–1997 del Sol Si	EH6

1996–2000 Civic Chassis Codes

1996–2000 Civic CX, DX Hatchback	EJ6
1996–2000 Civic DX Coupe	EJ6
1996–2000 Civic HX Coupe	EJ7
1996–2000 Civic EX Coupe	EJ8
1999–2000 Civic Si Coupe	EM1
1996–2000 Civic DX, LX Sedan	EJ6
1999–2000 Civic VP Sedan	EJ6
1996–2000 Civic EX Sedan	EJ8

numbers, aren't as readily available. In terms of engine swap practicality, they're every bit as accepting of any 2.0L or 2.4L K-series engine as any other Civic of the period and, like the Civic, many Integra components are easily transferable.

Although not nearly as popular of a candidate for a K-series engine transplant as other Civics may be, the del Sol shares the same pros and cons. Like the Civic, minor fabrication is required, ABS and hood-clearance challenges are present with most engine mount kits, and A/C is not compatible with right-hand-drive models.

1996–2000 Civic

When it comes to the sixth-generation Civic, there's a lot to choose from. Like the previous generation, Honda offered hatchback, coupe, and sedan models in a variety of trims. Like the previous generation, the 1996–2000 Civic shares much of its heritage with the 1994–2001 Integra, making the engine transplant process between the two similar. The sixth-generation Civic retains the model's famous double-wishbone suspension and features a more unique, rounded, and taller design.

Honda introduced its latest hatchback in two trims: DX and CX (EJ6). Like previous CX models, the 1996–2000 version is appointed with options sparingly, again making it the lightest of the bunch. Both were sold with the 106-hp D16Y7. Unfortunately, rear disc brakes were not an option for sixth-generation Civic hatchbacks but, as you'd expect, like all Civics of this era, Integra parts are easily transferable.

The Civic coupe is available in EX (EJ8), DX (EJ6), HX (EJ7), and Si (EM1) trims. The DX received the familiar 1.6L non-VTEC engine that the hatchback features while the HX was fitted with a slightly more powerful VTEC-E engine (the D16Y5), which is similar to the previous generation's VTEC-E power plant. It's no surprise that the EX was sold with Honda's higher-end single-cam VTEC D16Y8 that remained the most powerful Civic until the Si's introduction in 1999, which features the del Sol's 160-hp twin-cam B16A2 engine. The Si also features a number of performance add-ons, such as a close-ratio transmission, stiffer suspension components, rear disc brakes, and a front shock-tower brace.

Honda offered its sedan in several configurations, including EX (EJ8), LX, DX (EJ6), GX (EN1), and VP (EJ6) trims. EX and LX models feature the same engines as their coupe counterparts, as does the DX and Honda's new trim, the VP, which is a slightly upscale version of the DX. The GX model, which operates on natural gas was available for fleet purchase only and is a poor choice for any engine swap.

Chassis Pros and Cons

Like the fifth-generation Civic, the 1996–2000 body style is just as customizable and just as accepting for a K-series engine transplant. A more modern Civic also means slightly more weight but it's a small tradeoff for a newer chassis that arguably has accumulated fewer miles.

Unlike other Civics, the 1996–2000 body style does not require any cutting when performing a K-series engine transplant. In fact, it remains one of the few truly bolt-in K-series candidates. Like the previous Civic, A/C is not compatible with right-hand-drive models and the hood's underside must also be trimmed if power steering is retained. Models with ABS must also either convert to non-ABS braking systems or relocate their components because the system's pump interferes with the K-series exhaust manifold.

1994–2001 Integra

Acura's third-generation Integra was its final version for American consumers, only to be replaced by the RSX in 2002. Its eight-year production span was among the longest for any Honda product, though, partly because of its performance-orientated nature and entry-level cost. Introduced for the 1994 model year, the third-generation Integra was available to North American consumers in GS-R, GS, LS, RS, and Type R trims in both hatchback and sedan configurations.

1992–2000 CIVIC AND 1994–2001 INTEGRA

Although heavier than its Civic counterpart, the second-generation Integra remains one of the most popular Honda chassis. Every model features a twin-camshaft B-series engine, four-wheel disc brakes, and can accept almost any K-series powertrain. Minor fabrication is necessary when performing a K-series engine swap into any 1994–2001 Integra chassis. However, the process has long been perfected.

1994–2001 Integra Chassis Codes

1994–2001 Integra GS-R Hatchback	DC2
1997–2001 (exclude 1999) Integra Type R Hatchback	DC2
1994–2001 Integra LS Hatchback	DC4
1995–1996 Integra LS Special Edition Hatchback	DC4
1994–1999 Integra RS Hatchback	DC4
1997–2001 Integra GS Hatchback	DC4
1994–2001 Integra LS Sedan	DB7
1994–1996 Integra RS Sedan	DB7
1997–2001 Integra GS Sedan	DB7
1996 Integra LS Special Edition Sedan	DB7
1994–2001 Integra GS-R Sedan	DB8

Arguably the more popular of the two, Acura's three-door model was available in all five trims of which the GS, LS, and RS (DC4) are equipped with the entry-level 1.8L non-VTEC B-series engine, the B18B1. GS-R models (DC2) were sold with the more powerful B18C1 that benefits from VTEC (among other things) while the Type R (DC2), which was offered in limited quantities and only in a three-door layout in the United States, was sold with the 190-hp B18C5 engine and a close-ratio gearbox with a limited-slip differential.

Although the Integra sedan wasn't nearly as popular as the three-door, it shares a similar chassis, which means it benefits from the Integra's already adept suspension and powertrain. The same GS, LS, RS (DB7), and GS-R (DB8) trims are available, excluding the Type R, with the same 1.8L non-VTEC and VTEC engines.

Chassis Pros and Cons

All Integras are fitted with large four-wheel disc brakes from the factory (the Type Rs being the biggest) and one of the most impressive double-wishbone suspensions Honda has ever built. Such double-wishbone layouts allow for extensive suspension movement and articulation and lend themselves especially well to modifications.

Similar to the 1992–1995 Civic, minor fabrication is required and A/C is not compatible with right-hand-drive models. Unlike the Civic, though, the Integra offers the most space in front of the engine and the ability to use a full-size radiator and factory A/C condenser, even with a K-series engine transplant. Despite the Integra's alternate ABS pump location compared to Civic chassis, with most engine mount kits the ABS must either be removed, converted, or modified to clear the necessary right-side framerail bracket.

Engine and Transmission

Compared to B-series or H-series engine swaps, the K-series process is much more involved. The engine is rotated 180-degrees to whatever D- or B-series the car was originally sold with, which results in a number of aspects that must be customized that didn't need to be addressed with past engine swaps.

Choosing the right K-series engine can be challenging. Beyond cost, you have to consider horsepower, potential upgrades, ECU, engine wiring harness compatibility, and any clearance considerations. Selecting the right transmission is just as crucial. Not every aftermarket engine mount kit is compatible with every K-series transmission, so be sure to confirm whether or not a particular transmission may be used before moving forward.

Refer to Chapter 1 for help in selecting the engine and transmission that is right for you. Considerations such as horsepower, torque, type of i-VTEC, budget, and clearance issues must all be addressed before choosing an engine. Likewise, you must consider the number of gears, gear ratios, and budget when selecting a transmission. Once you address each of these considerations, you can select the appropriate engine mount kit. All popular engine mount kits, such as those from Hasport and Hybrid Racing, are compatible with almost any K-series engine and were designed to be used with a variety of different K-series-compatible transmissions, depending on the kit.

Mounts

Once you select an engine and transmission combination, you can choose the appropriate engine mount kit. Parts compatibility and installation processes vary slightly among each manufacturer's mounts, so checking with them first before ordering is a good idea. The following are some important points to consider.

1992–1995 Civic, 1993–1997 del Sol, and 1994–2001 Integra

Hasport offers three engine mount kits for these chassis: EGK1, EGK2, and EGK3. The EGK1 is the K-series engine mount kit in its simplest form and is compatible with 2002–2006 RSX, 2002–2005 Civic Si, 2001–2005 Civic Type R, 2001–2006 Integra Type R, 2006–2011 Civic Si, and 2007–2011 Civic Type R transmissions.

Hasport's EGK2 kit bolts up to the same transmissions but features two mounting positions for standard or lower engine placement, which allows 2.4L engine compatibility without having to modify the hood.

The EGK3 kit is a single-position kit, like the EGK1 but is compatible with 2003–2007 Accord, 2006–2008 Accord Euro R, and 2004–2008 TSX transmissions.

Regardless of which Hasport kit you select for these chassis, slight clearance adjustments must be made to the hood's underside if power steering is retained. Unlike other engine mount kits, Hasport's kits provide ample power steering rack clearance at the subframe in all positions, without modification. Finally, EGK1 and EGK3 kits require minor hood trimming when using 2.4L engines.

Retaining power steering or opting for a taller-deck 2.4L engine means hood clearance is sacrificed. The hood's underside structural webbing must be trimmed to allow clearance for the power steering pump pulley. In the case of 2.4L engines, it has to clear the valve cover and throttle body. Use an angle grinder to carefully cut the webbing free from the hood.

Hybrid Racing's engine mount kit for these chassis is also compatible with the same RSX, Civic Si, and Type R transmissions and offers two mounting positions but for altogether different reasons than

Hybrid Racing was the first company to offer a mass-produced engine mount kit designed for K-series engine swaps into the 1992–1995 Civic and 1994–2001 Integra chassis. The company's mounts have since been updated, are constructed of high-quality steel brackets and CNC-machined billet aluminum; they feature a variety of bushing hardnesses to suit any application. (Courtesy Hybrid Racing)

Left Side, Right Side: Which Is Which?

Right-hand-drive conversions as well as the prevalence of K-series engine swaps throughout the world make referring to either side of a vehicle by its driver- or passenger-side orientation confusing. For example, a North American Civic's driver-side engine mount is entirely different than a Japanese one. Driver-side configuration may change but a vehicle's left and right sides don't. A vehicle's layout can best be described from the perspective of sitting in either of its seats, which makes driver- or passenger-seat orientation irrelevant to the vehicle's left or right sides.

All of this makes describing locations within the chassis less confusing for everyone and relative to any chassis. ∎

1992–2000 CIVIC AND 1994–2001 INTEGRA

Hasport's kits. An alternate mounting position allows for additional clearance near the power steering rack, if equipped. Hood clearancing must also be performed if power steering or a larger-displacement 2.4L engine is used.

1996–2000 Civic

Hasport offers two engine mount kits for the later-model Civic: EKK1 and EKK2. The differences are simple: The EKK1 kit is compatible with the original subframe while the EKK2 kit was designed to be used with 1992–1995 Civic and 1994–2001 Integra subframes. Like Hasport's EGK2 kit for the older chassis, the EKK2 kit allows for additional clearance with 2.4L engines without having to modify the hood thanks to its dual-height design, which positions the engine 3/4-inch lower when mounted accordingly. Of course, you must carefully consider ground clearance before settling on any kit that positions the engine and transmission any lower. Both kits require hood modifications if power steering is retained.

Hybrid Racing also offers two engine mount kits for the 1996–2000 Civic, one that's compatible with the original subframe and the other with the older-style Civic or Integra subframe. Like the older chassis, both Hasport and Hybrid Racing kits allow ample power steering rack clearance and are compatible with the same RSX, Civic Si, and Type R transmissions.

For 1996–2000 Civic owners, there's another option that allows the less-expensive 2003–2007 Accord transmission as well as 2006–2008 Accord Euro R and 2004–2008 TSX gearboxes to be used in the sixth-generation Civic chassis. Provided the older-style Civic or Integra subframe is used, Hasport's EGK1, EGK2, and EGK3 kits designed for the 1992–1995 Civic are all compatible with the 1996–2000 Civic chassis once the subframe conversion has been completed and the appropriate left-side framerail bracket (Hasport PN EKLHB2) has been installed. Hasport's special bracket essentially converts any 1996–2000 Civic's left-side framerail to be more like the 1992–1995 styles.

Car Preparation

If you're planning a K-series engine swap, you need a certain level of mechanical competency, such as knowing how to remove the original engine. Still, there are several key points that wouldn't necessarily be addressed during a standard engine removal that apply to K-series engine conversions. The K-series engine transplant begins by removing the old engine and drivetrain.

Draining the Fluids

Start by draining the A/C refrigerant. A qualified professional should evacuate the system's contents appropriately and safely before moving on. Once the car is raised on jack stands or a lift, drain the transmission fluid, power steering fluid (if equipped), and coolant from the radiator. If the original engine will be stored for a significant period of time, recycled, or sold, drain the oil and coolant from the engine block.

Removing the Ancillaries

Disconnect and remove the battery, battery tray (1996–2000 Civic only), and bolts that connect the engine harness to the chassis. Next, disconnect the engine wiring harness from its connectors near the shock

Perhaps no other company is as synonymous with Honda engine swaps as Hasport. The Honda engine swap parts manufacturer offers more K-series engine swap solutions than anyone else, each of which are based on precision-cut steel brackets and CNC-machined billet aluminum mounts. Its 1996–2000 Civic kit was designed to allow almost any K-series engine to bolt into place without any cutting, welding, or fabrication.

Hasport is renowned for its unique solutions, including one-of-a-kind kits that allow less-expensive Accord-style transmissions to be used on 1996–2000 Civic chassis provided a 1992–1995 Civic or 1994–2001 Integra subframe has been swapped into place. Simple, bolt-on subframe conversions such as these are partially what make the sixth-generation Civic so popular.

HONDA K-SERIES ENGINE SWAPS

Company Profile: Hasport Performance Products

The Honda engine-mount business is a busy one these days. More than a dozen companies have come and gone over the years but none have outlasted one of the industry's pioneers: Hasport. For nearly 15 years Phoenix, Arizona-based Hasport has been conceptualizing, developing, and mass-producing Honda-specific engine transplant kits designed to retrofit larger, more powerful engines into smaller chassis.

Headed up by Brian Gillespie, the man responsible for the engine mount maker's marketing and product development, the company's first Honda engine swap took place in Hasport owner Keith Gillespie's (Brian's brother) nearby salvage yard, Honda Auto Salvage. It has since been shut down but in its prime, it provided the Hasport development team with just about any engine, transmission, and chassis it needed to not only devise new engine mount kits but also to ensure their compatibility with various body styles, trim levels, and chassis types. It's that sort of attention to detail, extensive lineup of engine mount kits, and the company's renowned customer service that have made Hasport the go-to engine mount solution for Honda fans across the globe.

Hasport has expanded beyond its precision-cut-steel and CNC-machined billet-aluminum engine mount kits to becoming the leader in engine swap solutions. Today, the company offers plug-and-play wiring harnesses, axles, shift linkages, cable-to-hydraulic transmission conversion kits, cooling system adapters, and much more. Over the years, Hasport has taken what was once a process reserved for skilled mechanics with high-end fabrication and welding equipment and turned it into a weekend project that even entry-level tuners may be able to take on.

Hasport makes full use of the latest technology and equipment to produce some of the industry's finest engine mounts. Each kit is designed in-house using industry-standard CAD software and then computer analyzed for structural integrity before being CNC machined on-site. Hasport mounts are machined from solid 6061-T6 aluminum at tolerances of less than .001 inch. All of this allows the company to offer a lifetime warranty on every engine mount kit it sells.

Hasport's loyalty to the Honda engine swap process doesn't end with its problem-solving brackets and mounts. Visit your favorite online Honda forum or pick up any Honda-related magazine and you're likely to see the Hasport name. Hasport and Gillespie are renowned for their willingness to share what was once considered top-secret engine swap information with the everyday Honda fan, helping ensure would-be engine swappers don't make the same sort of mistakes the pioneers once did. The world of high-performance Hondas is better for it. ■

Hasport continues to stay at the forefront of the Honda engine swap movement through its racing efforts. The company's road racing CRX has seen all manner of engine swaps, most recently a supercharged K-series engine (shown) that's since been replaced by a 60-degree, J-series V-6 power plant. (Photo Courtesy Hasport Performance Products)

Hasport's state-of-the-art facility and close relationship with local salvage yards allows the company to conceptualize, develop, and produce nearly any Honda-based engine mount kit in only a few days. In recent years, Hasport has been at the forefront of almost every new K-series and J-series Honda engine swap.

Before the engine and transmission can be pulled, the axles must be removed. Disconnect the outboard sides from each knuckle assembly and pry the inboard sides free from the transmission or intermediate shaft. To do this, the knuckles must be disconnected from the lower control arms and articulated away from the chassis, which allows each axle's outboard side to pull free.

The lower tie brace positioned in front of the subframe on the Integra chassis must be removed before installing a K-series engine and transmission. Clearance is minimal, which means that space must be provided for the larger K-series transmission. The B-series rear engine mount, heater hoses, and shift linkage are also waiting to be removed.

tower and from the underhood fuse box and remove the positive battery cable. Remove the wheels, shift linkage, exhaust A-pipe, catalytic converter, fuel feed and return lines, as well as the throttle cable.

Unlike other engine swaps, the radiator must also be removed along with the cooling fan and both radiator hoses. Both heater hoses exiting the heater core at the firewall as well as the brake booster vacuum hose must also be removed. Using a line-wrench, remove the hydraulic clutch line assembly that connects the clutch master cylinder to the clutch slave cylinder.

If A/C will be eliminated, remove the system's lines, condenser, wiring harness, and cooling fan. The compressor can remain attached to the engine. If power steering will be eliminated, remove the system's lines and reservoir. The pump can remain connected to the engine.

Removing the Axles

The axles must also be removed. There are two methods of doing so. Start by removing the axle-retaining nut located on the center of the knuckle's outboard side. Use a pneumatic air ratchet or large breaker bar to do this. Disconnect and remove the shock's lower fork from its lower control arm and set it aside. Next, remove the lower ball joint retaining nut and disconnect the ball joint using a ball joint separator or, the second method to reduce the risk of damaging the ball joint's grease boot is to use a dead-blow hammer to strike the side of the lower control arm near the ball joint. When struck properly, the ball joint dislodges from its knuckle, allowing the assembly to swing upward and outward. Once articulated appropriately and with the retaining nut removed, the knuckle assembly can be swung away from the axle's outboard side. Pry the axle's inboard side free from the transmission or intermediate shaft (depending on the side) and remove the axle.

Removing the Mounts

Disconnect the rear engine bracket along with the front engine and transmission brackets so that the engine and transmission are held in place by its left- and right-side mounts and remove the engine. With the engine removed, unbolt the rear engine mount that's positioned on the subframe and remove it along with the two front insulator mounts. All original engine and transmission brackets and mounts should be removed from the chassis before installing the new engine. On Integras, the tie brace that's positioned near the subframe must also be removed.

ABS Considerations

If the chassis is equipped with ABS, in most cases it must either be modified or removed. The exception is the 1998–2001 Integra, which was updated midway through its production cycle with a more compact ABS pump. With 1994–1997 Integras that feature the larger ABS pump you must either upgrade to the newer version, remove the ABS system entirely, or relocate the original pump away from the right-side framerail bracket.

Systems found on the 1992–1995 Civic and 1993–1997 del Sol, which are located near the firewall and interfere with K-series exhaust manifolds, must be removed entirely. Later-model 1996–2000 Civics that

CHAPTER 4

ABS clearance is a concern for almost every Integra chassis. Solutions include converting the braking system to a non-ABS system, relocating the ABS pump, or upgrading to the more compact pump found on later-model 1998–2001 Integras. The smaller pump allows necessary clearance for the right-side framerail bracket and mount assembly.

are equipped with ABS can, in some cases, retain them depending on the combination of exhaust manifold and engine mounts used.

Fortunately, each of these chassis are available in non-ABS configurations and that means the ABS conversion can be completed to factory specifications using parts sourced directly from Honda.

To eliminate ABS, remove the ABS pump from underneath the hood along with its lines and proportioning valve. Source the appropriate non-ABS proportioning valve from any non-ABS Civic, del Sol, or Integra and reconnect the master cylinder's and rear wheel's brake lines to it. Replace the two front wheels' lines with the shorter non-ABS versions and connect them to the new proportioning valve. Be sure to bleed the system according to the factory service manual.

Subframe Considerations

When swapping into a 1996–2000 Civic, whether or not to use a 1992–1995 Civic or 1994–2001 Integra subframe must be considered. Most aftermarket engine mount kits are compatible with the original later-model subframe; however, there are advantages to the older subframe. Additional clearance in front of the engine and the ability to use shorter, more optimally aligned axles are just two. A subframe swap also provides better weight distribution, especially over the front tires, because the engine and transmission are moved farther back; this allows almost any K-series intake manifold to fit, including the larger 2006–2011 Civic Si's.

If you plan to do a subframe swap, now is the time to do it. Any 1992–1995 Civic or 1994–2001 Integra subframe can be used along with the corresponding lower control arm assemblies, compliance arms and bushings, steering rack (manual or power-assisted), steering rack U-joint, and mounting bolts. Be sure to use the appropriate mounting bolts that correspond to the subframe; the 1996–2000 Civic's subframe mounting bolts are not compatible with older units. The original knuckle assemblies and lower shock forks can be retained.

For manual steering applications, any manual-steering-equipped 1992–2000 Civic subframe must be used because all Integra subframes of this period include provisions for power steering. For power-steering applications, select Civic subframes can be used; however, Integra subframes are preferred and provide the quickest steering ratio among all comparable chassis.

When removing the subframe, support it with a floor jack. Disconnect the lower control arms and mounting hardware and remove it from the chassis. Save all of the components and hardware until the new subframe is in place.

Clearance Considerations

The K-series is a tall engine, at least 2 inches taller than D-series and B-series engines. If mounted with factory ground clearance retained, the engine protrudes well above the hoodline. As such, aftermarket engine mount manufacturers have designed their kits to position the engine lower, allowing for clearance underneath the hood but with compromised ground clearance because the oil pan now sits lower than the subframe. Suspension ride height should be adjusted appropriately; take this into consideration once the engine has been installed.

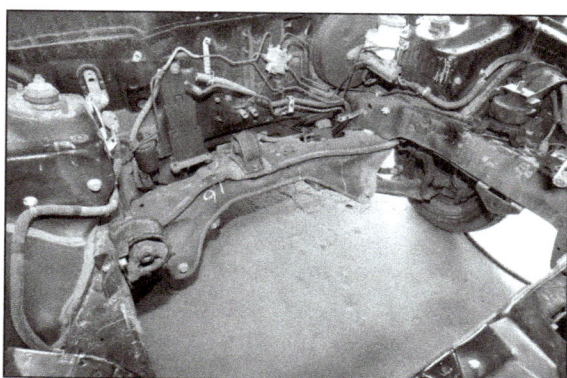

A number of aftermarket engine mount kits are compatible with the 1996–2000 Civic's original subframe (shown). However, swapping one from a 1992–1995 Civic or 1994–2001 Integra has its benefits, including increased clearance in front of the engine once installed and more optimally aligned axles.

1992–2000 CIVIC AND 1994–2001 INTEGRA

Larger-displacement 2.4L engines are 3/4 inch taller than 2.0L versions, such as this K20A3. Even with 2.0L engines, clearance is limited, and the hood's underside must be trimmed if power steering is retained. Be sure to consider ride height and hood clearance carefully before settling on a tall-deck engine.

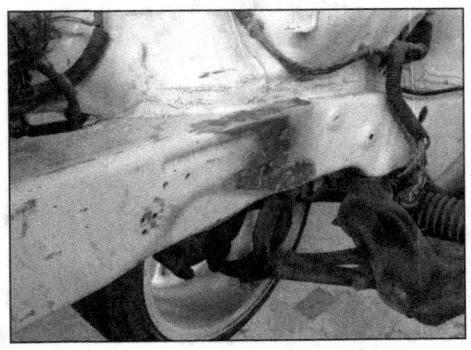

Once the original bracket has been removed, use an angle grinder to smooth the surface. To retain a factory appearance, use body filler to close up the openings from the original spot welding and sand the surface smooth. Finish up by masking off the area surrounding the bracket and prime and paint the area to avoid rust. (Photo Courtesy Hasport Performance Products)

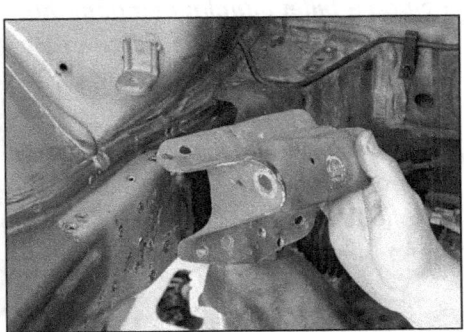

The right-side framerail bracket must be removed from every 1992–1995 Civic, 1993–1997 del Sol, and 1994–2001 Integra. Start by drilling out the bracket's spot welds and break it free using a pry bar. Avoid cutting the bracket off. A clean, smooth surface must be retained for the aftermarket bracket, which is installed next, to sit properly.

Larger 2.4L engines are even taller. Unless a dual-height engine mount kit, such as the one offered by Hasport, is used the hood's underside substructure must be trimmed near the valve cover and throttle body. Be sure to mark carefully and make any cuts after the engine's been installed to prevent removing too much material. Hood clearance must also be increased (regardless of engine type) if power steering is retained to allow clearance for the system's drive pulley. Again, mark and cut once the engine and power steering pulley are in place. For best results, remove the hood and carefully lay it on a soft surface before cutting. Use a grinder and make slow, careful cuts to avoid damaging the hood. Follow up with a sanding bit to deburr any sharp edges.

Right-Side Framerail Bracket

Regardless of the engine mount kit used, the right-side bracket located on the chassis of every 1992–1995 Civic, 1993–1997 del Sol, and 1994-2001 Integra must be removed. (When swapping into a 1996-2000 Civic chassis, this step can be skipped; instead, simply bolt the supplied bracket to the framerail.) Basic fabrication and cutting skills are necessary; you will also need a drill and angle grinder. Use a center punch to mark each of the existing bracket's spot welds and drill a hole through each of them using a 1/8-inch pilot drill bit. Follow up with a spot-weld-removing drill bit or standard 3/8-inch drill bit and remove the bracket using either a large pry bar or an air chisel.

If the bracket is stubborn and won't pry loose, check that each of the spot welds have been properly drilled out before continuing and risking damage to the framerail. Once the bracket is removed, use an angle grinder to clean up stray metal left by the drilling process and smooth the surface. Bare metal is now exposed; now's a good time to fill the original spot weld holes with body filler and prime and paint the area to avoid rust.

Hybrid Racing's kit requires an additional step that must be made to prepare the underside of the framerail. Drill out and remove the steel alignment tab that was originally used to locate the front transmission mount so that the framerail surface is completely flat. Follow the same procedure as above for drilling out the spot welds and painting the exposed surface.

Place the new right-side framerail bracket flush along the framerail so that its elongated holes on its bottom side are centered over what was previously the right-side insulator mount's mounting holes. Locate the two corresponding holes along the top of the bracket, mark their center-points using a punch,

CHAPTER 4

Once the new right-side framerail bracket has been properly positioned and the chassis has been modified, slip the supplied bolts through the framerail and thread them into the pre-existing framerail nuts. Use the provided nuts and washers to tighten the bracket to the pre-existing framerail nuts. This is a Hasport bracket; if a Hybrid Racing bracket is used, the raised section of metal on the framerail's underside must be drilled out and removed.

and drill 1/2-inch holes into the chassis, starting with a 1/8-inch pilot bit (the exact process may vary slightly between engine mount kits). Using the supplied hardware, slide the bolts through the holes, threading them into the pre-existing framerail nuts. Use the supplied nuts to secure the bolts from underneath.

Left-Side Framerail Bracket

When swapping into any chassis other than the 1996–2000 Civic, simply reuse the original framerail

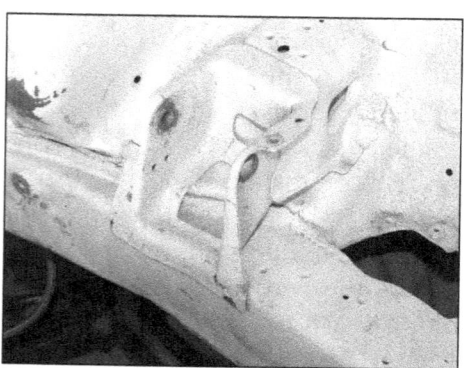

Later-model 1996–2000 Civics feature a removable left-side framerail mount that must be unbolted and set aside. Bolt the aftermarket framerail bracket in its place using the supplied hardware before installing the engine and transmission. (Photo Courtesy Hasport Performance Products)

bracket located on the left side of the engine bay.

Engine mount kits designed for the 1996–2000 Civic include the appropriate left-side framerail bracket, which simply bolts onto the framerail using the existing or supplied hardware.

Rear Subframe Bracket or Mount

Bolt the supplied aftermarket engine mount kit's rear brackets or mount (depending on the kit and chassis) to the car's rear subframe using the existing or supplied hardware (depending on the kit). If a 1992–1995 Civic or 1994–2001 Integra subframe is going to be used in a 1996–2000 Civic, it should already be in place.

Fortunately, every aftermarket engine mount manufacturer has designed its left-side mounts to be compatible with the left-side framerail bracket on 1992–1995 Civics, 1993–1997 del Sols, and 1994–2001 Integras. Nothing has to be modified. Simply remove the original D- or B-series mount to make way for the K-series version.

Depending on the manufacturer, a rear mount or bracket must be bolted onto the subframe. Hasport kits include a billet aluminum mount that bolts onto the subframe followed by an intermediary steel bracket that connects the mount to the transmission. Regardless of whether the engine and transmission will be installed from above or below, bolt the rear mount into place now.

Engine Preparation

Now's a good time to give the K-series donor engine a thorough review. It's easy for an engine to incur some damage during shipping or while in storage. Verify that each

Be sure to thoroughly inspect the engine before installing it. The throttle position sensor is one of the most common components damaged during storage or shipping. Not all K-series throttle position sensors are the same. Be sure to source the appropriate sensor from the same engine or source an aftermarket version from K-Tuned.

1992–2000 CIVIC AND 1994–2001 INTEGRA

As with damaged throttle position sensors, broken plastic thermostat housings are common. Be sure to source a replacement from the same engine. Several thermostat housings are available. They all bolt to the engine, but feature different outlets that direct the lower radiator hose into a variety of different directions.

Depending on which style of transmission is used, the aftermarket engine mount kit's rear bracket may be installed in two ways. For RSX-style transmissions (right), simply bolt the bracket onto the two exposed bolt holes, just below the vehicle speed sensor and to the left of the differential. For Accord-style transmissions (left), the bracket is fastened into place using the two bolt holes that normally attach the transmission to the engine block, just to the right of the differential.

Regardless of the transmission used, both 12-mm studs on top of the case must be removed to prepare for the aftermarket transmission bracket. The studs will not be reused and can be set aside.

Tall-deck 2.4L engines must use a different timing-chain-side engine bracket than that found on 2.0L engines. The bracket's hardware passes through the three exposed bolt holes (shown) in the timing chain cover then into the engine. Larger-displacement 2.4L engines can be distinguished by the bolt holes' nearly equal spacing between each other. The lower bolt hole on 2.0L engines is positioned higher.

sensor is in good condition before beginning. If the throttle position sensor is damaged, be sure to replace it with the appropriate sensor. Unlike older Honda engines, not all K-series throttle position sensors are alike.

Inspect the plastic thermostat housing; they can easily crack and, like the throttle position sensor, must be replaced with the appropriate piece for proper hose alignment.

Depending on the engine, the wiring harness may also need to be removed and fitted with the appropriate one. Be sure the harness is plugged into the appropriate connectors and temporarily tuck its ECU plugs out of the way.

Except for the right-side engine bracket that's located along the timing chain cover, remove all remaining mounting brackets from the engine and transmission. Temporarily remove the alternator for additional clearance as well as the exhaust manifold, if equipped; an aftermarket unit must be used, which should be installed after the engine is in place. If using Hasport's EGK3 kit with an Accord or TSX transmission, remove the two bolts fastening the engine block to the transmission near the differential. Hasport's rear bracket will attach here later.

Finish up by removing the two mounting studs on top of the transmission, no matter which kit or transmission is used.

Now's also a good time to clean the engine as well as the engine bay and perform any maintenance before setting it into place. If the clutch, flywheel, water pump, or any gaskets are in need of replacement, do so now. If a different intake manifold is going to be used, swap that into place now as well.

2.4L Engine Considerations

If a 2.4L K-series engine is going to be used, be sure that the

HONDA K-SERIES ENGINE SWAPS

appropriate right-side engine bracket is in place. Because of deck-height variations between 2.0L and 2.4L engines, a different bracket must be used. The 2002–2006 CR-V's K24A1 bracket (Honda PN 11910-PPA-000) must be used. Not all 2.4L brackets are the same, though. Be sure to order the appropriate one.

Engine Installation

If using an engine hoist, lower the engine and transmission into the engine bay. An optional load-leveler, which can be attached to almost any engine hoist, allows the angle of the engine and transmission to be adjusted while lowering the assembly into place, reducing the risk of damaging the car or the engine and simplifying the process. If a vehicle lift is used, simply lower the car onto the engine and transmission assembly.

An engine hoist may also be used to raise the vehicle so that the engine and transmission can be installed from underneath. If this method is used, be sure to securely connect the engine hoist to the car's front crossmember using a series of heavy-duty straps, spreading its load across the entire beam.

Left-Side Transmission Bracket and Mount

For 1992–1995 Civic, 1993–1997 del Sol, and 1994–2001 Integra chassis, position the left-side bracket on top of the transmission and fasten it using the supplied hardware. (The original mounting studs should have already been removed.) Some kits require a series of spacers, which are included along with instructions on where to position them. Next, slip the corresponding left-side mount into the car's framerail bracket using the original bolt and then onto the previously installed transmission bracket but don't tighten it.

Kits designed for the 1996–2000 Civic consist of a mount that bolts directly to the transmission, which slips into the already installed left-side framerail bracket.

Right-Side Engine Mount

Position the right-side engine mount into the already-installed framerail bracket and slide it onto the engine bracket's studs. The engine and transmission assembly may need to be rocked forward or backward to line up each hole. A jack can also be placed underneath the engine to help align everything. Use the supplied hardware to fasten the mount into place but don't tighten it completely.

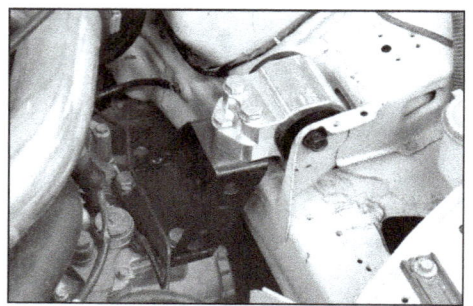

For 1992–1995 Civic, 1993–1997 del Sol, and 1994–2001 Integra chassis, once the engine and transmission have been positioned into the engine bay, fasten the aftermarket bracket to the transmission and its corresponding mount to the existing left-side framerail bracket. The transmission bracket can be installed before or after the engine and transmission have been lowered into position.

For 1996–2000 Civics, the left-side mount connects the transmission to the already-installed left-side framerail bracket. The mount and bracket are pre-installed because the engine and transmission assembly will be installed from underneath.

Installing the engine and transmission assembly from underneath is always easier. Position the assembly on a moveable cart and slowly lower the chassis onto it. When installing an engine from above, additional care must be taken to avoid harm to the chassis, engine, or transmission. The order in which brackets and mounts are installed also varies slightly depending on whether or not the assembly is lowered into place or installed from underneath.

The aftermarket right-side mount connects the already-installed right-side framerail bracket to the timing-chain-side bracket on the engine. Position a floor jack underneath the oil pan to gently raise or lower the engine, allowing the mount to properly align. This Hasport mount has been polished and upgraded with different hardware for a unique look.

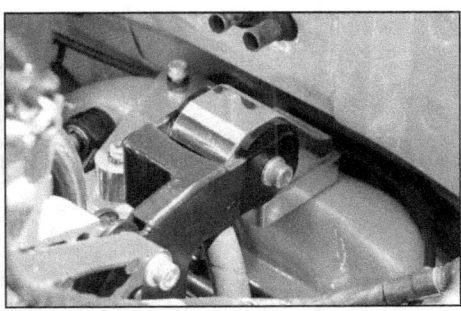

The Hasport rear bracket slips between the firewall and the engine, connecting the already-installed rear mount to the transmission. The bracket can be pre-installed on the engine before lowering the assembly into place or it can be slipped into position once the left- and right-side mounts are installed.

The donor engine's intermediate shaft may not always be compatible. Be sure to source one from a 2002–2006 RSX, 2002–2005 Civic Si, 2001–2005 Civic Type R, 2001–2006 Integra Type R, 2006–2011 Civic Si, or 2007–2011 Civic Type R originally equipped with a manual transmission.

Rear Engine Bracket or Mount

Adjust engine or vehicle height to allow room for the supplied rear engine bracket or mount (depending on the chassis or kit) to fit around the already-installed rear engine bracket or mount (depending on the chassis or kit) and attach it to the engine block or transmission (depending on the style of transmission and mounts) using the supplied hardware. Again, don't completely tighten any hardware yet.

Now the engine hoist can be released or the vehicle can be raised so that the mounts are fully supporting the engine and transmission. Tighten all engine and transmission mount and bracket hardware to the appropriate specifications.

Axles

Early K-series engine swap axles consisted of custom-made pieces that were made of 2002–2006 RSX or 2002–2005 Civic Si shafts, which share outboard spline patterns with Civics, del Sols, and Integras, modified with 1994–2001 Integra outboard joints. Both solutions work but keep in mind that they are factory components and most aftermarket axles are stronger, don't require modifying, and are only marginally more expensive. Today, piecing together axles makes about as much sense as fabricating your own engine mounts.

Hasport Performance, Hybrid Racing, and Driveshaft Shop each offer the appropriate axles that are as strong as or stronger than factory components. Whichever axles are chosen, start with a 2002–2006 RSX, 2002–2005 Civic Si, 2001–2005 Civic Type R, 2001–2006 Integra Type R, 2006–2011 Civic Si, or 2007–2011 Civic Type R intermediate shaft. It can be sourced from any manual transmission-equipped engine; then install the K-series axles similarly to how the original axles were removed.

Apart from custom axles, Karcepts offers another alternative. The company's replacement knuckles, which are compatible with the larger 29.5-mm spindles (36-mm socket) that can be found on the 2002–2006 RSX Type-S, for example, can be bolted onto any of the chassis in this chapter, expanding axle possibilities significantly. Karcepts' knuckles allow the larger-diameter 2002–2006 RSX Type-S, 2006–2011 Civic Si, and

Always replace the cotter pin at the lower ball joint when installing the axles and reassembling the knuckle assemblies. The cotter pin prevents the ball joint's retaining nut from loosening, which can lead to suspension failure. Whether or not the cotter pin is able to slip into place is also an indication of whether or not the retaining nut has been properly tightened.

1997–2001 Prelude base model axles to be used with little modification.

If experimenting with disassembling and reassembling CV joints sounds intimidating, the 2002–2006 RSX Type-S left-side axle can be used on the left side accompanied with either a 2006–2011 Civic Si right-side axle, 1997–2001 Prelude base model left-side axle, or 1997–2001 CR-V left-side axle for use on the right side.

Regardless of the method you choose, when installing new axles, be sure to use new cotter pins for each ball joint castle nut that was removed. Once the axles are installed, reconnect all removed suspension components, reinstall the wheels, and position the car back on the ground.

Throttle Cable

Almost any Civic or Integra throttle cable works; however, only the 1996–2000 Civic throttle cable is short enough to allow for a tidy look underneath the hood. The 1994–2001 Integra GS-R or 2002–2005 Civic Si throttle cables, which are also

With the exception of the 2002–2005 Civic Si, no Civic or Integra throttle cable is directly compatible with any K-series throttle body, which makes an adapter, such as this one from K-Tuned, so special. Simply bolt the bracket onto the throttle body to provide proper cable tension, which remains adjustable. (Photo Courtesy K-Tuned)

short, are also compatible. They connect at the firewall for a factory-like fit provided these chassis were originally equipped with manual transmissions. Any time any of these older Civic or Integra throttle cables are used (excluding 2002–2005 Civic Si), however, a special adapter bracket from K-Tuned must be positioned on the throttle body for compatibility.

Aftermarket cable assemblies are also available from K-Tuned. Simply connect any to the pedal assembly as usual and to the K-series throttle body.

Clutch Hydraulics

All of the chassis in this chapter feature clutch master cylinders that are compatible with the K-series hydraulic clutch system. The hydraulic clutch line assembly that spans from the car's clutch master cylinder to the K-series transmission's clutch slave cylinder must be modified or replaced to properly reach and connect to the K-series clutch slave cyl-

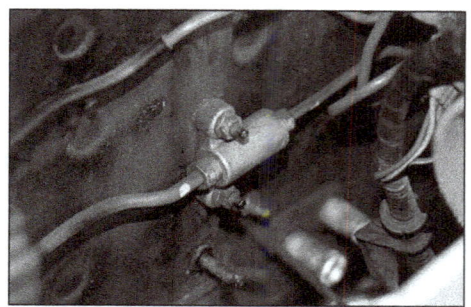

A number of ways are possible to connect any K-series transmission's clutch slave cylinder to the vehicle's clutch master cylinder. In one scenario, the chassis' joint pipe, which is located on the firewall, can be reused. Disconnect and discard the line on the left side and replace it with a section of steel-braided hose that spans to the clutch slave cylinder. The original hard line that spans from the joint pipe to the clutch master cylinder can remain intact.

inder. Hybrid Racing, Karcepts, and K-Tuned all offer clutch line assemblies that make the conversion a simple one.

A custom line made of Teflon-lined steel-braided hose along with the appropriate hose ends can also be used. Special inverted-flare metric adapters can be used to properly seal against the master cylinder or joint pipe and slave cylinder and allow for the new line to properly hook up. If a custom line is used, be sure to pressure test it before installing it and use at least one mounting clamp to attach it to the engine or transmission someplace mid-line to avoid flexing once the clutch pedal is depressed.

The original line can be reused in most cases. Start by disconnecting the line entirely on 1996–2000 Civics. On all other chassis, disconnect the two lines from the joint connector on the firewall and discard the

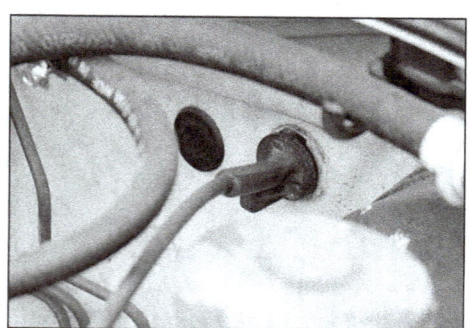

Choosing the right throttle cable can lead to a factory-like fit at the firewall. A number of different cables are compatible; however, shorter cables, such as those from the 1996–2000 Civic or 2002–2005 Civic Si, can lead to an even cleaner look underneath the hood.

A custom-made steel-braided hose can be used to connect the vehicle's clutch master cylinder to the K-series transmission's clutch slave cylinder, bypassing and eliminating the joint pipe at the firewall. The appropriate inverted-flare metric-to-AN adapters are needed to properly transition to the hose ends. (Photo Courtesy K-Tuned)

connector and the short line that originally connected to the master cylinder.

Connect the remaining line to the master cylinder and reshape it so that it routes properly toward the new slave cylinder. Use a small piece of tubing to carefully contour the line's bends to avoid kinking or damaging it. In most cases, the original line is too long and requires significant reshaping and bending to allow for a proper fit. Regardless of the method you use, once completed, be sure to bleed the hydraulic clutch system to ensure proper operation. Follow the standard procedure outlined in any Honda service manual to do this.

Brake Booster

The vehicle's brake booster vacuum hose must be replaced with any 2002–2006 RSX brake booster hose because the intake manifold now sits near the front of the vehicle. Be sure to route the hose away from any moving parts and connect it to the engine's distribution line or the vehicle's original check valve, located at the firewall, if a longer section of surplus hose is used.

Shifter Assembly

Unlike Civic, del Sol, and Integra rod-and-lever-style shift linkages, all vehicles with a K-series use cable-style mechanisms, much like those found in older F-series- and H-series-equipped Accords and Preludes. The cables link the in-car shift change lever sub-assembly (also called the shifter box) to the transmission's gear select levers. The key is being sure to use the right combination of shifter box and shifter cables; not all are compatible with one another or with every transmission.

For example, the popular 2002–2006 RSX shifter box is not compatible with 2003–2007 Accord or 2004–2008 TSX shifter cables. It also isn't compatible with all transmissions because the shift levers are reversed on some K-series transmissions, which can result in an oppositely oriented shift pattern. All of this should be taken into consideration before choosing a transmission.

Shifter box and shifter cable selection is crucial to any successful K-series engine swap. Not all shifter boxes are compatible with all shifter cables nor are they compatible with all transmissions. From left to right, here are shifter boxes from: 2006–2011 Civic Si, 2003–2007 Accord, 2002–2006 RSX, and 2002–2005 Civic Si.

Connecting the custom-made steel-braided hose at the clutch slave cylinder can be done in the same manner as connecting to the clutch master cylinder. Be sure to use the appropriate 90-, 120-, or 180-degree hose ends to route the hose away from any rubber hoses or moving parts but without kinking it. (Photo Courtesy K-Tuned)

A brake booster vacuum hose must span from an intake manifold vacuum source to the brake booster's check valve for the braking system to function properly. If the metal distribution line is present (upper right), connect the engine's brake booster vacuum hose to it at one end and use a section of surplus hose to span from the line's other end to the vehicle's brake booster check valve.

CHAPTER 4

Shifter box selection is determined by a particular transmission's shifter mechanism. Honda implemented two systems that work in opposition to each other. For example, first gear on one style of transmission lever is the result of an outward movement; it's an inward movement on the other style. If the wrong shifter box is used, proper gear engagement is impossible.

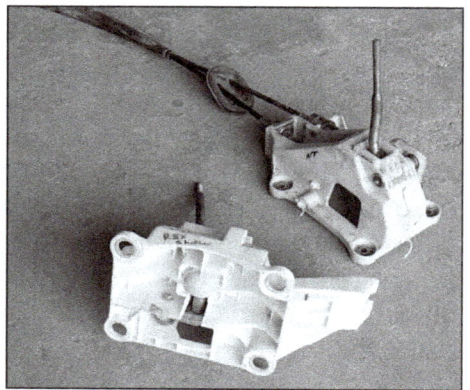

The two most popular shifter box styles are those from the 2002–2006 RSX (left) and the 2003–2007 Accord (right). The main difference lies in where the fulcrum is located on the individual shift levers; this results in an inward pull of the cable on one and an outward pull of the cable on another, even though the actual shifters are moving in the same direction.

Matching the appropriate shifter cables with the right shifter box is just as important as transmission compatibility. Accord-style shifter boxes, which can be used with 2003–2007 Accord, 2006–2008 Accord Euro R, 2004–2008 TSX, 2005–2011 Civic Si, and 2007–2011 Civic Type R transmissions, must be matched with shifter cables from any 2003–2007 Accord or 2004–2008 TSX.

Shifter Box

It all begins with the shifter box, which connects to the chassis in the cabin just below the shift boot. In the early days of K-series engine swaps, the solution was to fabricate a 2002–2006 RSX shifter box into the vehicle's center tunnel by means of a custom adapter plate. The process involves cutting and drilling, and is irreversible. Today, there are at least two alternate solutions, one of which allows the chassis to revert back to a stock-like condition and linkage-style shifter if necessary.

Before moving on, now is a good time to discuss the two types of K-series–compatible transmissions. Of course, more than two gearboxes are available but only two types of gear selectors are shared by all of them. The popular 2002–2006 RSX, 2002–2005 Civic Si, 2001–2005 Civic Type R, and 2001–2006 Integra Type R transmissions feature gear-select mechanisms that engage in the opposite direction compared to 2003–2007 Accord, 2006–2008 Accord Euro R, 2004–2008 TSX, 2006–2011 Civic Si, and 2007–2011 Civic Type R transmissions.

The RSX and similar transmissions mentioned above must be matched with a 2002–2006 RSX or 2001–2005 Civic (non-Si) shifter box. The 2003–2007 Accord and similar transmissions must be matched with a 2003–2007 Accord or 2004–2008 TSX shifter box. Each shifter box must also be matched with its corresponding shifter cables (discussed below). See page 27 in Chapter 1 for a complete list of compatible transmissions and their shifter boxes.

You can choose from three methods of installation: adapter plates, base adapter plates, and a no-cut solution.

Adapter Plates: The earliest method of retrofitting the K-series shifter mechanism into place is entirely custom. You start with a factory shifter box assembly. Because of the shape of Civic, del Sol, and Integra exhaust tunnels, an adapter must be used to mount the shifter box to any of the chassis in this chapter. Such adapters can be sourced from either Karcepts (only compatible with 2002–2006 RSX and 2001–2005 Civic shifter box) or K-Tuned (2006–2011 Civic Si version requires additional shifter cable conversion bracket).

Either adapter mounts the shifter box in the factory location and allows the interior to be put back to like-stock condition. That's mostly because the adapters position the shifter box partially underneath the exhaust tunnel, which means cutting the original sheet metal is required and exhaust clearance is minimized to roughly 1.5 inches. The good news is that the shifter cables can be routed underneath the chassis, eliminating the need to drill holes in the firewall.

First, remove the center console and shift boot so that the shifter opening is exposed. If a factory shifter

1992–2000 CIVIC AND 1994–2001 INTEGRA

Aftermarket adapter plates, such as this one from K-Tuned, allow the K-series shifter box to mount underneath the chassis, which means that the center console and shift boot can remain intact. The process can't be completed without fabrication, and reverting back to the original rod-and-lever style shift linkage also can't be done without even more fabrication. (Photo Courtesy K-Tuned)

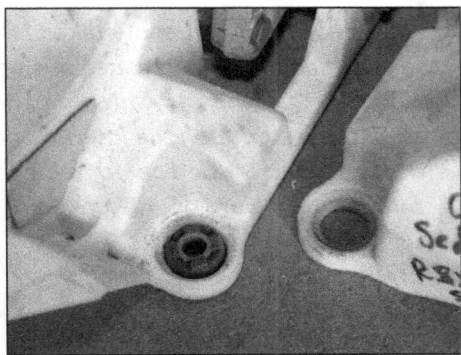

Before the shifter box can be mounted onto the adapter plate, its four rubber bushings must be removed and discarded. Use a flathead screwdriver to pry them away and prepare the shifter box for installation.

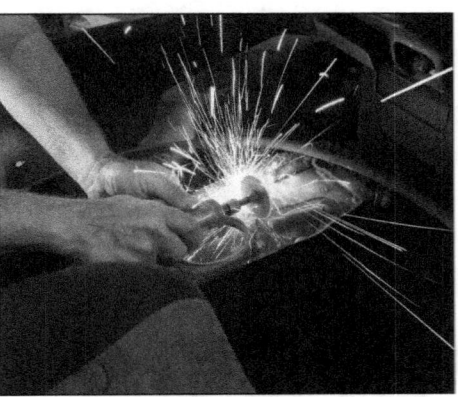

Every aftermarket adapter plate requires permanent modifications to the chassis. Use the manufacturer's supplied template and an angle grinder to cut away the raised shifter opening along the exhaust tunnel. It's a necessary procedure to allow the shifter assembly to sit flat and protrude into the interior. (Photo Courtesy Hasport Performance Products)

box is going to be used, it must be trimmed to fit through the opening. Both kits provide instructions that outline exactly where to cut.

If using a 2002–2006 RSX or 2001–2005 Civic shifter box, trim the small raised region on the right side of the box, near the neutral return

Hasport's prototype adapter plate allows the seldom-used but significantly less expensive Accord-style shifter box to mount underneath. Best of all, Hasport's design retains the cables' original rubber seal, resulting in a factory-like fit.

spring, and near the lower right corner of the assembly. If using a 2003–2007 Accord or 2004–2008 TSX shifter box, trim the right-side cable holder and along the two left-side mounting holes. If equipped, remove the metal or rubber bushings from each corner of the shifter box.

Both kits include a rear bracket that bolts to the two original shift-linkage mounting holes and a main adapter plate, which mounts to the bracket. Bolt the main adapter plate into place and position it up against the chassis, marking the two bolt holes with a center punch or felt-tip pen from underneath. Using a 1/8-inch pilot drill bit, drill holes into the exhaust tunnel. From inside the car, position the supplied template over the rear bracket's bolts, which should protrude into the cabin, and tape it into place. The 1/8-inch pilot holes should line up with the holes on the template. Verify that they do, remove the template, and enlarge both holes using a 9/32-inch drill bit. Reinstall the template, mark the area to be cut, and cut out the appropriate section using an angle grinder or sheet metal cutter.

Once cut and deburred, install the shifter cables onto the box and bolt the complete assembly into place from underneath. Generally, the mounting hardware is made up of nuts and bolts that traverse from the inside of the vehicle to its underside. You need a helper to hold onto either the nut or bolt, depending on which side they're on, to keep the hardware from spinning while tightening.

Finally, test the shifter and be sure that each gear engages properly. To ensure against air leaks within the cabin, use caulking to seal the area around the shifter box from underneath.

Base Adapter Plates: This is a similar albeit simpler solution. A billet aluminum adapter plate is bolted on top of the exhaust tunnel where the original shifter was located that features provisions for either style shifter box, depending on the adapter. Of course, the base plate adapter mounts the shifter

CHAPTER 4

Base adapter plates, such as these from K-Tuned, make shifter box installation easy although not nearly as elegant as other solutions. That's because such plates mount on top of the exhaust tunnel, below the shifter box, which means any interior panels can't be retained. The shifter cables must also pass through the interior and out through the firewall. It's a solution best reserved for dedicated track cars or custom applications where missing interior pieces are of little concern. (Photo Courtesy K-Tuned)

assembly higher than the adapter kits just mentioned, which means any interior panels that were removed will not go back into place; however, because nothing's mounted underneath, ample exhaust clearance is retained.

K-Tuned offers two versions of the base plate adapter for both styles of transmission that are manufactured from billet aluminum and include all necessary mounting hardware. The cables must also be routed through the firewall when using these plates.

Base plate adapters like these are popular because they are among the easiest ways to install the popular

Honda's 2006–2011 Civic Si transmission is a special case. It shares the same mounting points as RSX-style transmissions but features a gear selector mechanism comparable to the Accord's. Shifter cables from any 2003–2007 Accord or 2004–2008 TSX may be used; however, a special conversion bracket from K-Tuned that allows them to bolt to the transmission is necessary. (Photo Courtesy K-Tuned)

2006–2011 Civic Si gearbox into any of these chassis with limited modifications. Simply use the 2003–2007 Accord or 2004–2008 TSX shifter box and shifter cables, which are oriented in the same direction as the Civic Si transmission, along with K-Tuned's special transmission conversion bracket that allows the cables to properly fit up to the gearbox.

No-Cut Solution: Both Hybrid Racing and K-Tuned offer versions of a no-cut shifter box that leave the factory exhaust tunnel intact, which means the original D- or B-series engine, with their rod-style shift linkages, can be easily swapped back into place. No-cut shifter boxes also allow all interior pieces, including the center console, to remain in place.

Both kits are compatible with 2002–2006 RSX, 2002–2005 Civic Si, 2001–2005 Civic Type R, and 2001–2006 Integra Type R transmissions. Kits are also available that are compatible with 2003–2007 Accord, 2006–2008 Accord Euro R, 2004–2008 TSX, 2006–2011 Civic Si, and 2007–2011 Civic Type R gearboxes.

Similar to the adapters mentioned earlier, no-cut shifter boxes mount from underneath, which means exhaust clearance is compromised but the interior can be put back to stock condition. The shifter cables can also be routed underneath the vehicle, which means no additional holes must be cut in the firewall.

No-cut shifter boxes are comprehensive solutions, which means the shifter itself is included; there's

Perhaps the most finessed shifter box solution is the no-cut shifter box, such as those offered by K-Tuned or Hybrid Racing. Like the previously mentioned adapter plate, the K-Tuned assembly (shown) mounts from underneath but without any cutting or fabrication. Notice that the original raised opening along the shifter tunnel has been retained; it must be cut away when following other methods.

no need to source an RSX shifter box when going this route.

Both kits offer an adjustable throw to suit the driver's specific preference, bolt up to the chassis through existing holes, and remain hidden once the interior is reassembled. They're also compatible with 2002–2006 RSX shifter cables and, of course, each company's own line of shifter cables.

Shifter Cables

If a 2002–2006 RSX, 2002–2005 Civic Si, 2001–2005 Civic Type R, or 2001–2006 Integra Type R transmission is going to be used with a 2002–2006 RSX, 2001–2005 Civic, or aftermarket no-cut shifter box, the preferred cables include those

1992–2000 CIVIC AND 1994–2001 INTEGRA

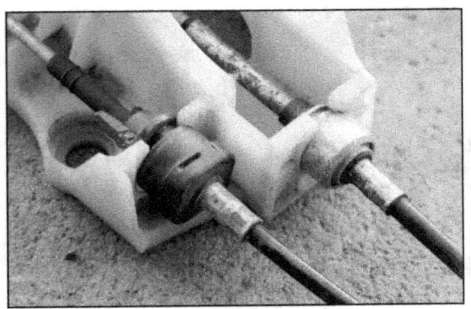

Generally, sourcing cables from the same chassis as the shifter box is ideal. This ensures compatibility with each other at the shifter box. Be sure to use the original retaining clips when securing the cables to the shifter box.

from the 2002–2004 RSX or even the later-style 2005–2006 RSX, which require a bit of modifying to fit, specifically, small metal weights at each cable's end. These must be cut off to work regardless of the shifter box or transmission that is going to be used.

Both Hybrid Racing and K-Tuned also offer their own versions of RSX shifter cables that feature solid aluminum bushings instead of the factory plastic ones and an overall stronger, more durable design. (K-series shifter cables have been reported to break.)

The 2003–2007 Accord or 2004–2008 TSX shifter cables must be used if any of the previously mentioned Accord or TSX shifter boxes are used along with a 2003–2007 Accord, 2006–2008 Accord Euro R, 2004–2008 TSX, 2006–2011 Civic Si, or 2007–2011 Civic Type R transmission. Hybrid Racing also offers its own line of aftermarket cables that are compatible.

If using an adapter kit or no-cut shifter box, the cables can be routed underneath the chassis, directly to the transmission's gear selector. If using a base adapter plate, the cables must be routed through the firewall.

Cut a 1.5-inch hole in the floor in front of the shifter or down low on the firewall and route the shifter cables into the engine bay. Be sure to allow clearance between the cables and the catalytic converter, exhaust, and anti-sway bar (if equipped) if they are routed underneath. For race applications that won't retain the heater core, simply slip both cables through the heater hose opening in the firewall. Whichever way the cables are routed, be sure to do so smoothly and to avoid harsh bends, which can result in binding.

When attaching shifter cables to the transmission and shifter box assembly, locate the cables in their respective brackets before attaching their rod ends to their respective levers. Use a hammer to tap the retaining clips into place and be sure to use the appropriate washers and cotter pins to ensure that nothing comes loose. Once fastened into place, test the shifter for proper engagement.

When using a base adapter plate to mount the shifter box, the cables must span through the interior, past the firewall, and into the engine bay. A 1.5-inch hole must be drilled in the firewall to allow the cables to pass through. Locate the hole in an inconspicuous place, such as in the center of the firewall, near the floor. Be sure to drill the hole from the engine-bay side before installing the engine and transmission. (Photo Courtesy Hasport Performance Products)

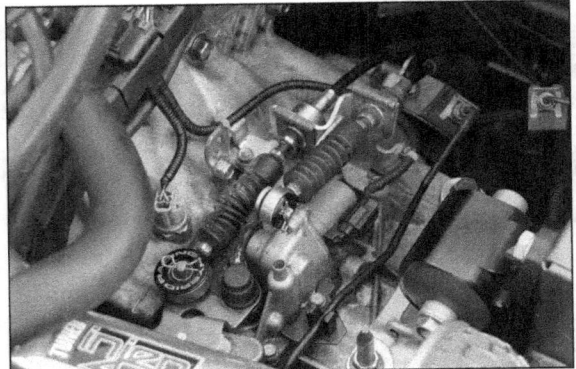

Aftermarket shifter cables, such as these from Hybrid Racing, are compatible with factory and aftermarket shifter boxes including their own. K-series shifter cables can stretch or even break, which makes a stronger, more durable set such as this even more appealing. Purchasing aftermarket shifter cables also eliminates the guesswork that's often involved when sourcing used parts from the salvage yard that can be difficult to distinguish from one another.

Fuel System

K-series-equipped vehicles all have returnless fuel systems, which means that unlike older Hondas and Acuras, only a single line traverses from the fuel tank to the engine. Their fuel pressure regulators are also mounted within their gas tanks. All of the chassis in this chapter feature return-style fuel systems, which can be retained but require some modification.

Fuel Rail and Fuel Pressure Regulator

Retaining the older Civic, del Sol, and Integra return-style fuel system

CHAPTER 4

starts with a bypass-type aftermarket fuel pressure regulator suitable for fuel injection applications matched with the factory fuel rail or an aftermarket fuel rail that features inlet and outlet ports.

Stock Fuel Rail, Aftermarket Fuel Pressure Regulator: The most cost-effective method is to retain the factory fuel rail. However, because K-series fuel rails feature only a single inlet port, a bypass-type adjustable fuel pressure regulator with at least two inlet ports and a single outlet port must be adapted into the system to allow unused fuel to travel back to the tank.

To adapt the factory fuel rail to an aftermarket fuel pressure regulator, simply slip a section of 5/16-inch fuel injection hose over the fuel rail's inlet barb and connect it to one of the fuel pressure regulator's upper ports using the appropriate fittings. To do this, the plastic connector must be cut away from the fuel rail's inlet barb.

Fuel pressure regulators can vary widely depending on the model but generally consist of -6 or -8 female O-ring-sealed AN ports. Simply source the appropriate male-to-male union and thread it into place along with the corresponding AN female-to-male-barb adapter. Next, slip the fuel injection line over the barb and secure it using fuel injection hose clamps. The remaining upper port must connect to the vehicle's original fuel feed line, which is located at the top of the fuel filter. Carefully cut the original line away from the banjo connection, and expose the hose barb. Next, slip a section of fuel injection hose over the barb and connect it to the remaining inlet port at the fuel pressure regulator using the same series of fittings. Alternatively, the original fuel feed line can be cut in half, and a 5/16-inch male-to-male barb can be used to join the two lines together.

For a cost-effective fuel system, disassemble the vehicle's original fuel feed line that spans from the fuel filter to the fuel rail and retain its banjo-to-barb hose end. You need an angle grinder or hack saw to break it free from its crimped-on metal collar. Once completed, reattach the banjo to the fuel filter and slip inexpensive rubber fuel injection hose over its barb, spanning to the aftermarket fuel pressure regulator. (Photo Courtesy Hasport Performance Products)

A return line must also span from the fuel pressure regulator's lower exit port to the fuel return hard line located near the firewall. A similar male-to-male AN union and AN female-to-male-barb adapter must be used along with 1/4-inch fuel injection hose and the appropriate clamps. Be sure that the original fuel-return hose has been removed from the hard line and slip the new hose into place, fastening it using fuel injection hose clamps.

Aftermarket Fuel Rail, Aftermarket Fuel Pressure Regulator: Although the previous method is cost-effective and proven to work, for applications that require additional fuel flow, bypassing the inlet stream through the fuel pressure regulator isn't always a good idea and can pose restrictions. An aftermarket fuel rail that features both an inlet and an outlet port is the solution.

Here, a feed line spanning from the fuel filter to the fuel rail's inlet port can be made following the same procedures outlined above that allow unobstructed flow into the fuel rail. Connect the fuel injection hose to the fuel filter and source the appropriate AN-to-barb adapter to connect it to the fuel rail. The fuel pressure regulator can either be mounted directly to the opposite end of the fuel rail by means of the appropriate union or externally, using similar AN-to-barb adapters and fuel injection hose. Connect the fuel pressure regulator's lower return port to the factory fuel return line as outlined above.

Fuel systems that include an aftermarket fuel rail, such as this one from Hybrid Racing, and high-performance AN fittings and hose are more common. It's easier to retain the vehicle's return-style fuel system because, unlike K-series fuel rails, aftermarket fuel rails feature both inlet and outlet ports. (Photo Courtesy K-Tuned)

When transitioning to an aftermarket fuel rail, be careful not to damage the O-rings when removing the fuel injectors. Use a small amount of liquid hand soap to lubricate the O-rings before reinstalling them. Avoid most spray lubricants; some can damage a fuel injector's seals over time. Use a twisting motion while pulling or pushing when removing and reinstalling fuel injectors. All of this helps reduce the risk of damaging them and allows them to slip out and back in more easily.

Install the aftermarket fuel rail using either the supplied hardware or the engine's original hardware. When reconnecting the engine wiring harness' connectors to the fuel injectors, be sure to connect the ground wire to its original location. Whichever method is chosen, be sure to leave the fuel pressure regulator's vacuum reference port open; K-series engines do not require this feature.

Specialty Fittings and Lines

Chances are that some sort of high-quality anodized-aluminum AN fittings and steel-braided specialty hose will be used regardless of the type of fuel pressure regulator and fuel rail chosen. Hybrid Racing, Karcepts, and K-Tuned each offer hose-and-fitting kits that eliminate the challenge of figuring out exactly what's needed. Each kit includes the appropriate -6 AN fittings and line along with a special -6 male-to-banjo adapter that can be used with the factory fuel filter or an inline fuel filter that allows for additional clearance at the firewall. Because of fuel rail and fuel pressure regulator differences as well as the variety of AN fittings and adapters, many methods can be used.

Fuel Pump

The remainder of the fuel system can remain stock until further modifications are made to the engine. This includes the factory K-series fuel injectors, fuel filter, and the type of fuel pump originally installed in the vehicle. With that said, high-mileage Civics and Integras of this era are likely in need of a fuel pump replacement whether or not a larger, more powerful K-series is being dropped into place. Aftermarket in-tank fuel pumps from AEM, DeatschWerks, and Walbro are all worth considering and are a small investment to make considering the scope of the entire engine swap.

Early K-series engine swaps were based on the del Sol's smaller (half-size) radiator that was either relocated or modified to fit. This aftermarket aluminum version has been modified so that the radiator's upper water neck doesn't interfere with the intake manifold. Typically, the radiator's water neck is directed perpendicularly to the one shown here.

Hybrid Racing offers turnkey fuel systems that include everything needed for a K-series engine swap into any older non-native chassis. Kits include a high-flow fuel rail with inlet and outlet ports, an adjustable fuel pressure regulator, and all of the lines, fittings, and hose ends necessary to complete the system. (Courtesy Hybrid Racing)

Cooling System

As you'd expect, there are a number of ways to complete the cooling system on any of the chassis in this chapter. Over the years, various methods have been implemented, most of which I cover here.

Radiator

Early cooling solutions were based on the 1994–1997 del Sol VTEC's dual-row half-size radiator, which features large-diameter inlets and outlets that match the K-series engine's water necks, or an aftermarket aluminum version thereof.

Because of the K-series engine's orientation, the radiator must be repositioned onto the opposite side of the engine bay so that its hoses can be routed efficiently, allowing for clearance between the intake manifold and the upper radiator inlet. The original lower radiator support brackets must be cut off, similar to how the right-side framerail bracket was removed, and welded onto the opposite side of the core support. Alternate methods include cutting off the inlet and outlet necks from aftermarket aluminum radiators and

CHAPTER 4

When reusing a radiator that was designed for the chassis and not the engine, it must be relocated. Drill out and remove the two lower radiator mounts (similar to how the right-side framerail bracket was removed) and weld them into place at the opposite end of the core support. The core support behind a properly drilled-out series of spot welds should look like this.

K-Tuned offers its own radiator solution that retains the original placement, making use of the chassis' original lower radiator mounts. The upper water neck has also been reconfigured so it doesn't interfere with the intake manifold. Because of this, custom radiator hoses or those from K-Tuned must be used. (Photo Courtesy K-Tuned)

The 2002–2006 RSX or 2002–2005 Civic Si (shown) radiators can be popular solutions for Integra chassis because of their integrated provisions for the radiator fan switch. Any of these chassis' lower radiator mounts must be relocated or an aftermarket mounting kit from Hybrid Racing or K-Tuned can be used to complete the swap.

reorienting them for an appropriate fit. Fortunately, a number of alternate methods are available today, most of which require little to no fabrication.

Hybrid Racing and K-Tuned once again offer the simplest solutions. Hybrid Racing's half-size radiator mounts in any of these chassis' orig-

Today, all sorts of radiator solutions are available. Hybrid Racing's half-size radiator was designed to mount in the A/C condenser's original location, which means that drilling and welding are not required. Since it's positioned on the opposite side of the core support, the upper water neck doesn't interfere with the intake manifold. (Courtesy Hybrid Racing)

inal A/C condenser locations and includes the appropriate bracket to fasten it into place. Despite the radiator sitting where the A/C condenser once resided, A/C is still fully compatible. K-Tuned's solution retains radiator placement on the right side of the engine bay but because of its unique reoriented inlets and outlets, clearance between the engine is retained. Both are simple bolt-in solutions that are no more complex than removing and replacing the original radiator.

Another solution from K-Tuned is its relocation kit, which positions any half-size Civic radiator on the left side of the engine bay, similar to Hybrid Racing's kit. Because of its placement, the orientation of the original inlet and outlet can remain intact.

For those looking to maximize cooling or Integra owners who don't wish to downgrade to a half-size radiator, K-Tuned and Hybrid Racing each

offer solutions. K-Tuned's solution is simple but available only for 1994–2001 Integra and 1996–2000 Civic chassis. A series of brackets and hardware allow placement of any full-size 2002–2006 RSX or 2002–2005 Civic Si radiator without fabrication.

Hybrid Racing's solution includes its own custom radiator with

Many aftermarket radiators designed for K-series engine swaps feature provisions for the radiator fan switch, similar to 2002–2006 RSX or 2002–2005 Civic Si radiators. Simply thread the original D- or B-series radiator fan switch into the bung. Don't forget the original O-ring, which can typically be reused if it isn't torn or visibly damaged. (Photo Courtesy K-Tuned)

applications compatible with every chassis in this chapter. On Civic applications, the radiator features provisions to mount onto one of the original A/C condenser tabs as well as the original right-side radiator mount. Integra applications bolt onto the original radiator mounts. Reoriented inlets and outlets ensure against any clearance issues between the radiator and the engine.

Be aware of the donor engine's upper coolant outlet pipe. Multiple versions are available but there are only two distinct styles; each determines which upper radiator hose may be used. Side-mount water necks (left) require an entirely different shape of hose than front-mount water necks (right). (Photo Courtesy Hasport Performance Products)

Cooling Fan

Regardless of the chassis, radiator, or engine combination chosen, cooling fan clearance is minimal. An aftermarket, 12-inch-diameter fan must be used and, in the case of the 1996–2000 Civic, must be positioned on the opposite side of the radiator.

Under normal conditions, the cooling fan is positioned on the radiator's engine side and is designed to pull air past itself. Airflow must continue to move in that same direction, even once the fan's location has been reversed.

Locate the two wires connected to the fan's motor and carefully connect them to the battery terminals to verify which direction the fan will spin once mounted. Adjust the polarity of the two wires so that, once mounted onto the opposite side of the radiator, the fan may push instead of pull. (Be sure that whatever fan you plan to use features blades that are designed to push or pull, depending on which side of the radiator it's mounted on.) Once verified, cut the original fan's two-pin connector off with at least 4 inches of wire exposed and solder it to the new fan's wires, taking into account the appropriate polarity. All of this allows for a plug-in connection on the vehicle for easy removal later.

Radiator Hoses

Early K-series engine swaps generally made use of a 2002–2006 RSX Type-S or 2002–2005 Civic Si upper radiator hose and a cut-to-fit 1994–2001 Integra radiator hose down below. A number of aftermarket manufacturers, such as Hybrid Racing and K-Tuned, now produce engine swap-compatible hoses that are designed to work with almost any radiator and will likely outlast any factory hose.

Before moving on, it's important to mention the two types of upper coolant outlet pipes, or water necks that determine which radiator hose must be used. First, all K20A2, K20Z1, K20A, K20A3, and K24A1 engines share a similar design that integrates the water neck onto the front of the cylinder head. (All other engines listed in Chapter 1 feature a water neck that's fitted onto the side of the cylinder head.)

The lower water necks that are integrated into each engine's thermostat housing are also different and are

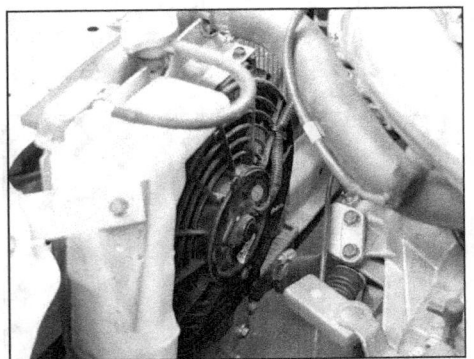

Every K-series engine swap into any non-native chassis requires a slimmer aftermarket cooling fan. With the exception of the 1996–2000 Civic, the fan can be mounted in its original location on the radiator's engine-bay side. Most aftermarket fans have the ability to either pull or push air past the radiator, depending on the polarity of their wires. When mounting on the engine-bay side, be sure that the fan pulls air past the radiator when spinning.

A number of different lower water necks that attach directly to the thermostat housing are also available. Lower radiator hose selection is generally dependent on the engine's lower water neck. Any lower water neck may be swapped onto any engine; however, its corresponding thermostat housing must always be used with it.

associated with the same engines as above. Generally, RSX-style (K20A2, K20Z1, K20A, K20A3, and K24A1) thermostat housings are preferred because of how they orient the lower radiator hose. Be sure to consider which thermostat housing is present before purchasing a lower radiator hose.

If a Civic-style radiator is going to be relocated onto the opposite side of the engine bay by means of custom fabrication, silicone radiator hose kits from Hybrid Racing or K-Tuned make for a simple installation. The same is true if Hybrid Racing's full-size radiator will be used. Instead of cutting and attempting to modify an RSX hose to fit, each kit's upper hose routes underneath the intake pipe for a tidy factory-like fit. While both companies' hoses are compatible with most K-series engines, only Hybrid Racing offers an upper radiator hose that is also compatible with side-mount water necks. Installing them is easy.

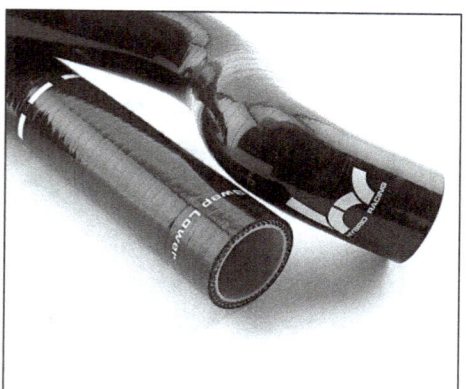

Silicone radiator hoses, such as these from Hybrid Racing, can take the guesswork out of determining factory hoses' compatibility with various water necks and radiators. Hybrid Racing's hoses are compatible with multiple configurations; simply install them as they are or trim along the white dotted lines for alternate fitments. (Courtesy Hybrid Racing)

Applications where K-Tuned's half-side radiator is used in the original location must also use hoses from K-Tuned, albeit a slightly different application, which are not compatible with side-mount water necks.

Finally, if a 2002–2006 RSX or 2002–2005 Civic Si radiator is used, K-Tuned also has the solution with silicone hose applications compatible with both styles of cylinder head.

Cooling Electrical

Unlike with B-series engine swaps, the radiator fan switch and coolant temperature sensor (thermo unit) must both be addressed. On K-series-equipped chassis, the switch that triggers the cooling fan is integrated into the radiator and the accompanying coolant temperature sensor isn't able to communicate with any of these chassis' instrument clusters. The original D- or B-series coolant temperature sensor must be integrated so that the instrument cluster's temperature gauge functions properly. The radiator fan switch must also be reused so that the cooling fan can turn on as needed.

If a 2002–2006 RSX or 2002–2005 Civic Si radiator is used, simply thread the radiator fan switch into the designated location. Hybrid Racing radiators also feature provisions for the radiator fan switch.

The fact that a factory Civic radiator without provisions for the radiator fan switch will be used presents a problem. The solution isn't difficult and there are at least two different ways to address all of this. Start by removing the original D- or B-series coolant temperature sensor and radiator fan switch; alternatively, purchase them from a Honda dealership or salvage yard. Depending on the sub-harness, you may need to save

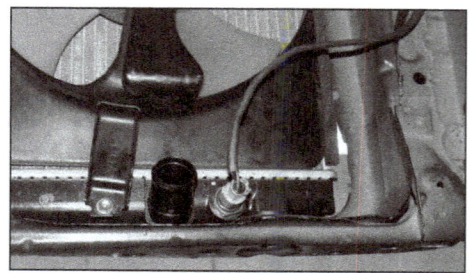

A radiator fan switch should be integrated into the cooling system and wired into place. Here, it's threaded directly into a 2002–2005 Civic Si radiator. If you are making your own sub-harness, you need the electrical connector from the original D- or B-series engine wiring harness. Pre-made aftermarket sub-harnesses include the appropriate connector for an easy plug-in solution. (Photo Courtesy Hasport Performance Products)

their corresponding electrical connectors with at least 4 inches of wire intact (these must be soldered onto the wiring harness later).

A hose insert that has provisions for the coolant temperature sensor

Often, a radiator may be used without provisions for a radiator fan switch. This adapter from Hasport is spliced into the lower radiator hose. The adapter features a threaded bung for the radiator fan switch along with the necessary grounding terminal. An optional provision is also included for the coolant temperature sensor, which may also be mounted at the intake manifold.

and radiator fan switch must be placed in-line along the lower radiator hose. Hasport and Hybrid Racing both offer inserts that feature threaded provisions for both sensors. When splicing into the cooling hose using Hasport's or Hybrid Racing's in-line adapters, be sure to ground them to the engine or transmission using the supplied grounding posts.

K-Tuned offers another solution: Its radiator hose kit for left-side-mounted radiators features provisions for the radiator fan switch; however, the coolant temperature sensor must still be located elsewhere.

Although many kits offer provisions for mounting the coolant temperature sensor at the lower radiator hose, when possible, the sensor should be mounted up high for greater accuracy. Hybrid Racing and K-Tuned have special adapter fittings designed to replace the unused idle air assist valve located on the intake manifold and feature provisions for the coolant temperature sensor.

Simply thread the adapter into the coolant port located on the intake manifold and thread the corresponding sensor into the adapter. This method can be used along with the previously mentioned lower radiator hose adapter for the radiator fan switch; simply plug the coolant temperature sensor port in the adapter because it'll be located elsewhere.

It doesn't matter where the sensors are mounted; simply connect them to the sub-harness when performing necessary wiring connections later. The coolant temperature sensor is a single-wire connection while the radiator fan switch must be grounded to the engine or chassis and its remaining wire connected at the sub-harness.

Most engine management systems, such as Hondata's K-Pro, can activate the cooling fan through the ECU based on coolant temperature within the cylinder head. If this method is selected, the radiator fan switch doesn't need to be installed. Instead, the fan can be triggered by the engine coolant temperature sensor (which is already integrated into the engine wiring harness) that communicates directly with the ECU, and can be programmed to activate at any temperature. However, whenever possible, the cooling fan should be activated by the radiator fan switch (as outlined above); K-Pro's feature should generally be used only as an emergency backup.

Heater Hoses

The two heater hoses that span from the heater core and its valve assembly at the firewall must connect to the engine in order for the heater to function properly. If interior heating will not be retained, simply bypass the inlet and outlet on the engine side.

To retain the heater, use 5/8-inch (16-mm) cooling hose to connect the heater hose outlet and water valve inlet at the firewall to the heater hose inlet and outlet on the engine. In most cases, surplus 180-degree hose can be used to connect to the water valve to avoid contact with the exhaust manifold. A number of hoses work for this, some of which may even be sourced from the original D- or B-series engine. Alternatively, the water valve inlet can be removed from its bracket and positioned inline, reoriented so it faces away from the exhaust manifold.

For greater accuracy, the coolant temperature sensor that communicates with the instrument cluster should be mounted high. Remove the unused idle-air assist valve at the intake manifold and thread into place the appropriate adapter from K-Tuned or Hybrid Racing that features provisions for the coolant temperature sensor. The sensor's single wire must use its connector from the original D- or B-series engine wiring harness if a sub-harness will be made from scratch or connected to an aftermarket sub-harness' provided connector. (Photo Courtesy Hasport Performance Products)

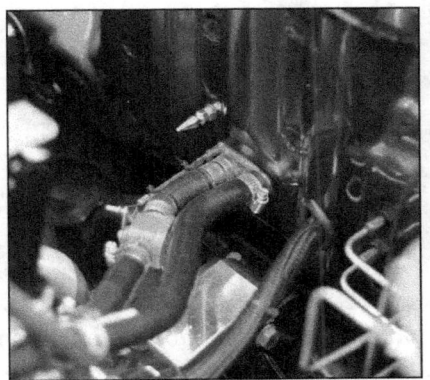

A number of ways are possible to route the two heater hoses exiting the chassis' heater core outlet and water valve inlet to the engine. Whichever method is chosen, the hoses must be carefully routed away from the exhaust manifold. Here, the valve assembly has been removed from its bracket at the firewall, allowing two relatively straight sections of hose to be used. The result positions both hoses safely away from any hot exhaust components.

CHAPTER 4

Every K-series engine features 16- and 19-mm nipples that must connect to every non-native chassis' 16-mm heater core outlet and water valve inlet nipples. To transition from 16 to 19 mm, the smaller-diameter hose can be carefully stretched over the larger-diameter nipple or an adapter from K-Tuned can be used that splices the two appropriately sized hoses together. If climate control won't be retained, simply loop the two nipples on the engine together or plug their respective inlets and outlets on the engine.

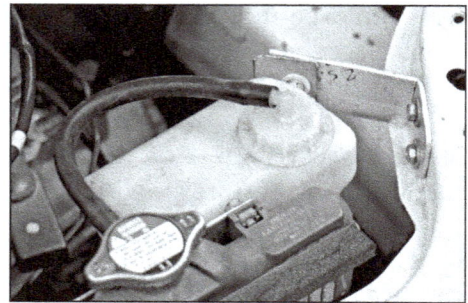

In most cases, the coolant overflow reservoir must be relocated. Here, a simple bracket was made to relocate it onto the opposite side of the engine bay. Be sure to connect the reservoir's nipple to the radiator using 5/16-inch hose and mount it high enough in the engine bay for it to work effectively.

Whichever method is chosen, it's important to know that all K-series engines feature 16- and 19-mm connections compared to the 16-mm nipples on all of the chassis in this chapter. The 5/8-inch hose must be stretched over the larger nipple or installed in two sections using a 5/8- to 3/4-inch brass reducer. K-Tuned offers its own version that features a hard-anodized black finish that makes the seam difficult to spot. Whichever method is chosen, be sure to avoid kinking the hoses, and route them away from hot exhaust components.

Overflow Reservoir

In almost every case the radiator overflow reservoir must be relocated someplace near the left-side transmission mount. A custom bracket can be made or sourced from Kar-cepts and a section of 5/16-inch hose must span from the reservoir's nipple to the radiator. The reservoir is often eliminated to retain an uncluttered look or because there's seemingly no place to mount it. Don't do that. The reservoir serves several key functions and plays its own role in an engine operating at its ideal temperature.

A/C and Power Steering

Both A/C and power steering are compatible with any of the vehicles covered in this chapter, providing they're not right-hand drive. Configuring the systems isn't as easy as it was with B- or H-series engine swaps, though. A number of custom and aftermarket components must be used and the processes vary depending on whether or not A/C and power steering is retained separately, together, or eliminated entirely.

A/C and Power Steering Delete

Before getting into A/C and power steering conversions, let's first go over what's required if neither is chosen. The K-series drive belt doesn't just rotate the water pump and alternator but also the A/C compressor and power steering pump. An automatic belt tensioner that passes through a series of five other pulleys ensures that everything operates appropriately. As such, when removing the A/C compressor or power steering pump, the belt that's left is too long.

The solution lies in the 2002–2005 Civic Si K20A3 engine's electric power steering system that features an idler pulley where the power steering pump is normally located. This, in combination with a custom-length seven-rib accessory belt that accounts for the missing

The K-series drive belt is responsible for a whole lot more than any D-, B-, or H-series engine's is. Driven by the crankshaft pulley (far left), a single belt rotates the power steering pump or idler pulley (top), alternator (right center), water pump (lower center), and A/C compressor (right lower). A hydraulic tensioner connected to its own pulley (upper center) ensures that the belt remains taut and functional.

1992–2000 CIVIC AND 1994–2001 INTEGRA

The first step to eliminating power steering is to source the 2002–2005 Civic Si idler pulley. The seventh-generation Civic Si features an electric power steering system that isn't driven by the crankshaft. As such, an idler pulley was developed specifically for the Si K20A3. Be sure to source its corresponding bracket, bearing cover, bolt, and belt to complete the conversion.

A/C and Power Steering Delete Parts

2002–2005 Civic Si idler pulley (Honda PN 31190-PRA-000)
2002–2005 Civic Si idler pulley bracket (Honda PN 31175-PRA-000)
2002–2005 Civic Si bearing cover (Honda PN 31185-PCX-003)
2002–2005 Civic Si flange bolt (Honda PN 90031-PRA-000)
Seven-rib, 50.5-inch accessory belt (Dayco PN 5070505)

A/C compressor pulley, is the first of many solutions. Belt length can vary significantly depending on engine type and crankshaft pulleys; however, 2.0L engines typically accept a 50.5-inch belt while 2.4L engines use a slightly longer 52-inch belt.

Finally, be sure to source the appropriate idler pulley bracket, bearing cover, and mounting bolt. They can be purchased from Honda and bolted up in a stock-like manner.

An alternate method involves eliminating the A/C compressor and power steering pump as well as the belt tensioner mechanism and using a shorter belt that spans only around the crankshaft pulley, water pump, and alternator. A larger-diameter aftermarket alternator pulley, such as one from AEM (PN 23-7032), designed for the 2002–2005 Civic Si K20A3, must be used to prevent the belt from rubbing against itself and, to provide tension, the alternator must be shimmed away from the engine block using a series of washers at each of its mounting bolts. Because of different-sized K-series crankshaft pulleys, exact belt length varies between applications but is approximately 39 inches. Although this method eliminates both A/C and power steering, it's generally not recommended because of the inability to properly tension the belt.

Of course, the aftermarket has its own solutions; ones that provide for a cleaner look and eliminate the need for the K20A3 idler pulley altogether. Hybrid Racing's auto-tensioning A/C and power steering removal kit is compatible with all K-series engines and is based on a spring-loaded automatic belt tensioner that replaces the factory unit and allows for both the A/C compressor and power steering pump to be removed, allowing the included shorter drive belt to route around the crankshaft pulley, water pump, and alternator.

The kit also relocates the alternator to the A/C compressor's original location for additional chassis clearance, which is, perhaps, its best benefit. K-Tuned and Karcepts offer similar kits that also relocate the alternator and are based on manual tensioners. To install either style of tensioner, be sure to remove the factory A/C compressor, alternator, power steering pump, and belt tensioner first. It's easiest to do all of this before installing the engine.

Keep in mind that any time power steering components are removed from a vehicle originally equipped with it, the steering rack should be swapped for a manual version or its inlets and outlets appropriately looped together using a short section of hose. This prevents debris from entering what was once an otherwise closed system.

Power Steering Delete with A/C

Hybrid Racing also has a solution when A/C is retained without power steering. You begin with the same K20A3 idler pulley along with the necessary hardware. The factory K20A3 accessory belt must be used, allowing the K-series A/C compressor to be installed in stock configuration.

Hybrid Racing's kit makes use of a 1996–2000 Civic A/C condenser that can be mounted in the radiator's original location (not compatible with full-size radiators or right-side-mounted radiators) and the 2002–2006 RSX or 2002–2005 Civic Si A/C compressor (or equivalent). Other compressors may also be compatible; however, both of these lend themselves well to proper hose orientation and feature the necessary single-wire thermal protection switch connector (other compressors feature three-wire connectors). Integras may retain their original A/C condensers when using this kit.

Hybrid Racing's kit uses a combination of the Civic or Integra original A/C lines and its own custom-made ones that complete the conversion.

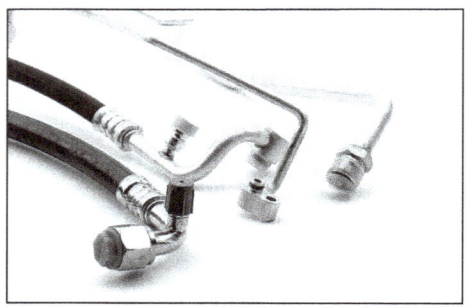

Retrofitting any non-native K-series chassis to be compatible with A/C isn't easy. However, Hybrid Racing has done its part to make the conversion more manageable. Its kits include all necessary lines and instructions on how to integrate them with the Civic, del Sol, or Integra chassis. Custom lines can also be made; however, a fair amount of crimping, brazing, and line bending is required. (Courtesy Hybrid Racing)

The A/C condenser and its cooling fan must be retained if A/C will be integrated. Hybrid Racing offers a kit that's based on the smaller A/C condenser of the 1996–2000 Civic. Custom mounts and brackets, such as these, can be made to mount the assembly.

The whole process can be done without the help of a kit but custom lines have to be fabricated as well as a significant amount of brazing.

When retaining A/C, begin by removing the battery, battery tray assembly, and the front bumper cover, including any fog lights or turn signal assemblies that may be attached. This is most easily done before the engine and radiator are in the car.

Bolt the 1996–2000 Civic condenser into place using Hybrid Racing's brackets. Remove the suction pipe assembly that spans from the firewall to the condenser along with the discharge line and suction hose that connect to the A/C compressor. On Civic chassis, the short condenser pipe must also be eliminated from the system. Be sure to save all of the hardware since some of it may need to be reused.

Hybrid Racing's kit supplies the appropriate pieces that allow the K-series A/C compressor to integrate within Civic, del Sol, and Integra chassis. A custom cooling fan that mounts to the front side of the condenser must also be used because of clearance issues. Be sure to source a unit that flows at least 1,000 cfm. Mount it to the condenser using a standard cooling fan mounting kit and position the assembly on the vehicle's right side.

When installing Hybrid Racing's A/C lines, be sure to lubricate the O-rings appropriately and reuse the original mounting hardware when possible. Be sure that the lines don't rub against the engine or transmission and carefully bend them away if necessary.

In terms of wiring, the compressor's thermal protection switch and condenser's cooling fan switch must both be addressed. Hybrid Racing provides the specific wiring diagrams for each chassis but plan on lengthening the one-pin A/C compressor connector to reach the new compressor's location on the opposite side of the engine bay. In addition, when using a factory ECU, wire the included relay to the appropriate 12V power source, ground, and two accessory pinouts located at the ECU.

If using K-Pro, Hybrid Racing provides the appropriate instructions for connections that must be made between the ECU plugs of both the factory chassis wiring harness and the K-series engine wiring harness. Similar to the radiator cooling fan, cut off the original A/C condenser fan's two-pin connector with at least 4 inches of wire exposed and solder it to the new fan's wires for a plug-and-play connection with the existing wiring harness. Be sure that the fan spins in the appropriate direction before finalizing its wiring.

A/C Delete with Power Steering

If power steering is retained but not A/C, start with a 2002–2004 RSX power steering pump. Such pumps are proven to offer the most clearance; however, there are other options that also may work. To allow additional clearance on 1992–1995 Civic chassis where hood space is at a premium, the answer lies with Jackson Racing, whose smaller-diameter supercharger pulley (PN 052-154) fits as if it were made for this.

Belt length may vary significantly depending on crankshaft pulley and power steering pump pulley diameter. With the A/C compressor removed, simply route the new belt following the same path. Next, a high-pressure feed hose from the 2002–2004 RSX bolts up to the pump, as you'd expect, and also bolts directly to the rack without any modifications. The remainder of the system includes the reservoir and low-pressure lines. The chassis' original reservoir can be reused or get one from any RSX. Connect the reservoir's two ports to the rack's two ports using 3/8-inch hose

A number of different K-series crankshaft pulleys are available, many of which are of different diameters. Of course, crankshaft pulley diameter directly affects drive belt length. To determine the appropriate belt length when using mismatched combinations of pulleys or those of unknown origins, route a section of string along the drive-belt path, cut it to length, and measure it. Provide the measurement and appropriate number of ribs to your local auto parts store for a compatible belt, which may or may not be a K-series engine belt.

Like the coolant overflow reservoir, the power steering reservoir may also have to be relocated. Here it's been mounted near its original location; however, its lines have been properly routed to the opposite side of the engine bay where the K-series power steering pump is mounted. The choice is yours: Relocate either the reservoir or the lines.

and the appropriate factory clamps where necessary.

It's important to know that some subframes feature three inlets and outlets, in which case a corresponding Civic power steering reservoir should be used to make the conversion easier. For even more hood clearance, unbolt the low-pressure return hose connection from the pump and reorient it for more space.

Hybrid Racing's power steering kit is based on the 2002–2004 RSX power steering pump and crankshaft pulley but belt selection is entirely custom. A seven-rib 53.5-inch belt must be used. This kit includes everything needed to adapt power steering to any of the Civic, del Sol, or Integra steering racks listed in this chapter. The appropriate power steering fluid cooler and overflow reservoir is also included with each kit for easy installation and, because of the kit's special low-profile fitting, hood clearance can be retained without cutting.

Hybrid Racing's power steering kit was designed around the power steering pump and crankshaft pulley of the 2002–2004 RSX and includes a low-profile adapter that allows for additional hood clearance. A high-pressure line that's compatible with the Civic, del Sol, and Integra power steering rack on one end and the RSX power steering pump on the other is what makes the kit truly worthwhile. (Courtesy Hybrid Racing)

Be sure that when using the RSX Type-S power steering pump the appropriate Type-S crankshaft pulley is used to prevent over-spinning and damaging the pump.

A/C with Power Steering

If A/C and power steering are retained, start with the appropriate power steering pump and crankshaft pulley and use the same combination of Hybrid Racing and factory components outlined above. Belt selection is easy; it's whatever the donor engine originally called for. (For specifics on hooking up power steering and A/C components, see previous sections.)

Intake and Exhaust Systems

K-series engine transplants are much more involved compared to older B- or H-series engine swaps where ancillaries, such as throttle bodies and exhaust manifolds, are rarely of concern. Because of drive-by-wire electronics that newer K-series engines feature as well as general chassis constraints, a number of issues must be addressed.

Throttle Body

Many K-series donor engines are equipped with drive-by-wire electronic throttle bodies. (See Chapter 1 for details on what type of throttle body each popular K-series engine features.) Before beginning the transplant on any of the chassis included in this chapter, an older cable-style throttle body must be swapped into place. The engine's intake manifold determines which throttle body may be used because bolt patterns differ among them.

Aftermarket throttle body adapters from Hybrid Racing and Karcepts that allow cable-style throttle bodies

CHAPTER 4

Unless a major electrical overhaul is planned that includes an unprecedented amount of wiring and a completely updated pedal assembly, be sure that the donor engine is equipped with a cable-driven throttle body. The large plastic housings and connectors easily distinguish electronic drive-by-wire versions.

Not all K-series intake manifolds are compatible with all K-series throttle bodies. Because of different bolt patterns, cable-driven throttle bodies may not always be used with newer intake manifolds that are normally matched with electronic drive-by-wire versions. Adapters, such as this one from K-Tuned, make compatibility easy. Here, a series of flush-mount bolts mount the flange to the intake manifold's unique bolt pattern, which allows the throttle body to bolt onto the flange's second set of properly oriented bolt holes.

Retaining the chassis' original evaporative emissions canister is important if you plan to retain emissions-legal status. The canister's lines must span to the connections at the throttle body or the plastic fitting located near the intake manifold, depending on the engine. Longer bulk hose will be required since the K-series throttle body is positioned on the opposite side of the engine bay.

to be bolted onto intake manifolds that accept drive-by-wire throttle bodies are also available.

If connecting the evaporative emissions system canister for an emissions-legal engine transplant, connect the canister's lines to the throttle body's nipples or the plastic connector located near the valve cover, depending on the engine.

Intake Piping

Once the engine is in place and the appropriate throttle body and intake manifold has been selected, an intake pipe and air filter must be added. Factory components may work but a cold-air unit from Hybrid Racing, AEM, Karcepts, or K-Tuned should be used. Hybrid Racing's cold-air intake was designed for K-series-swapped Civics and Integras and features high-end glass-reinforced silicone construction and stainless steel T-bolt clamps.

A number of aftermarket short-ram intake systems designed for the 2002–2006 RSX or 2002–2005 Civic Si as well as the 2004–2006 TSX, depending on which intake manifold is present, may also be used. Regardless of which intake system is chosen, be sure to install the intake air temperature sensor into the tubing and connect it to the engine wiring harness.

Exhaust Manifold

The exhaust system starts with the header. None of the factory K-series exhaust manifolds are compatible with any of the Civic, del Sol, or Integra chassis in this chapter, which means an aftermarket header must be used. Again, Hybrid Racing, K-Tuned, DC Sports, and PLM offer their engine swap headers in various configurations. They bolt directly onto any K-series engine, clearing the car's subframe and other components. Factory K-series exhaust manifolds are somewhat restrictive, so adding any of these aftermarket headers doesn't just allow for the appropriate clearance but can significantly increase horsepower when matched with the appropriate intake and exhaust system.

Intake piping solutions are no longer custom when it comes to K-series engine swaps. Systems such as this one from K-Tuned include everything necessary: the appropriate silicone couplers, clamps, mounting brackets, pipe, and filter. K-Tuned's intake systems are also available in a variety of finishes. (Photo Courtesy K-Tuned)

An aftermarket exhaust manifold specifically designed for K-series engine swaps into any of these chassis is mandatory to allow proper clearance at the firewall and subframe as well as underneath the chassis. In most cases, however, no exhaust manifold bolts directly to the exhaust system. The exhaust tubing directly following the exhaust manifold must be cut and shortened to fit using the appropriate flange.

Once the header is in place, bolt up a compatible exhaust system and muffler. Be sure to choose a system that features piping no smaller than 60 mm. Almost any exhaust system does fine here; what's important is the diameter of its piping. The K-series engine is significantly larger than the engine originally installed in any of these chassis. This means that a larger-diameter aftermarket version is mandatory if all of the engine's benefits are to be met without restriction.

With the exhaust and header installed, an aftermarket catalytic converter can be fabricated into place or an adjustable-length mid-pipe, such as that offered by Hybrid Racing, can be set to the appropriate size and bolted up, eliminating the need for fabrication or welding.

ECU Selection

The appropriate ECU should be chosen early on but selecting the right one isn't as easy as it is with B- or H-series engine swaps. Most modern Honda ECUs are equipped with immobilizers, which are designed to render the vehicle's electronics useless unless they're matched with their corresponding transponder key and receiver. The key, immobilizer system indicator, ECU, and immobilizer control unit (located at the ignition switch), must all work together. Of course, this presents a problem because none of the vehicles in this chapter are equipped with this.

Fortunately, there are three popular solutions. The simplest is to source a Japanese-spec 2001–2005 Civic Type R or 2001–2006 Integra Type R ECU. Earlier Type R ECUs like these feature immobilizers that can easily be bypassed; however, Type R ECUs are also costly and hard to source. They're also (unless modified) only suitable for 2.0L performance i-VTEC engines, such as the K20A2.

To bypass the immobilizer, the main relay must simply be grounded on its own, not through the ECU. Simply cut ECU wire E7 and appropriately ground the wire's main relay side to the chassis.

ECU selection is critical to a successful K-series engine swap, but choosing the right one can be confusing. Japanese-spec ECUs, such as the PRC computer from the Integra Type R, are among the most popular choices. Such computers can be rid of their anti-theft immobilizers relatively easily and are directly compatible with Hondata's K-Pro engine management system.

The second solution is Hybrid Racing or K-Tuned immobilizer bypass units, which are simple circuit boards enclosed in small plastic cases that can be spliced directly into the engine wiring harness to disable the immobilizer.

Compatible ECUs include those from the 2002–2004 RSX Type-S for performance i-VTEC engines, 2002–2004 RSX base model for economy i-VTEC engines using the dual-stage intake manifold, 2002–2005 Civic Si for economy i-VTEC engines not using the dual-stage intake manifold, and 2002–2006 CR-V for 2.4L economy i-VTEC engines. (Note that 2005–2006 RSX ECUs are not compatible.)

Although the Accord or Element ECUs may seem like viable options for 2.4L engine swaps, they feature entirely different pinouts and cannot be easily rid of their immobilizers. The CR-V ECU shares its pinouts with the RSX, which means wiring harness selection just got a whole lot easier.

Once an immobilizer bypass unit is sourced, disabling the immobilizer

Honda integrated the anti-theft immobilizer system into every vehicle that's native to the K-series engine. The results render every K-series ECU useless if the immobilizer isn't addressed. K-Tuned's Immobilizer Bypass eliminates the immobilizer by connecting its four wires at the ECU. (Photo Courtesy K-Tuned)

is easy and involves tapping four wires into the ECU's A and E connectors, which are outlined in both companies' instructions.

Any of the above ECUs can be used on either 5-speed or 6-speed gearboxes; however, when using an ECU from a 5-speed vehicle with a 6-speed transmission, the reverse-gear lockout must be addressed in order for shifting to remain smooth and for reverse gear to be engaged. A momentary switch can be hard-wired into place to override the reverse gear solenoid.

Hondata's K-Pro is the third, and perhaps most elegant, solution aside from a stand-alone engine management system. K-Pro not only disables the ECU's immobilizer, it also eliminates the secondary oxygen sensor and offers several other features, such as fuel and ignition tunability, cam angle control, data-logging, and pre-installed base maps. K-Pro-modified ECUs can also be configured to work with any K-series engine or transmission and the appropriate outputs are provided for reverse-gear lockout functionality with 5-speed ECUs.

A working K-series ECU must be provided to Hondata to have it converted. K-Pro is currently compatible with the following manual-transmission-style ECUs: 2002–2004 RSX base model, 2002–2004 RSX Type-S, 2001–2006 Integra Type R, 2001–2005 Civic Type R, 2002–2006 CR-V, and 2002–2005 Civic Si.

Transmission Considerations

Transmission options must be considered carefully when selecting an ECU. Unlike older D- and B-series transmissions that feature similar vehicle speed sensors, Honda made two sensors available to K-series gearboxes: low frequency and high frequency. Low-frequency vehicle speed sensors, such as those found in 2002–2004 RSX, 2002–2005 Civic Si, 2001–2005 Civic Type R, and 2001–2006 Integra Type R transmissions communicate with the ECU and instrument cluster through a low-frequency signal that initiates at the transmission's final-drive gear.

High-frequency vehicle speed sensors, such as those found in 2005–2006 RSX, 2003–2007 Accord, 2006–2008 Accord Euro R, 2004–2008 TSX, 2006–2011 Civic Si, and 2007–2011 Civic Type R transmissions, communicate with the ECU only, which then sends the signal to the instrument cluster through a high-frequency signal that initiates at the transmission's third gear.

For the ECU and instrument cluster to properly interpret vehicle speed and for VTEC to work, the transmission, vehicle speed sensor, ECU, and engine and chassis wiring harnesses must all be compatible with one another.

The easy solution is to use a low-frequency-type transmission along with the appropriate 2002–2004 RSX or 2002–2005 Civic Si ECU. When matched with the right engine wiring harness, the process is nearly plug-and-play. High-frequency-type transmissions can be used, and fortunately any of their shortcomings can be corrected through K-Pro or with a supplemental device like K-Tuned's Adjustable Speed Converter.

K-Tuned's converter allows transmissions with high-frequency speed sensor signals that none of the vehicles' instrument clusters in this chapter would otherwise be able to communicate with to do so properly. K-Tuned's solution must be wired into the engine wiring harness near the ECU and allows transmissions such as the 2005–2006 RSX, 2003–2007 Accord, 2006–2008 Accord Euro R, 2004–2008 TSX, 2006–2011 Civic Si, and 2007–2011 Civic Type R to be

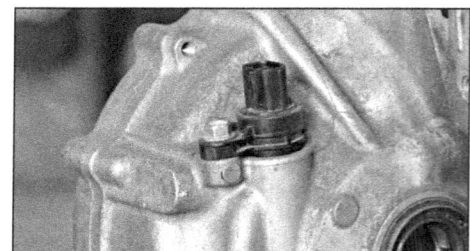

Vehicle speed sensors, such as these from 2002–2004 RSX, 2002–2005 Civic Si, 2001–2005 Civic Type R, and 2001–2006 Integra Type R transmissions, communicate using a low-frequency signal that initiates at the transmission's final-drive gear. Selecting an ECU that's compatible with that same low-frequency signal is critical.

Hondata's K-Pro is arguably the most popular tool for K-series ECU tuning. It plugs directly into appropriate K-series engine wiring harnesses, which means that no additional wiring is necessary, the immobilizer is disabled, and it provides the same tuning capabilities you typically find with higher-end, stand-alone engine management systems.

1992–2000 CIVIC AND 1994–2001 INTEGRA

Vehicle speed sensors, such as these from 2005–2006 RSX, 2003–2007 Accord, 2006–2008 Accord Euro R, 2004–2008 TSX, 2006–2011 Civic Si, and 2007–2011 Civic Type R transmissions, communicate using a high-frequency signal that initiates at the transmission's third gear. When matched with the wrong ECU, vehicle speed doesn't register appropriately and VTEC doesn't function.

used on older chassis as well as with any of the engine swap-compatible ECUs mentioned earlier. Wiring connections aren't complicated and are limited to 12V ignition power, ground, vehicle speed signal input, and vehicle speed signal output.

Wiring

Once a particular engine and transmission has been chosen, wiring can begin. K-series engine swap wiring has three major components: engine harness, sub-harness, and charge harness.

Hybrid Racing's Vehicle Speed Converter allows ECUs and vehicle speed sensors that weren't initially compatible with each other to work together. The converter reinterprets the high-frequency signal to accommodate the ECU and instrument cluster. Hondata's K-Pro also has the same capabilities. (Courtesy Hybrid Racing)

Engine Harness

Unlike older Honda engine swaps where the original engine wiring harness can be reused and modified, with K-series engine swaps into older chassis like those in this chapter, everything starts with a K-series engine wiring harness sourced from any manual-transmission-equipped 2002–2004 RSX, 2002–2005 Civic Si, or 2002–2006 CR-V (automatic versions can be converted). Later-model 2005–2006 RSX harnesses may also be used but extensive modifications must be made to them. Also, be sure to select a harness from a left-hand-drive vehicle; right-hand-drive engine wiring harnesses are not directly compatible.

Each of the above harnesses plug directly into any previously mentioned K-series ECU's A and B connectors, which means that any necessary wiring takes place at the harness' 20-pin connector and the ECU's E connector. Overall, the 2002-2004 RSX Type-S harness has proved to be the most popular; it's compatible with either 5-speed or 6-speed transmissions because of its reverse-gear lockout connector and offers the most flexibility.

The engine wiring harness should already be connected to the engine and routed through the original hole in the chassis, located below and behind the battery. The fuse box, battery, and battery tray must be removed to access this. Save and reuse the original wiring harness grommet for a factory-like fit. To remove and reuse the grommet, slit its side open so that the original harness can be pulled out; secure it to the new harness with electrical tape.

The harness can also be routed into the cabin elsewhere along the firewall for a cleaner look. Simply drill the appropriate-size hole and reuse the original grommet in the new opening. Be sure to plug any unused wiring harness openings on the firewall to avoid fumes and debris from entering the cabin. Once completed, retrieve the engine wiring harness from inside the cabin, plug its A and B connectors into the ECU, and reinstall the battery, battery tray, and fuse box.

Finally, be sure that the engine is grounded to the chassis in at least three locations and that the engine wiring harness is grounded to the engine. An improperly grounded engine can lead to all sorts of trouble, which can often be difficult to trace. Appropriate grounds include those from the timing chain cover and the transmission case.

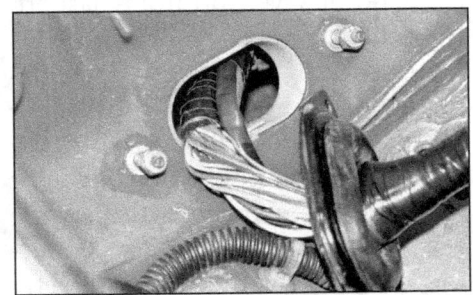

When routing the K-series engine wiring harness into the chassis, follow the existing wiring harness path through the firewall. Here, the original D-series engine wiring harness' firewall grommet has been retained and integrated onto the new harness. The results are a factory-like appearance and reduced chances of engine bay fumes entering the interior.

CHAPTER 4

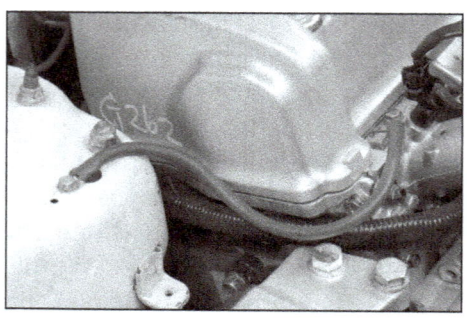

Improper grounding is one of the leading causes of what may appear to be an engine wiring harness or sub-harness problem. Be sure to ground the engine to the chassis in at least three locations. The engine wiring harness must also be grounded to the engine using the harness' internal grounding connectors.

Sub-Harness

The sub-harness is the intermediary between the K-series engine wiring harness, the ECU, and the car, including the instrument cluster. It allows everything to communicate with one another. You can make your own sub-harness, which requires a significant amount of electrical know-how, or you can purchase a plug-and-play version from Hasport, Hybrid Racing, Rywire, or K-Tuned.

A typical sub-harness includes six major components: the E connector that plugs directly into the ECU's remaining slot, a connector that plugs directly into the engine wiring harness' open 20-pin connector, a connector that plugs directly into the chassis wiring harness, an oxygen sensor connector, an oxygen sensor relay, and either a data link connector for monitoring error codes or another chassis wiring harness connector, depending on the vehicle.

Before moving on, some wiring procedures must be addressed that are common to all sub-harnesses, regardless of the manufacturer. First, the previously installed radiator fan switch, whether threaded directly into the radiator or into a lower radiator hose adapter, must be appropriately wired into place.

Cut the radiator fan switch connector from the car's original engine wiring harness, leaving at least 4 inches of wire exposed, and plug it into the radiator fan switch if the appropriate connector is not already provided on the sub-harness. Splice the connector's signal wire to the specified wire on the sub-harness and the other to any suitable chassis ground. Follow the same procedure for installing the coolant temperature sensor, connecting its single signal wire to the appropriate wire on the sub-harness.

A number of additional connections must be made that are vehicle-specific. Appropriate wires must be located on the underdash harness' original ECU plugs (which no longer plug into the ECU), and properly connected to the sub-harness so that the fuel pump, malfunction indicator lamp, electronic load detector, tachometer signal, and data link connector all function appropriately. The process and number of connections that must be made varies among chassis.

Next, plug the sub-harness' E connector into the ECU and the

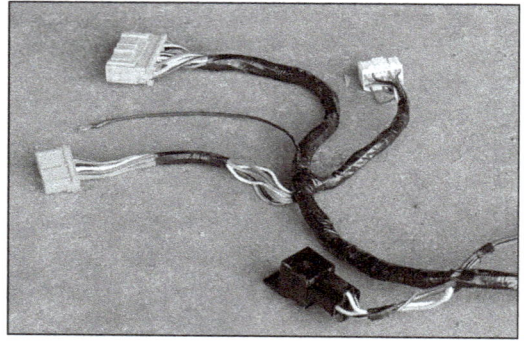

The sub-harness is the intermediary between the ECU, engine wiring harness, and chassis. The 20-pin connector (upper left) plugs directly into the engine wiring harness. If you make your own sub-harness, you need to source this connector and direct each of its wires to the appropriate locations.

sub-harness' 20-pin connector to the one on the engine wiring harness inside the vehicle. A final wire must be spliced into the engine harness' B connector at the ECU that controls the battery light at the instrument cluster. Do not cut this wire. Use a wire splice to connect it. Find a suitable place to mount the ECU, data link connector, and oxygen sensor relay, and move on to the driver's side to finish the wiring.

Regardless of which chassis is used, the primary oxygen sensor must also be connected. Route the plug through the existing hole in the floor, if equipped, or drill a suitable hole somewhere on the center tunnel underneath the dash. If K-Pro or some other engine management system isn't being used and OBD-II is retained, a secondary oxygen sensor must also be wired into place. Source the connector from the car's original engine wiring harness and connect its four wires to the sub-harness' remaining four wires according to the instructions.

Gain access to the chassis wiring harness near the left-side shock tower and follow the instructions for the sub-harness for making the appropriate connections. Once the appropriate connectors have been located, connect them to the new sub-harness. Be sure to secure the sub-harness and its connectors with electrical tape and zip ties where necessary.

Most plug-and-play sub-harnesses aren't expensive but assembling your own can reduce the overall cost of the project. You need the appropriate service manual for your chassis as well as one for the K-series ECU you plan to use. Refer to the wiring diagram on page 42. If you plan on attempting your own wiring conversion. The ECU's E plug connector and engine wiring harness' 20-pin connector must be manually wired into place. The appropriate connectors can be sourced from any 2002–2004 RSX or 2001–2005 Civic chassis wiring harness.

Charge Harness

The K-series charge harness spans from the positive battery terminal to multiple locations: alternator, knock sensor, starter, fuse box, and engine wiring harness. On K-series-equipped vehicles the fuse box is located near the front bumper, which means the harness must be lengthened to reach the fuse box, which is located near the firewall. Connectors attached to the fuse box must also be swapped for ones compatible with any of the chassis in this chapter.

To do all of this, a combination of the car's original charge harness and the K-series engine's charge harness must be used. Doing so eliminates unnecessary customization. Once completed, the new charge harness should span from the positive battery terminal to the starter, from the positive battery terminal to the fuse box, and from the fuse box to the alternator.

Suspension and Braking

Even the heaviest K-series engines weigh only marginally more than B-series engines that are, of course, native to Civics and Integras of this period. As such, suggested suspension and braking modifications aren't much different than are otherwise recommended.

The most dramatic suspension improvement that can be made is to invest in a proper set of tires. The appropriate compound along with the widest set that fits without rubbing against the chassis is ideal. If the goal is to maximize handling, avoid excessive lowering, which limits shock travel, and keep suspension camber close to factory recommendations, erring slightly on the negative side. Excess negative camber and incorrectly sized tires, which is a growing phenomenon among the non-performance-oriented Honda community, only hurts a car's handling capabilities by significantly reducing the tires' contact patches.

In terms of braking, Honda did its homework when determining what its Civic, del Sol, and Integra lineup required. Any time performance is increased and excess vehicle speeds are achieved (which is, after all, why most K-series engines are swapped into place), more capable braking components should be considered. You need only look to the 1994–2001 Integra or the 1999–2000 Civic Si. Both chassis are equipped with rear disc brakes that can be swapped among all Civic and Integra chassis for instant upgraded stopping power.

If extensive track time is planned, cross-drilled or slotted rotors along with more aggressive pads and steel-braided brake lines that can withstand the hotter fluid temperatures are upgrades that should be considered. For this, look to companies such as Power Slot, EBC Brakes, and Hawk Performance for components that may be used on the street as well as the track.

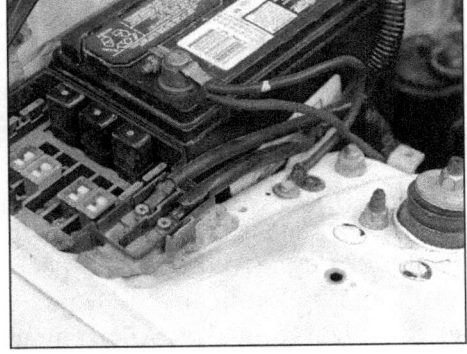

A charge harness must be made that directs current from the battery throughout the engine bay. The K-series charge harness may seem to be a direct fit, but it isn't. It's too short and its electrical connectors at the fuse box's terminals are incompatible. The two connectors must be sourced from the original D- or B-series charge harness and grafted onto the K-series harness.

Most braking upgrades for Civic and del Sol chassis can be sourced from higher-end models that feature rear disc brakes from the factory, including any 1999–2000 Civic Si, del Sol VTEC, or third-generation Integra. Further upgrades can be made with the addition of slotted or cross-drilled rotors that allow for better cooling and high-performance pads. In most cases, though, a four-wheel-disc changeover is more than sufficient.

CHAPTER 5

1988–1991 CIVIC AND 1990–1993 INTEGRA

In 1987, Honda Motor Company did something right, something that forever changed the way the automotive performance rank and file viewed the brand. On the heels of a global car market that had shifted from thrilling albeit environmentally careless domestics to more Earth-loving yet characterless subcompacts, Honda introduced the world to the greatest trade-off yet: the fourth-generation Civic. Consider the foundation for Honda performance officially laid.

The 1988 model year Civic was Honda's sleekest to date; its hoodline lowered, its glass expanse increased, its wheelbase longer. This new Civic's aerodynamic adeptness and no-nonsense rigid structure yet light weight was something special, typically uncharacteristic of cars of its class. Fuel injection was now standard for all U.S.-bound trims, and a new-for-1988 sedan was introduced, accompanying revved hatchback, wagon, and CRX models. But if it hadn't been for Honda's thoroughly reinvented double-wishbone suspension and all-new 4-cylinder D16A6 engine, it's unlikely any of us would be babbling on about the Japanese auto firm's fourth-term Civic a quarter of a century later.

To this day, few suspension configurations are as tidy, as well packaged, and as formidable as Honda's unequal-length A-arm arrangement (also known as a double-wishbone suspension). The now-historically validated layout features single upper and lower A-arms (wishbones) for each front corner and a multi-link trailing arm rear suspension that each pivots against the chassis and suspension members. Compared to older Civics' timeworn front torsion bar suspensions, double-wishbone lay-outs allow for improved handling

The Honda 1988–1991 Civic and CRX aren't the easiest chassis for a K-series powertrain swap. Compared to later-model Civics, these engine bays are considerably smaller. A significant amount of fabrication is also necessary to complete the conversion. However, the results of swapping such an engine into any of these lightweight chassis is nothing short of remarkable.

Part of what has made the 1988–1991 Civic and CRX such special cars is their double-wishbone front suspensions. Unequal-length upper and lower A-arms link together at the knuckle assembly, allowing for a significant amount of travel and articulation. Thanks to years of aftermarket support, Honda's famed front suspension may be upgraded in numerous ways.

and better stiffening in factory form and yield far more options in terms of performance improvements. Honda employed its famed double-wishbone suspension on the Civic line for 13 model years until adopting its current MacPherson strut layout.

Club racers immediately latched onto this alternative race car, not just because of its forward-thinking suspension but also because of the Civic Si hatchback's and CRX Si's D16A6 power plant that set the pace for more performance-minded engines that were later developed. Honda's most powerful, most durable SOHC Civic engine yet, the D16A6 was also its largest, pushing a class-leading 106 hp thanks to more cubic inches, a 9.1:1 compression ratio, and a 7,100-rpm redline that was made possible from a thoughtfully configured 1.52:1 rod/stroke ratio. The Si's 16-valve cylinder head with its redesigned water jackets provided more predictable cooling for racers and featured one of Honda's most optimally designed intake and exhaust ports; ones that were straighter and capable of flowing better than even later VTEC heads. All of this was for the Si, a no-nonsense sporty sort of car that didn't waste itself on accouterments such as power steering or an automatic transmission.

Honda's 1988–1991 Civic must also be credited for the Honda engine swap revolution's humble beginnings. Early tuners looked to the Japanese market's twin-cam ZC engine and began transplanting them into place before the body style's four-year lifespan was fulfilled. As the fifth-generation model was introduced, those same tuners began experimenting with the more complex, 160-hp B16A transplant, which was also sourced from Japan-specific trims. Those early B-series engine swaps are undoubtedly responsible for the next 20-some years' worth of transplanting, building, tuning, and racing, all in the name of Honda's Civic.

It doesn't make sense to discuss the 1988–1991 Civic without including the 1990–1993 Integra. The similarities between the two are seemingly endless. Honda's early lineup of Civics and its second-generation Integra remain popular among tuners more than 25 years after their introduction for a number of reasons. Their double-wishbone suspensions, lightweight structures, and cross-compatibility with one another are partially why. The 1988–1991 Civic and 1990–1993 Integra aren't the most accepting in terms of K-series engine swaps. Their engine bays afford less space than later Civics and Integras and their cable-style clutch mechanisms and pre-OBD electronics present further obstacles that are exclusive only to such older chassis. However, after all is said and done, and the K-series is in place, none of this really matters. After all, few cars are as powerful or as fast as a 220-hp K20A positioned inside of an 1,800-pound CRX.

1988–1991 Civic

The fourth-generation Civic was made in three flavors (hatchback, sedan, and wagon) and in a number of trim levels, including EX, Si, LX, DX, and Std. A special 4WD version was also available exclusively for wagon models. With the exception of the five-door wagon's slightly shorter engine bay, all 1988–1991-model Civic chassis feature similar engine bays and remain different from one another mostly by engine and transmission selection as well as by amenities. Although the fourth-generation Civic's engine bay isn't a mirror image of the 1990–1993 Integra's, it's close enough that B-series engines and transmissions transfer over with relative ease.

None of this makes the K-series engine transplant any easier but it does reveal how (as with B-series engine swaps) the K-series transplant process doesn't differ much between the two chassis.

Honda released its Civic hatchback in 1987 for the 1988 model year in two trim levels: DX and Std (ED6). During the model's second year of production, Honda then released its top-of-the-line Si. The ED7 Civic Si was sold with the popular D16A6, a 106-hp SOHC power plant that predated VTEC, while DX and Std models were equipped with slightly less-powerful 1.5L engines. Si models feature the sort of creature comforts that are expected of any entry-level car by today's standards but are no

1988–1991 Civic Chassis Codes

1988–1991 Civic DX, Std Hatchback	ED6
1989–1991 Civic Si Hatchback	ED7
1988–1991 Civic DX, LX Sedan	ED3
1990–1991 Civic EX Sedan	ED4
1988–1991 Civic DX Wagon	EE2
1988–1991 Civic 4WD 1600 Wagon	EE4
1988–1989 Civic Wagovan	EY2

match for the lightweight DX and Std chassis.

The Civic sedan was reintroduced for the 1988 model year in LX and DX (ED3) trims and then in EX (ED4) form beginning in 1990. From the firewall forward, little distinguishes four-door models from hatchbacks. Honda outfitted its sedan models with the same D-series engines with rear disc brakes exclusive to the 1990–1991 EX.

Once again, a five-door wagon model was also introduced, which was available in DX (EE2), 4WD 1600 (EE4), and Wagovan (EY2) configurations. Honda's fourth-generation Civic wagons feature marginally shorter engine bays compared to their counterparts but are still worthwhile K-series engine transplant candidates and were originally offered with the same 1.5L and 1.6L non-VTEC D-series engines.

Chassis Pros and Cons

The fourth-generation Civic chassis is, arguably, where the Honda performance story begins. It was the first Civic to receive any sort of engine swap on a wide scale as well as the first with the ability to share many of the Integra's suspension and braking components. The fourth-generation Civic chassis is also light, measuring as few as 1,933 pounds, which makes it a swap worth considering, despite any additional work that may go along with it.

However you manage to get it in there, hood clearance is going to be a problem once the K-series is in place. Power steering clearance is also limited for the few models that are so equipped and don't retrofit easily. Unlike 1992-and-newer chassis, the fourth-generation Civic's engine bay is small. Despite all of that, hatchback chassis in particular remain favorites among longtime Honda enthusiasts. Aftermarket components are also limited for such engine swaps. With the appropriate pieces, though, K-series transplants into these chassis aren't out of reach for those with intermediate skills; however, a fair amount of fabrication and electrical modifications must be made compared to newer chassis. Cutting, grinding, and welding should all be expected when performing any K-series engine swap into any 1988–1991 Civic. Finally, the battery must be relocated to the trunk for ideal engine fitment.

1988–1991 CRX

For many, the CRX defined the Honda performance movement. For some, it still does. The two-seater CRX is built on the same platform as the hatchback and sedan, but benefits from a lighter-weight chassis and a more performance-oriented nature. Its options are limited and include the Si (ED9), DX, and HX (ED8). All three are structurally similar but feature different engines and transmissions. The Si shares the same 106-hp D16A6 as the hatchback while DX models are fitted with the less-powerful D15B2. Lightweight HF models, which boast fuel consumption ratings better than many of today's hybrids, are equipped with the highly efficient D15B6. Like the hatchback, Si models feature many of the accouterments that Honda owners have come to expect but at the expense of added weight, including rear disc brakes on 1990–1991 models and a sliding sunroof. In terms of lightweight fourth-generation Civics, nothing beats the CRX HF.

Equal in popularity to the hatchback, the 1988–1991 CRX is for many the epitome of Honda performance. Here, a K20A engine and transmission have been swapped into place. The K-series engine swap process is similar for every Civic and CRX of this generation.

1988–1991 CIVIC AND 1990–1993 INTEGRA

1988–1991 CRX Chassis Codes

1988–1991 CRX DX, HF	ED8
1988–1991 CRX Si	ED9

1990–1993 Integra Chassis Codes

1990–1993 Integra GS, LS, RS Hatchback	DA9
1991–1993 (exclude 1992) LS Special Edition Hatchback	DA9
1992–1993 Integra GS-R Hatchback	DB2
1990–1993 Integra GS, LS, RS Sedan	DB1

Chassis Pros and Cons

Perhaps the CRX's best feature is its light weight, with its HF model weighing just over 1,800 pounds and its heaviest of all Si still less than 2,200 pounds. As with the Civic, hood clearance is also an issue with the CRX; K-series engine swap components aren't as readily available as they are for later-model chassis. Because of the fourth-generation Civic and CRX pre-OBD electronics, a fair amount of wiring is necessary. Fortunately, aftermarket-wiring solutions are available, which can simplify the process. Getting the engine and transmission into place is just as challenging. Intermediate fabrication skills are necessary as is the ability to weld one of the engine's mounting brackets to the chassis. Finally, the battery must be relocated to the trunk to avoid interference with the engine.

1990–1993 Integra

The second-generation Integra was offered in hatchback and sedan configurations in trim levels ranging from GS-R, GS, LS, to RS.

Introduced for the car's final two years of production, the three-door hatchback's GS-R model (DB2) featured North America's first taste of DOHC VTEC engines except for the arguably unobtainable NSX C-series. The GS-R B17A1 engine featured a dynamically adjustable valvetrain, much like the D16Z6 but produced significantly more power, 160 hp to

Be sure to select the appropriate engine and transmission before ordering any accompanying parts. A number of factors must be considered, all of which can affect whether or not mounts, radiator hoses, and ECUs, for example, may or may not be compatible. When selecting an engine, don't immediately dismiss less-expensive, economy i-VTEC versions. A 160-hp K20A3 can be a significant upgrade from the D-series or non-VTEC B-series engine that is being replaced.

be exact. GS, LS, and RS hatchbacks (DA9) and sedans (DB1) shared the less-powerful non-VTEC B18A1 engines and longer-ratio gearboxes, which, to be fair, still managed to produce more power than any Civic engine could yield to date.

All second-generation Integras feature Honda's double-wishbone suspension up front and, for the first time for the Integra, include a fully independent suspension in the rear. Four-wheel disc brakes are also standard on all Integras of the period.

Chassis Pros and Cons

Unlike the Civic and CRX, hood clearance isn't an issue with the Integra. Here, any 2.0L K-series engine drops into place with room to spare between it and the hood. The same fabrication procedures are required with the second-generation Integra as with the fourth-generation Civic, and wiring can be just as complicated. Because of the car's production span, electronics vary between pre-OBD and OBD-I; however, the overall wiring process differs little between the two. Although the battery must also be relocated to the trunk, Integras afford slightly more room up front between the intake manifold and the radiator.

Engine and Transmission

The K-series engine and transmission you choose affects a number of aspects of the swap. Civics and Integras of this era are among some of the lightest. It's important to not forget that when selecting the engine. For example, a 160-hp K20A3 might not seem very powerful when considering the base model RSX (from which it came) but when you place that much horsepower and

CHAPTER 5

142 ft-lbs of torque under the hood of a 2,200-pound CRX it's an entirely different story.

Mounts

After you decide on an engine and transmission, you can choose the appropriate mount kit. The choices are few, as are the number of transmissions compatible with any of the chassis in this chapter.

1988–1991 Civic and 1988–1991 CRX

Engine mount selection is limited when it comes to any fourth-generation Civic or second-generation CRX chassis. Hasport's EFK1 engine mount kit allows any K-series engine to bolt into place along with the appropriate 2002–2006 RSX, 2002–2005 Civic Si, 2001–2005 Civic Type R, 2001–2006 Integra Type R, 2006–2011 Civic Si, or 2007–2011 Civic Type R transmission. Unlike alternate engine mount kits that are available for later-model Civics, Accord and TSX transmissions are not compatible. Moreover, unlike with newer Civic chassis, hood clearance is minimal and a taller Japanese-spec SiR front-end-conversion or SiR-style hood that's compatible with the North American-spec front end must be used regardless of the K-series engine that is selected. Taller-deck 2.4L engines require even more clearance, in which case a custom hood must be sourced.

In addition, Hasport's EFK1 engine mount kit is only compatible with North American-spec vehicles that were not originally equipped with B-series engines.

And, finally, because of clearance issues, power steering is not compatible.

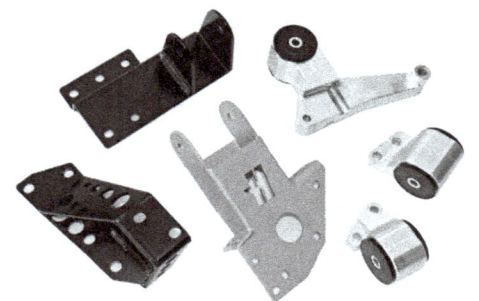

Hasport is among the few manufacturers to offer engine mount kits specifically for the 1988–1991 Civic and CRX as well as for the 1990–1993 Integra. The company's right-side framerail bracket must be welded to the chassis. Because of this, Hasport provides an unfinished piece (center) that's free of paint and ready for the process.

1990–1993 Integra

Mount choices are just as few for the second-generation Integra. Once again, though, Hasport offers the appropriate solution. The company's DAK1 kit is the bolt-in solution for all trim levels and is compatible with the same series of transmissions as the previously mentioned Civic and CRX models. For transplants where power steering is retained, slight clearance adjustments must be made to the hood's underside to allow space for the system's pump and drive pulley.

Although taller-deck 2.4L engines are compatible with Hasport's DAK1 engine mount kit, hood clearance is compromised because of the larger engine. The hood's substructure must be cut away to allow clearance near the valve cover and throttle body.

Car Preparation

If you've never removed an engine, familiarize yourself with Chapter 4 where a more detailed explanation of the process is laid out

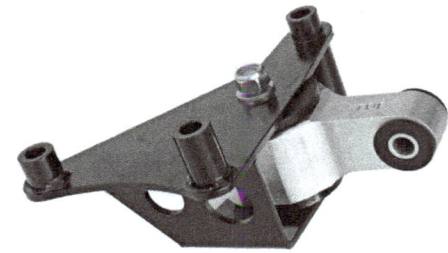

Hasport's Integra-based engine mount kits are similar to the Civic and CRX kits. However, they differ in exactly how they attach to their rear subframes. Both kits feature a bracket that mounts onto the subframe, but only Integra kits include a "dog bone" mount that connects to its corresponding steel transmission bracket.

for the later-model Civic and Integra. The overall process is similar; however, there are a few considerations that remain specific to older chassis.

As with any engine swap, it begins with removing the old engine and transmission. Be sure to remove each of the engine and transmission mounts and brackets and set them aside; none of them are needed when performing the transplant.

Compared to other engines that have typically found their way into the fourth-generation Civic and second-generation Integra engine bays, fitting the K-series into place isn't easy. Thankfully, the aftermarket has sorted all of this out, making fitment relatively straightforward, albeit tight. Remember, unlike other engine swaps, the K-series sits 180-degrees opposed to the D- or B-series originally in your car. As such, aspects that you normally don't worry about must be addressed.

Draining the Fluids

Not every chassis covered in this chapter features A/C but for those

1988–1991 CIVIC AND 1990–1993 INTEGRA

that do, the system must be drained before proceeding. A professional with the appropriate equipment should evacuate the system. Once drained, raise the car and drain the remaining fluids, including the transmission fluid, power steering fluid (if equipped), coolant, and engine oil.

Removing the Ancillaries

Begin by disconnecting and removing the battery and battery tray. Disconnect the engine wiring harness connectors from the chassis and from the underhood fuse box. Be sure that all ground wires have also been disconnected from the chassis. Remove the wheels, shift linkage, exhaust A-pipe, catalytic converter, fuel feed and return lines, as well as the throttle cable.

The radiator must also be removed along with its cooling fan and the two heater hoses that exit from the heater core at the firewall. Disconnect the clutch cable from the transmission and temporarily secure it out of the way using zip ties. If A/C won't be added or retained, remove the system's lines, condenser, wiring harness, and cooling fan now.

Because of limited clearance, power steering is not compatible with Civic or CRX chassis. If equipped, or for Integra chassis where it will be eliminated, be sure to remove the system's components once the engine and transmission have been taken out.

Finally, remove the MAP sensor and purge control solenoid valve assembly from the firewall along with the supporting bracket and vacuum lines. Each of these is self-contained and is included with whichever K-series engine you've chosen.

Removing the Axles

As with any engine transplant, the axles must be removed before moving forward. Refer to Chapter 4 for the appropriate procedure or consult a service manual. Remove the lower shock forks, and with the ball joints properly disconnected, rotate the knuckle assemblies outward and remove the axles.

Removing the Mounts

Unbolt and remove the front transmission mount and then disconnect the rear engine bracket from its mount and from the transmission. Support the engine and transmission with the appropriate hoist or platform and then disconnect and remove the left- and right-side mounts before removing the entire assembly. Once the engine has been removed, unbolt the rear engine mount from the subframe.

Finally, unbolt and remove the front crossmember along with the two radius rods that connect to

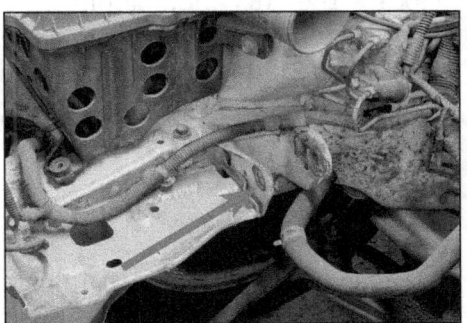

The right-side framerail bracket on every Civic, CRX, and Integra of this era must be removed. A fair amount of fabrication is involved. Be sure to remove the battery tray to its left along with the factory airbox above. The chassis wiring harness that's attached to the chassis should also be temporarily unclipped and moved out of the way. (Photo Courtesy Hasport Performance Products)

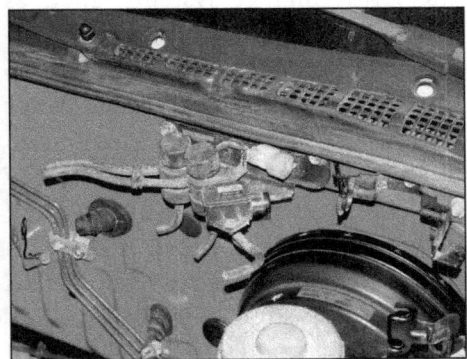

When preparing the engine bay, remove the firewall-mounted MAP sensor and remove the solenoids and their corresponding bracket. All of this is integrated into the K-series engine, which means none of this will be reinstalled. (Photo Courtesy Hasport Performance Products)

When preparing a 1988–1991 Civic or CRX engine bay for any other engine swap, it should typically look like this. However, K-series engine swaps require so much more to be removed, including the shift linkage, battery tray, fuel filter, heater hoses, and charge harness. Be sure that the rear mount has also been removed from the subframe and that the crossmember and its radius rods have been unbolted and set aside. (Photo Courtesy Hasport Performance Products)

CHAPTER 5

the lower control arms. Two framerail brackets, which are welded directly to the chassis, are all that should remain.

ABS and Other Brake System Considerations

The ABS system must be addressed on Integra models that are so equipped (the U.S.-spec Civic and CRX do not feature ABS). The system must either be relocated or removed. Relocate the ABS modulator, accumulator, and pump away from the engine or source the appropriate non-ABS lines and proportioning valve from any 1990–1993 non-ABS Integra. Whichever strategy is chosen, bleed the system according to the factory service manual.

Civic, CRX, and non-ABS Integra chassis have their own brake system clearance issues. In both cases, the brake-proportioning valve interferes with engine placement. Fortunately, modifying and relocating the valves isn't difficult. Start by removing the evaporative emissions canister and unbolting the fuel filter bracket from the firewall. Next, simply unbolt the proportioning valve and wiring harness bracket from the framerail. Use locking pliers to clamp the proportioning valve together and remove its mounting bracket.

Reorient the bracket and mount it to the opposite side of the proportioning valve. Once reattached, remove the locking pliers. Gently bend the brake line assembly so that the proportioning valve may swing toward the firewall, where it ultimately mounts to the fuel filter bracket's original location on Integra chassis and a pre-existing stud on Civic and CRX chassis.

The fuel filter and its bracket must also be relocated. Consider where the K-series exhaust manifold will be positioned before settling on a location. This fuel filter was raised and mounted closer to the shock tower with the help of a spacer, away from the heat of the exhaust system. (Photo Courtesy Hasport Performance Products)

Be sure to remount the fuel filter with its bracket nearby, far away from where the exhaust manifold is ultimately positioned.

Crossmember Considerations

Regardless of the chassis you choose, an aftermarket tubular-style crossmember allows for more clearance. Aftermarket systems, such as those from K-Tuned, feature adjustable radius rods, which can help improve traction and allow for better overall clearance. The original crossmember may be reused with any of the chassis covered in this chapter; however, the process of getting it to fit on Civic and CRX chassis versus the Integra is slightly different.

When it comes to the Civic and CRX, the factory crossmember and radius rods may be retained and reinstalled in their original locations. The crossmember must be modified, though, to allow clearance for the K-series oil pan. Once the engine and transmission have been installed, set the crossmember in place and mark

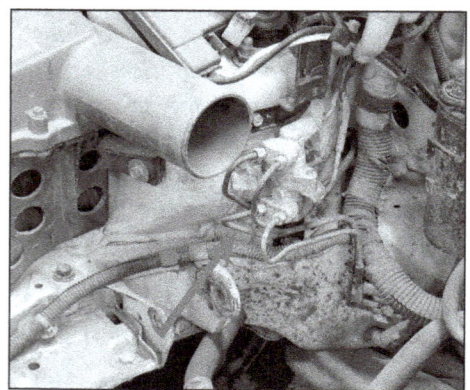

Before the engine and transmission can be installed, the brake's proportioning valve must be relocated on every Civic, CRX, and non-ABS-equipped Integra to allow clearance for the donor engine's valve cover. Start the procedure by unbolting the proportioning valve's bracket from the shock tower. Be sure to set 6-1.0-mm bolts like these aside; they may prove useful later on. (Photo Courtesy Hasport Performance Products)

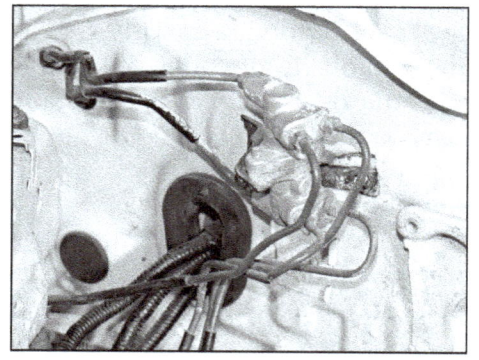

Carefully rotate the proportioning valve along with its brake lines toward the firewall. The brake lines should remain connected during the process, which means the system doesn't require bleeding once completed. However, take care when bending the lines; careless, harsh bends can result in kinked lines, which must be replaced. On Civic and CRX chassis, an existing 6-1.0-mm stud located on the firewall can be used to secure the proportioning valve. (Photo Courtesy Hasport Performance Products)

1988–1991 CIVIC AND 1990–1993 INTEGRA

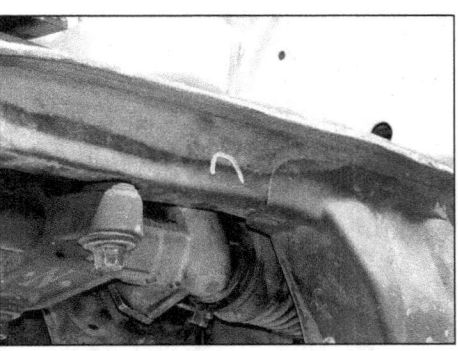

In some cases, the factory crossmember may be retained, but clearance is minimal on these chassis. An aftermarket, tubular crossmember, such as this one from K-Tuned, doesn't just result in additional clearance, it also stiffens the chassis and the suspension with its adjustable-length radius rods. K-Tuned crossmembers also feature optional radiator mounts, which can simplify the cooling system significantly. (Photo Courtesy K-Tuned)

The subframe must be clearanced on 1988–1991 Civic and CRX chassis to allow room for the transmission. Use a ball-peen hammer and place a 1/4-inch-deep dent within the marked area shown here. The lip directly above the mark must also be bent flat. Use a ball-peen hammer to conform it to shape. (Photo Courtesy Hasport Performance Products)

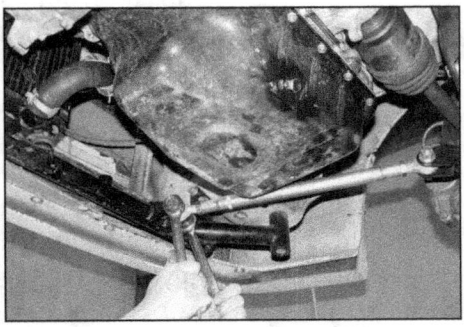

When retaining the original crossmember on the 1988–1991 Civic or CRX, it must be modified to make room for the K-series oil pan. Tubular crossmembers require no fabrication. Notice the built-in radiator mount on the left and the adjustable-length radius rod being tightened into place. Radius rods, when properly set up, reduce the front-to-back motion of the tires when launching, which significantly improves traction. (Photo Courtesy Hasport Performance Products)

The 1990–1993 Integra's radius rods interfere with the K-series transmission housing. Hasport's specially designed radius rods take care of this and are compatible with the factory crossmember. The radius rods must be replaced with Hasport's or those that accompany any aftermarket tubular crossmember in order for the transmission to clear. (Photo Courtesy Hasport Performance Products)

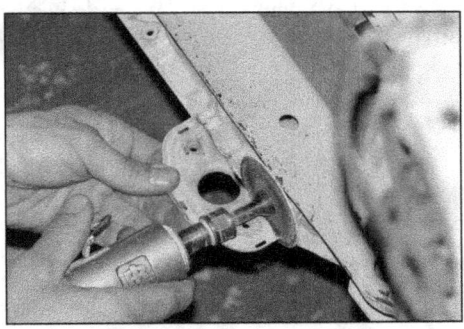

In most cases, the factory radiator mounts must be cut off to allow clearance for custom brackets or an aftermarket tubular crossmember that features its own mounts. Use an angle grinder to cut along the lower core support. Be sure to deburr the exposed sheet metal when finished to avoid sharp edges. (Photo Courtesy Hasport Performance Products)

where it interferes with the oil pan. Use an angle grinder to notch the crossmember, allowing ample clearance between itself and the oil pan.

The crossmember solution for the second-generation Integra is slightly simpler. Here, radius rods interfere with the transmission, not the crossmember itself. Once again, Hasport has the solution with its reshaped K-series-compatible radius rods. Simply bolt them to the crossmember and lower control arms for a factory-like fit.

Clearance Considerations

Unfortunately, clearance modifications don't end with the crossmember. For starters, the battery must be relocated to the trunk. Be sure to use an appropriate mounting kit and a minimum of 2-gauge wire to run from the fuse box underneath the hood to the battery. The ground wire can connect to any suitable location within the trunk.

Next, clearance must be made on Civic and CRX chassis at the subframe. Carefully estimate where the transmission's differential will be located and dent the subframe using a ball-peen hammer. A 1/4-inch-deep dent must be placed approximately 2.5 inches from where the lower control arm's mounting brace attaches to the subframe. The lip located directly above this location must also be bent upward to allow for additional clearance.

Up front, the original radiator supports must be cut off unless you use a custom radiator that's designed to sit in the factory location.

Additional modifications must be made to Civic and CRX chassis to retain appropriate drive belt and alternator clearance. Remove the right-side headlight assembly and trim the sheet metal near where the alternator pulley will be positioned. From inside the engine bay looking toward the headlight opening, trim near the lower-right region. This step can be skipped if the alternator is relocated using the appropriate method.

As is the case with newer chassis, ground clearance and hood clearance are also at minimums once the K-series engine transplant is in place. Hasport has yet to release a dual-height kit for any of these chassis, which would allow for additional hood clearance. This means that there's only one way to mount the engine in any of these chassis. As such, ground clearance may be retained as much as possible but hood clearance is at a minimum.

Larger, 2.4L engines pose even more of a problem, further reducing space between the engine and the hood. Integra chassis, which are the only ones in this chapter that may retain power steering, face similar hood clearance issues.

When making clearance modifications to the hood's substructure, be sure to make the appropriate marks after the engine has been installed; remove the hood, and place it on a soft surface. Cut slowly and carefully to avoid removing excess material. Finish with a sanding bit to deburr any sharp edges.

Right-Side Framerail Bracket

The right-side bracket located on the framerail of every 1988–1991 Civic and CRX as well as every 1990–1993 Integra must be removed before proceeding. You need a drill and an angle grinder to do this.

Start by using a center punch to mark each of the existing bracket's spot welds. Drill out the bracket's spot welds using a 1/8-inch pilot drill bit and follow up with a spot-weld-removing drill bit or standard 3/8-inch drill bit. Once each spot weld has been drilled away, remove the bracket using a large pry bar or air chisel. Be sure that each spot weld has been properly drilled out before continuing and risking damage to the framerail.

Once the bracket has been removed, use an angle grinder to clean up stray metal left by the drilling process and smooth the surface.

If the K-series alternator is going to remain in its original location, the chassis on 1988–1991 Civics and CRXs must be modified near the right-side headlight. Clearance must be made for the alternator pulley and drive belt. Use an angle grinder to trim along the housing's side closest to the engine bay. Today, a number of alternator relocation kits are available, so this step could be skipped. The section above the headlight has also been trimmed to allow clearance for a supercharger pulley. (Photo Courtesy Hasport Performance Products)

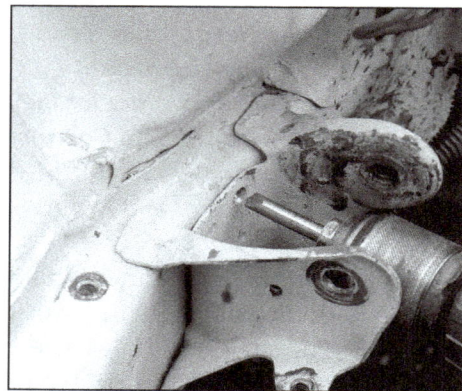

The right-side framerail bracket must be removed on every chassis in this chapter. Start by drilling out the spot welds, which allows the bracket to break free from the chassis. Here, a special spot weld–removing drill bit is used to quickly detach the bracket. (Photo Courtesy Hasport Performance Products)

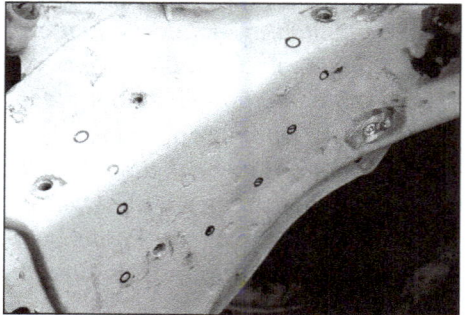

Once the right-side framerail bracket has been removed, position the Hasport bracket onto the framerail and mark the chassis through each of its holes using a felt-tip pen. To properly locate the bracket, Hasport has added two holes that allow it to temporarily bolt to two of the battery tray's original mounting holes. These holes must only be used to locate the bracket; do not rely on them to support the engine and transmission assembly. (Photo Courtesy Hasport Performance Products)

1988–1991 CIVIC AND 1990–1993 INTEGRA

Finish by filling the original spot weld holes with body filler to prepare for later priming and painting to avoid rust.

Position the Hasport bracket on the right-side framerail and bolt it to two of the original battery tray's existing bolt holes. It's important to note that these bolts are used only to properly locate the bracket and do not support the engine alone. Once positioned, use a felt-tip pen to mark the framerail through each of the remaining exposed holes. Remove the bracket and strip each of the marked areas to bare metal.

Finally, reinstall the bracket and rosette weld each of the bracket's holes to the framerail. The perimeter of the bracket may also be welded to the framerail instead of or in addition to the rosette welds. Be sure to strip the framerail appropriately if you choose to do so.

Left-Side Framerail Bracket

The original left-side framerail bracket must remain intact; it is reused once the new engine and transmission go into place.

Rear Subframe Bracket

Position the supplied rear engine bracket on top of (Civic and CRX) or below (Integra) the subframe and bolt it into place using a combination of the original bolts and provided hardware. Don't tighten the hardware until all of the brackets and mounts have been installed.

Engine Preparation

As you would do before any engine transplant, inspect the engine and transmission for any damaged parts before preparing it for installation. It's easy for sensors and ancillaries to be damaged during the removal process, during shipping, or while in storage. If the appropriate engine wiring harness isn't already installed, remove the harness that came with the engine and install the correct harness. Remove each of the engine's and transmission's brackets and mounts except for the right-side engine bracket, located on the timing-chain side of the engine.

Next, remove the two studs from the transmission that hold its mount assembly in place. If you don't have access to a stud extractor, use the

This left-side transmission bracket is being bolted onto the transmission. The left-side framerail bracket can remain unmodified. Unlike the right-side framerail bracket that would otherwise interfere with the K-series engine, the left-side framerail bracket is positioned well out of the way. (Photo Courtesy Hasport Performance Products)

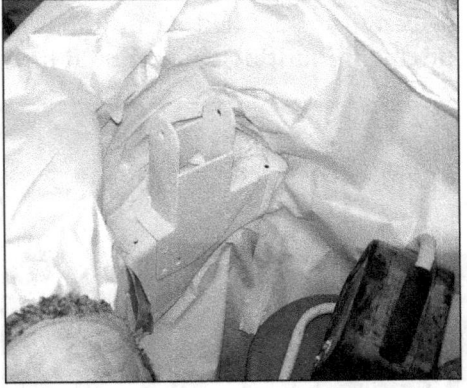

Once the Hasport bracket has been installed and welded into place, mask off the surrounding area and prepare it for priming and painting. For best results, be sure to fill any of the exposed spot welds with body filler before beginning. Don't skip this step. Hasport's bracket is untreated to simplify the welding process. If left unpainted, the bracket can corrode over time. (Photo Courtesy Hasport Performance Products)

Before installing the engine and transmission assembly, bolt the rear bracket to the subframe. The process differs slightly between chassis. This Hasport bracket is being mounted to a Civic- and CRX-style subframe. (Photo Courtesy Hasport Performance Products)

When preparing the donor engine for installation, all but one factory mount or bracket should be removed. The exception is the right-side engine bracket located at the timing chain cover. This particular bracket was designed specifically for taller-deck 2.4L engines. Be sure that the appropriate bracket is in place before installing the engine.

Most engine mount kits require removal of the pair of 12-mm mounting studs on top of the transmission before installing the engine. A stud remover works well here but so do two nuts of equal size. Simply thread both nuts onto the stud, tighten them against each other, and loosen the stud by turning the lower nut. If properly tightened, the upper nut prevents the lower nut from spinning, effectively turning the stud into a bolt.

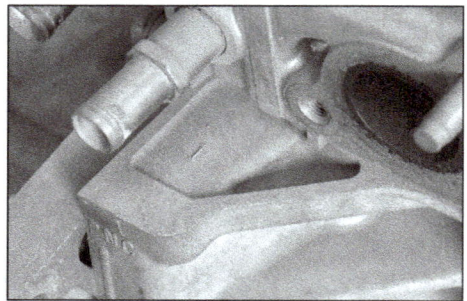
Few characteristics distinguish 2.0L engines from larger-displacement 2.4L ones other than the engines' identification code. This semi-triangular-shaped recessed section on the exhaust side of every 2.0L engine near the transmission appears shallow when compared to 2.4L engines.

Larger-displacement 2.4L engines can be identified by their deep, recessed sections located on the exhaust side, near the transmission. The deeper groove, when compared to 2.0L engines, is the result of the blocks' increased deck heights.

double-nut method: two nuts are threaded onto the stud, tightened together, and used in conjunction with a wrench or socket to remove the stud.

You also need to remove the exhaust manifold and downpipe that came with the engine. There are no factory components compatible with any of the chassis listed in this chapter.

Finally, remove the alternator for additional clearance during installation and take a few minutes to degrease the engine before getting started. Now is also a good time to perform any routine maintenance, such as replacing the water pump, performing a valve adjustment, and upgrading the clutch and flywheel.

2.4L Engine Considerations

Because of limited hood clearance, taller-deck 2.4L engines aren't nearly as popular as 2.0L engines with any of these chassis but they may still be used. When performing a 2.4L transplant, be sure that the appropriate right-side engine bracket is used. The 2.4L engine's taller deck height means it mounts slightly differently in the engine bay. As such, the 2002–2006 CR-V's K24A1 bracket (Honda PN 11910-PPA-000) must be used.

Engine Installation

If you don't have access to a lift, which allows you to install the engine and transmission from underneath, you must use an engine hoist. An optional load leveler can make the process simpler and safer. Once attached to the engine hoist, the load leveler allows the angle of the engine and transmission to be adjusted. All of this can make installing the assembly much easier and reduce the risk of damaging the chassis.

Alternatively, an engine hoist may also be used to raise the vehicle, which allows the engine and transmission to slide in from underneath. Be sure to connect the engine hoist securely to the car's front crossmember using heavy-duty straps so that its load is distributed across the entire beam.

Left-Side Transmission Bracket and Mount

Position the left-side bracket on top of the transmission and fasten it using the supplied hardware. (The original mounting studs should have

Hasport's steel bracket must be bolted onto the transmission before being connected to the billet aluminum mount at the framerail. For best results, be sure that each bolt has been threaded into place before tightening any of them. Until all three mounts have been installed, leave all engine and transmission brackets and mounts loose. (Photo Courtesy Hasport Performance Products)

already been removed.) Finish by slipping the supplied left-side mount into the car's framerail bracket and then onto the previously installed transmission bracket, also using the supplied hardware. Be sure to leave everything finger-tight for now.

Right-Side Engine Mount

Position the right-side engine mount into the already-installed framerail bracket and slide it onto the engine bracket's studs. Frequently, the engine and transmission may need to be rocked forward or backward for each hole to line up. A jack can also be placed underneath the engine. Use the supplied hardware to fasten the mount into place but don't tighten it down completely.

Rear Engine Mount

For the Civic and CRX, use a jack to raise or lower the engine assembly or the vehicle to allow room for the supplied rear engine mount to fit around the already-installed rear engine bracket. Attach it to the rear of the transmission using the supplied hardware. Again, don't completely tighten any hardware yet.

For the Integra, raise or lower the engine assembly or vehicle to allow room for the supplied rear engine mount and transmission bracket. Attach the bracket to the rear of the transmission using the supplied hardware. Slide the provided mount through the already-installed subframe bracket, into the just-installed engine bracket, allowing the assembly to be bolted together.

With all three mounts in place, remove the engine hoist or raise the vehicle so that the mounts are fully supporting the engine and transmission. Tighten all engine and transmission mount and bracket hardware to the appropriate specifications.

Axles

With the abundance of durable, custom-fit aftermarket axles, retrofitting your own custom-made pieces is no longer the only option. Hasport and Driveshaft Shop have the solution. Their customized axle sets, available for Civic, CRX, and Integra chassis, are lighter and stronger than factory components and take the guesswork out of fitting the appropriate shafts into place.

Select Civic Std and CRX HF models present a problem that none of the other trims do. Such models were fitted with front knuckle assemblies that accept their own unique small-spline axles. Swap any other 1988–1991 Civic, CRX, or 1990–1993 Integra knuckle assemblies into place before moving forward.

As with later-model Civics and Integras, though, factory components may also be used. Here, 2002–2006 RSX or 2002–2005 Civic Si axles, which share outboard spline patterns with all of the chassis in this chapter, can be installed without modification. If larger-diameter 2002–2006 RSX Type-S axles are used, the outer

Hasport supplies a billet aluminum engine mount that connects the already-installed right-side framerail bracket to the timing-chain-side engine mount. Be sure that the correct timing-chain-side engine mount has been installed. An incorrect bracket can lead to an engine that sits too high or two low, depending upon bracket type and engine deck height. (Photo Courtesy Hasport Performance Products)

Once the left- and right-side brackets and mounts have been connected, the rear engine mount can be slipped into place. Unlike any of the swaps detailed in Chapter 4, on earlier model Civic and CRX chassis such as these, the mount connects directly to the transmission and the bracket connects to the subframe. (Photo Courtesy Hasport Performance Products)

The second-generation Integra's rear mount assembly is made up of three pieces: a subframe bracket that should have already been bolted into place, a transmission bracket that can be bolted up before or after the engine assembly has been installed, and a dog bone–style mount that connects the two together. (Photo Courtesy Hasport Performance Products)

joints must be swapped for Integra axles, which are able to slip into the Civic, CRX, and Integra knuckles.

Karcepts' replacement knuckles may also be used. They are compatible with the larger 29.5-mm spindles (36-mm socket) that can be found on the 2002–2006 RSX Type-S, for example, and can be bolted onto any of the chassis in this chapter, expanding axle possibilities significantly. Karcepts' knuckles allow the larger-diameter 2002–2006 RSX Type-S axles to bolt up without modification.

Whichever axles are chosen, be sure to use an intermediate shaft sourced from any manual-transmission 2002–2006 RSX, 2002–2005 Civic Si, 2001–2005 Civic Type R, 2001–2006 Integra Type R, 2006–2011 Civic Si, or 2007–2011 Civic Type R and replace the cotter pins for each ball joint castle nut that was removed. With the axles installed, the suspension components and wheels can be reinstalled and the car can be positioned back on the ground.

Throttle Cable

As with most K-series engine swaps, a number of throttle cables are compatible. Nearly any Civic or Integra throttle cable works but only the 1996–2000 Civic's is short enough to look like it belongs. Also compatible are the 1994–2001 Integra GS-R or 2002–2005 Civic Si throttle cables, which are also short and connect at the firewall for a factory-like fit on all of these chassis provided they were originally equipped with manual transmissions. Simply add the appropriate K-Tuned throttle cable bracket to adapt any of the non-K-series-native throttle cables to any K-series throttle body.

Aftermarket cable assemblies are also available from K-Tuned. (Converting any of these chassis to be compatible with an electronic, drive-by-wire throttle body would be a labor-intensive, unnecessary procedure. Be sure you always use a cable-driven throttle body and one of the previously mentioned throttle cables.)

Speedometer Cable

Every chassis covered in this chapter features a cable-driven mechanical speedometer (excluding 1992–1993 Integras). There are two ways to allow the chassis' instrument cluster to communicate with the transmission's vehicle speed sensor. One is to simply swap the original mechanical speed sensor from any 1988–1991 Civic or CRX onto the K-series gearbox and hook the speedometer cable up as you normally would (Integra sensors feature larger housings that interfere with the K-series engine block).

Selecting the proper intermediate shaft is crucial. The shorter 2006–2011 Civic Si intermediate shaft (left) is among the most popular solutions. Most aftermarket axles have been designed specifically for Civic Si shafts (like these or ones of similar length).

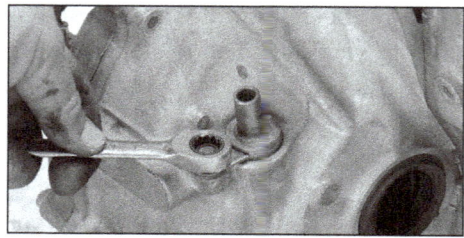

Pre-OBD chassis, including every Civic, CRX, and Integra in this chapter, with the exception of the 1992–1993 Integra, present a unique problem. Older chassis rely on cable-driven mechanical vehicle speed sensors that communicate directly with the instrument cluster. Fortunately, any D-series vehicle speed sensor of the same era bolts directly to any K-series transmission. You need the original retaining clip and an 8-1.25-mm bolt to hold the sensor in place. (Photo Courtesy Hasport Performance Products)

If you plan to convert to an electronic vehicle speed sensor, such as the K-series is equipped with, the instrument cluster must be swapped for a compatible unit, such as one from any duly equipped Japanese-spec Civic or CRX SiR.

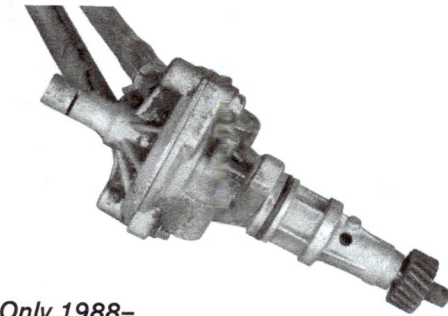

Only 1988–1991 Civic and CRX vehicle speed sensors may be used when converting a K-series transmission to communicate with any of these chassis' older instrument clusters. Mechanical vehicle speed sensors from any 1990–1991 Integra feature larger housings that interfere with the K-series engine block.

1988–1991 CIVIC AND 1990–1993 INTEGRA

Clutch Hydraulics

If 1988–1991 Civic, CRX, and 1990–1993 Integra K-series engine swaps differ from later-model chassis in any way, it's in their clutch mechanisms. Like almost every other pre-1992 Honda, early Civic and Integra platforms are not equipped with hydraulic-operated clutch systems and instead feature a cable-driven assembly that spans from the pedal assembly to the clutch fork. Of course, all K-series transmissions are based on hydraulic clutch systems; that means something must be converted.

Hasport once again has the solution with its specialized clutch master cylinder adapter. Simply bolt the adapter to any rigid surface near the clutch fork and adapt any 1992–1995 Civic hydraulic clutch master cylinder and reservoir to it.

Next, a hydraulic clutch line must be fabricated that connects the new clutch master cylinder to the

Hasport's cable-to-hydro adapter allows any hydraulic clutch–style K-series transmission to be used in any of these Civic or Integra chassis that are native to cable-operated clutch mechanisms. The conversion is based on a hydraulic clutch master cylinder that's actuated by the vehicle's original clutch cable. This means that the pedal assembly can remain intact: a significantly simpler solution than earlier conversions.

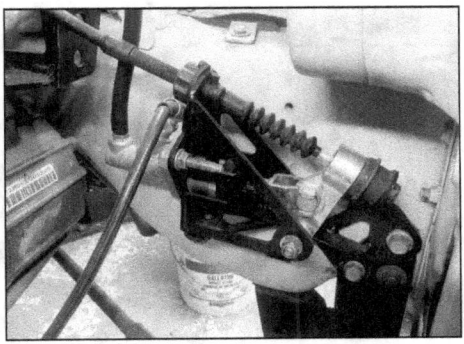

When using a cable-to-hydro transmission adapter, such as Hasport's, be sure to mount it securely to the chassis or transmission. A flexible hydraulic line must also span from the adapter's clutch master cylinder to the K-series transmission's clutch slave cylinder. Finally, a low-pressure hose must also span from the clutch master cylinder to a remotely mounted fluid reservoir. (Photo Courtesy Hasport Performance Products)

K-series transmission's clutch slave cylinder. A custom line can be made from Teflon-lined steel-braided hose along with the appropriate hose ends and inverted-flare metric adapters that thread into the master cylinder and slave cylinder. Be sure to pressure test the line before installing it.

Finally, connect the car's original clutch cable to the Hasport bracket's cable mechanism. Once properly installed, the cable appropriately engages the system's arm, which counteracts against the master cylinder.

Brake Booster

A section of 3/8-inch rubber hose must be used to span from the brake booster check valve to the intake manifold vacuum source or distribution line. Be sure to route the hose away from any moving parts and leave the check valve in its original orientation, in-line with the hose. If you retain the distribution line on the engine, the brake booster line from any 2002–2006 RSX also works.

Shifter Assembly

Similar to the Civic and Integra chassis covered in Chapter 4, those in this chapter feature rod-and-lever-style shift linkages that aren't compatible with K-series transmissions. All K-series-equipped vehicles use cable-style shifter mechanisms that, with the help of the aftermarket, can be retrofitted into just about any Civic or Integra.

Shifter Box

The conversion starts with the shifter box, which connects to the chassis in the cabin underneath the shift boot. Like other aspects of the chassis covered in this chapter, the solutions here are few albeit effective.

Unlike with later-model Civics and Integras, available engine mount kits for any of the chassis covered in this chapter restrict them to the select number of transmissions mentioned earlier. The limitations don't end there, though. Honda introduced two different gear selector mechanisms for its K-series-compatible transmissions that operate in opposition to one another.

All of this means that the appropriate shifter box must be matched with the appropriate transmission in order for everything to work as planned. This is important to keep in mind when selecting the appropriate shifter box and shifter cables. If using a 2002–2006 RSX, 2002–2005 Civic Si, 2001–2005 Civic Type R, or 2001–2006 Integra Type R transmission, a 2002–2006 RSX or 2001–2005 Civic (non-Si) shifter box must be used and matched with the appropriate cables.

Clutch Bleeding Basics

Any time a pressurized hydraulic clutch system is opened, such as when performing an engine swap, it must be properly bled. Releasing pressure from the system exposes it to oxygen, which introduces air bubbles that can cause the clutch mechanism to malfunction or fail. Of course, the system also needs to be properly bled on chassis that weren't originally equipped with such hydraulics but have been converted during the K-series engine swap process.

Start by removing any stray particles or contaminants from the clutch fluid reservoir. Add a small amount of fluid and stir to break up any sediment; remove using a turkey baster or vacuum bleeder. Use a lint-free rag and thoroughly wipe down the reservoir. Keep in mind that brake fluid is a solvent and can remove paint and other finishes if they come in contact with one another. Clean up any spills quickly with water and a soft towel.

Bleeding can be accomplished several ways using expensive, specialized equipment. It can also be done quickly and inexpensively with a helper.

Fill the clutch fluid reservoir with the appropriate DOT 3 brake fluid. To ensure that the system doesn't run dry during the bleeding process (which means that you have to start over), turn a full bottle of fresh fluid upside down onto the reservoir to make sure the reservoir doesn't run dry. Place a bucket or tray below the clutch slave cylinder, have a helper depress and release the clutch pedal three or four times, and open the slave cylinder's bleeder valve while the clutch pedal is still fully depressed. Once opened, the clutch pedal depresses farther, allowing a stream of fluid to exit the system.

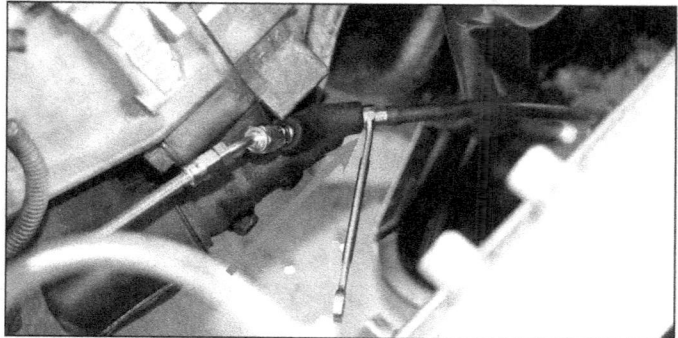

Any time a hydraulic clutch or braking system has been disassembled, it must be bled of excess air. Every hydraulic-style Honda transmission features a fluid bleeder valve at its clutch slave cylinder. Simply open the valve using an 8-mm line wrench to release fluid, and air, from the system. A conventional box-end wrench may be used; however, it may round the valve's hex-shaped head, making it difficult to tighten or remove. A line wrench reduces this risk.

Close the valve and repeat the process multiple times until the stream is clear, smooth, and free of any visible air bubbles.

Finally, do not pump the pedal excessively far; it can damage the master cylinder's internals from sediments or deposits that may have built up over time. Place a small block of wood underneath the pedal to prevent this from happening. Once completed, a properly bled hydraulic clutch system allows for a firm yet consistent pedal. Be sure to top off the reservoir when finished. ∎

Be sure to avoid any of the Accord or TSX components mentioned in Chapter 4, as they are not compatible.

If a 2006–2011 Civic Si or 2007–2011 Civic Type R transmission is chosen, a 2003–2007 Accord or 2004–2008 TSX shifter box along with their matching cables must be used.

You can choose from three methods of installation: adapter plates, base adapter plates, and a no-cut solution.

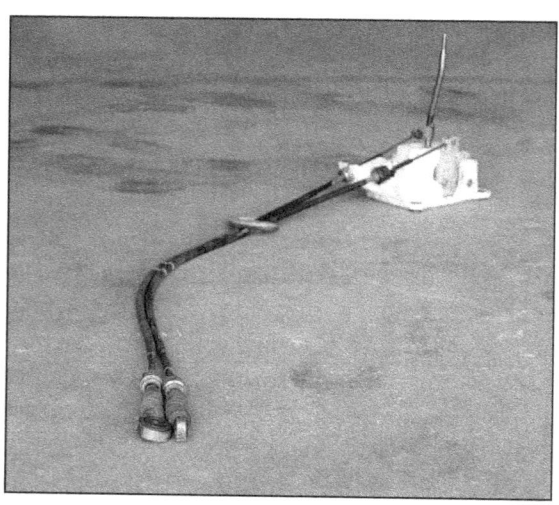

Because of limited engine mount kit selection for older chassis, including those in this chapter, less expensive Accord-style transmissions may not be used. Be sure to avoid the popular Accord shifter box and its cables, which are not compatible with the RSX-style transmissions that must be used here. Instead, look to the often-used RSX shifter box and its cables, such as this one.

1988–1991 CIVIC AND 1990–1993 INTEGRA

Adapter Plates: Early K-series engine swaps into any of these chassis meant retrofitting the shifter mechanism into place was a custom procedure. It still is somewhat common but Karcepts makes the process a whole lot easier with its adapter plate, provided a 2002–2006 RSX or 2002–2005 Civic (non-Si) shifter box is used.

Karcepts' adapter is based on the factory shifter box assembly and acts as an intermediary between the shifter and the chassis. The adapter allows the shifter box to bolt up underneath the chassis, which means the center console along with all of its interior components can be retained. The exhaust tunnel's sheet metal must be cut; this means that the process is irreversible without welding. Clearance underneath is also significantly compromised. Still, Karcepts' adapter is one of the most straightforward shifter solutions there is.

When using a shifter box adapter plate, the exhaust tunnel must be modified. Templates that outline exactly where to cut accompany kits such as those from Karcepts. In short, a rectangular section must be removed from the tunnel that includes the circular raised opening that's occupied by the original shift lever. (Photo Courtesy Hasport Performance Products)

Installing the Karcepts adapter plate into any of these chassis is similar to later model Civics and Integras covered in Chapter 4.

Remove the shift knob, shift boot, center console, original shifter assembly, and center console's mounting bracket. The shifter assembly must be trimmed before going into place. Karcepts provides instructions that outline exactly where to cut. Trim the small raised region on the right side of the box, another spot near the neutral return spring, and also near the lower right corner of the assembly so that it may fit within the opening.

Also, if equipped, remove the metal or rubber bushings from each corner of the shifter box. (See Chapter 4 for more details on the process.)

Karcepts' adapter includes a rear bracket that bolts to the two original shift-linkage mounting holes and a main adapter plate that mounts to the bracket. Before the rear bracket goes in place, a small section of sheet metal must be removed for the bracket to fit. Test-fit the bracket, use a felt-tip pen to mark its location, and remove a small section of the outer layer of the tunnel's two-layer structure. Use a small die grinder and pry bar. The remainder of the process is similar to that outlined in Chapter 4.

Bolt the adapter into place, mark the appropriate holes, drill, and fasten the template into place. Verify that the fitment is appropriate and cut the required hole into the tunnel. Be sure to deburr the cut before installing the shifter cables and shifter box assembly from underneath.

Finally, test the shifter and be sure that each gear engages properly. To ensure against air leaks within the cabin, use caulking to seal the area around the shifter box from underneath.

Once the shifter box has been properly mounted to its adapter plate, its cables may span toward the engine bay and above the subframe. Be sure to avoid kinking when routing them toward the transmission. It's easiest to connect the shifter cables to the shifter box before mounting it to the chassis. (Photo Courtesy Hasport Performance Products)

Base Adapter Plates: A marginally less-expensive and slightly less-complex solution is the base adapter plate, which allows the shifter assembly to bolt on top of the exhaust tunnel. Of course, space underneath is preserved but any interior components surrounding the shifter don't easily go back into place.

The plate must be fashioned from scratch and is typically nothing more than a square section of 1/8-inch steel plate that's large enough for the shifter box to bolt onto. Drill the appropriate holes in the plate and the chassis so that the shifter box can bolt to the plate and the plate can then bolt to the chassis. Four small sections of steel tubing should be positioned between the plate and the chassis where the bolts will be placed that allow the assembly to sit slightly above the shifter opening, preserving it in the event that the original engine must be reinstalled.

Base adapter plates like these are popular because until recently

CHAPTER 5

Custom base adapter plates are significantly easier to install than any adapter plate that positions the shifter box underneath the chassis. A simple plate has been cut out that bolts to the exhaust tunnel using a series of spacers, and features four additional bolt holes that allow the shifter box to mount onto the plate. No interior components around the shifter may be retained here. However, the shifter cables can now follow a much smoother path toward the transmission. (Photo Courtesy Hasport Performance Products)

Mounting the shifter box to a custom base adapter plate like this is easy. Simply bolt it in place using the appropriate-length hardware. Notice how the shifter cables follow a straight and direct path, toward the firewall, which reduces the chances of any kinking or binding. (Photo Courtesy Hasport Performance Products)

they were the only way to allow the 2006–2011 Civic Si gearbox to be used in any of these chassis. All that's needed are the 2003–2007 Accord or 2004–2008 TSX shifter box and shifter cables, which are oriented in the same direction as the Civic Si transmission, and K-Tuned's special transmission conversion bracket that allows the cables to properly fit up to the gearbox.

No-Cut Solution: An alternative solution that involves little fabrication comes by way of Hybrid Racing and K-Tuned. Both leave the exhaust tunnel and shifter opening intact, which means the original engine can be reinstalled relatively easily. No-cut shifter boxes also allow all interior pieces, including the center console, to remain in place. Both kits are compatible with the 2002–2006 RSX, 2002–2005 Civic Si, 2001–2005 Civic Type R, and 2001–2006 Integra Type R transmissions but only

K-Tuned also offers a no-cut shifter box solution for any 1988–1991 Civic or CRX and 1990–1993 Integra chassis, which can significantly simplify installation and shorten the parts list. Simply use the provided shifter box, shifter cables, and mounting mechanism. No cutting or permanent modifications are required. (Photo Courtesy K-Tuned)

Hybrid Racing offers an additional kit that works with the 2006–2011 Civic Si's gearbox.

Like the Karcepts adapter, no-cut shifter boxes mount from underneath, which means exhaust clearance is compromised at the expense of a fully retained interior. The shifter cables can also be routed underneath the vehicle, which means no additional holes must be cut in the firewall.

Both companies' solutions are comprehensive and come with everything needed, including the shifter box, and are compatible with either 2002–2006 RSX shifter cables or 2003–2007 Accord, 2004–2008 TSX, or 2006–2011 Civic Si shifter cables, depending on the shifter box used, as well as each company's own line of shifter cables.

Shifter Cables

With the exception of the 2006–2011 Civic Si transmission and its corresponding Accord or TSX cables, shifter cable selection is limited to those from the 2002–2006 RSX, 2001–2005 Civic, or aftermarket versions thereof. Later-model 2005–2006 RSX shifter cables may also be used but require modifying to fit. The cables' metal weights that are positioned at their ends must be cut off for appropriate clearance.

Hybrid Racing and K-Tuned also offer their own versions of RSX shifter cables that feature solid aluminum bushings instead of the factory plastic ones and an overall stronger, more-durable design.

Again, unless a 2006–2011 Civic Si transmission is used, avoid any cables that were originally designed for any Accord or TSX chassis.

If a shifter box adapter kit is used, route the cables underneath

1988–1991 CIVIC AND 1990–1993 INTEGRA

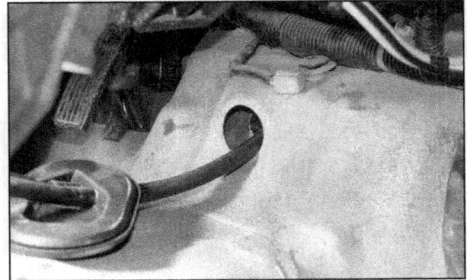

When mounting the shifter box inside by means of a base adapter plate, the shifter cables must be routed through the firewall. Drill a 1.5-inch hole directly in front of the shifter box, near the floor. For best results, drill a pilot hole from inside the chassis and finish it off from the engine bay side using a hole saw, before the engine and transmission have been installed. (Photo Courtesy Hasport Performance Products)

Just how short 1988–1991 Civic and CRX chassis are is evident by how long the K-series shifter cables appear once installed. Gradual loops (shown) help avoid kinking or binding, which can impair the shifting process. (Photo Courtesy Hasport Performance Products)

the chassis toward the transmission's gear selector. For all other methods, the cables must be routed through the cabin and out the firewall. Cut a 1.5-inch-diameter hole in the floor in front of the shifter or through the firewall and route the cables through. When routing the cables underneath the chassis, you must be sure to account for appropriate clearance between the cables and the exhaust system and its components as well as any chassis braces, if equipped.

Whichever method is used, avoid harsh bends, which can impair proper shifting.

Once the cables are connected to the shifter box and routed into the engine bay, connect them to their respective brackets and levers on the transmission. Tap the cables' retaining clips into place using a hammer and secure them using the original washers and cotter pins. Once everything is fastened in place, test the shifter for gear engagement and potential binding.

Fuel System

Like the majority of older Hondas and Acuras, the 1988–1991 Civic and CRX as well as the 1990–1993 Integra, feature the return-style fuel systems where unused fuel at the fuel rail is recirculated back into the fuel tank. All K-series-equipped vehicles feature return-less fuel systems, which means K-series engines only feature inlet ports at their fuel rails, not inlets and outlets as with older engines.

All of this presents a problem for vehicles with fuel tanks that expect a stream of fuel to make its way back toward the tank through the fuel return line. An aftermarket fuel rail and adjustable fuel pressure regulator offer the easiest solution.

Fuel Rail and Fuel Pressure Regulator

The older Civic and Integra return-style fuel system can be retained with a bypass-type aftermarket fuel pressure regulator. It should be suitable for fuel injection applications and matched with the factory fuel rail or an aftermarket fuel rail with the appropriate inlet and outlet ports. Refer to Chapter 4 for details that are universal to practically every K-series engine swap and read on for those specific to the vehicles in this chapter.

Stock Fuel Rail, Aftermarket Fuel Pressure Regulator: The least-expensive method is to retain the factory fuel rail. The factory K-series fuel rail presents a problem for return-style fuel systems, though: It features no outlet port through which unused fuel may be transported back to the fuel tank.

The solution lies with a bypass-type adjustable fuel pressure regulator that features at least two inlet ports and a single outlet port. This doesn't just integrate a fuel pressure regulator into the system, which must be in place, it also serves as a distribution block, allowing fuel to pass through itself and be distributed to the fuel rail or back to the fuel tank.

Cut away the plastic connection from the fuel rail's inlet barb and slip a section of 5/16-inch fuel injection hose over it. Next, connect the hose to one of the fuel pressure regulator's upper ports with the appropriate fittings. All of this can vary significantly depending on the fuel pressure regulator but typically consist of -6 or -8 female O-ring-sealed AN ports.

Thread the appropriate male-to-male union into place along with its corresponding AN female-to-male-barb adapter. Slip the fuel

Automatic to Manual Conversions

Starting with a manual transmission–equipped chassis always makes the most sense. Every K-series engine mount kit was designed around such platforms and is only compatible with 5- or 6-speed K-series gearboxes. However, the perfect donor vehicle isn't always native to a manual transmission. Frequently, it's an automatic transmission-equipped chassis. Fortunately, converting almost any vehicle covered in this book to accept a manual transmission is a tried-and-proven process.

It all begins with gathering the right parts from any similar manual transmission-equipped vehicle. For late-model chassis that would normally use a hydraulic-clutch-style transmission, source the appropriate pedal assembly, clutch master cylinder, clutch fluid reservoir, and associated hydraulic lines and brackets. In most cases, provisions for each of these components are already located on the firewall and chassis, which means installing them is simple and requires no more than potentially drilling a few holes.

Older chassis that typically use cable-clutch-style transmissions are slightly different. Here, the K-series swap already requires a hydraulic-clutch conversion that works in tandem with the car's original clutch cable and pedal assembly. Source the appropriate clutch cable and pedal assembly from any similar manual transmission–equipped chassis and bolt them into place along with all necessary components to complete the cable-to-hydraulic clutch conversion.

Finally, the electrical system must be addressed to complete the conversion, regardless of the chassis used. The reverse light connection normally positioned at the automatic shift lever must be rerouted to the transmission's sensor. The shift-lock solenoid must also be removed from the ignition so that the key may be removed once turned off. ■

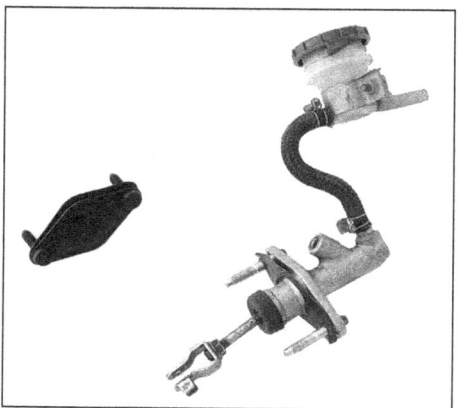

Every conversion from automatic to manual transmission starts by gathering the right parts. Source the appropriate components from the manual transmission counterpart of the chassis you have. The clutch master cylinder and clutch fluid reservoir on the right has been sourced from a 1992–1995 Civic. The block-off plate on the left was unbolted from the automatic chassis' firewall, revealing mounting provisions for the clutch master cylinder. It shows how easy the conversion can be.

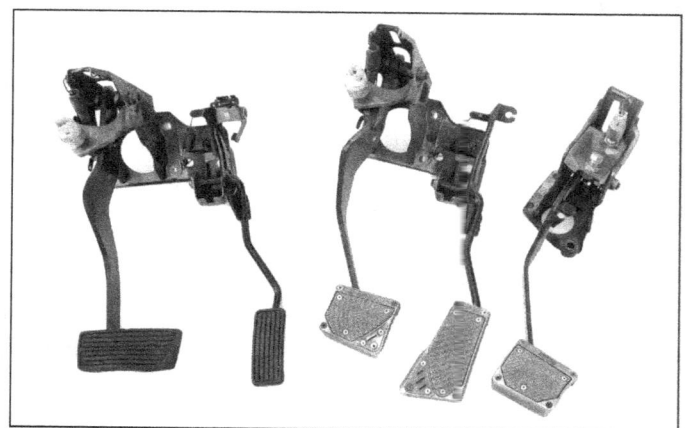

The appropriate pedal assembly must also be sourced when completing a conversion from automatic to manual transmission. Source the correct pedal assembly from any manual-transmission-equipped, similar chassis.

injection line over the barb and secure it using fuel injection hose clamps. The fuel pressure regulator's remaining upper port must connect to the vehicle's original fuel feed line, which runs from the fuel filter.

However, the line must be modified first. Cut the original line away from its banjo connection using a sharp blade, exposing the hose barb.

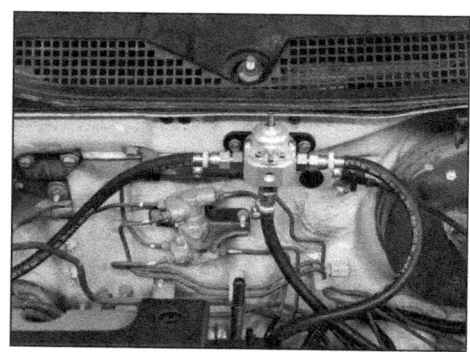

An aftermarket fuel pressure regulator with multiple inlet ports has been attached to the firewall. The line on the left spans from the fuel filter and directs fuel into the regulator. The line on the right directs fuel to the fuel rail. The line on the bottom directs excess fuel back to the gas tank, where it's recycled and ultimately sent back to the fuel filter.

Next, slip a section of 5/16-inch fuel injection hose over the barb and connect it to the fuel pressure regulator's upper port using the same series of fittings as before. Be sure to secure both ends with the appropriate hose clamps.

The return line must also be addressed. A section of 1/4-inch fuel injection hose must span from the fuel pressure regulator's lower exit port to the fuel return hard line that's located near the firewall. Use a similar male-to-male AN union and AN female-to-male-barb adapter with the appropriate fuel injection hose clamps to finish it off.

Aftermarket Fuel Rail, Aftermarket Fuel Pressure Regulator: The original K-series fuel rail may work and prove to be cost-effective but it isn't the ideal solution. Because the fuel stream must pass through the fuel pressure regulator before entering the fuel rail, it poses a restriction. As horsepower increases along with a demand for more fuel, it poses a problem. The solution is an aftermarket fuel rail that features its own inlet and outlet ports.

A line must span from the fuel filter to the fuel rail's inlet port. Follow the same procedure at the fuel filter and source the appropriate AN-to-barb adapter, which must thread into the fuel rail. Mount the fuel pressure regulator to the opposite end of the fuel rail using the appropriate union or externally with the same AN-to-barb adapters and hose used (as outlined previously) with the factory fuel rail.

Any time an aftermarket fuel rail is used, be careful to preserve the O-rings when removing the fuel injectors. A small amount of liquid hand soap applied to the O-rings when reinstalling them can keep them from tearing. Install the fuel rail using the recommended hardware, connect the fuel injectors to the engine wiring harness, and be sure to connect the ground wire to its original location.

Regardless of the method chosen, when using an aftermarket fuel pressure regulator be sure to leave its vacuum reference port open. K-series engines do not require this.

Specialty Fittings and Lines

Although more cost-effective, rubber fuel injection hose and conventional fuel injection hose clamps may be used, high-quality anodized-aluminum AN fittings and steel-braided specialty hose is typically more common.

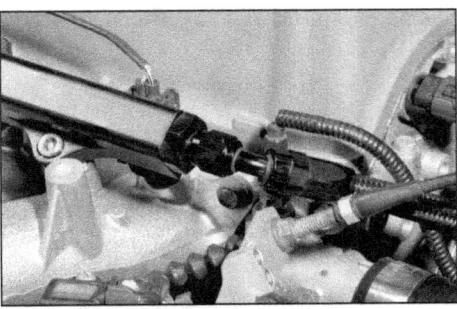

The world of high-performance plumbing can be confusing. All sorts of fittings, adapters, hose ends, and hoses, as well as a variety of finishes, are available. In most cases, -6 hose is recommended for fuel lines, which is equivalent to 3/8-inch; it's slightly larger than any of Honda's fuel feed lines that travel throughout the chassis.

Hybrid Racing, Karcepts, and K-Tuned each offer hose-and-fitting kits that eliminate the challenge of figuring out exactly what's needed and include the appropriate fittings and line to make everything work. Because of fuel rail and fuel pressure regulator differences as well as the variety of AN fittings and adapters, you have many options.

Fuel Pump

Provided the engine remains relatively unmodified, the rest of the fuel system can remain stock. This includes the fuel injectors, fuel filter, and fuel pump. However, high-mileage Civics and Integras of this era are likely in need of a fuel pump replacement whether or not a larger more-powerful K-series is dropped in.

Aftermarket in-tank fuel pumps from AEM, DeatschWerks, and Walbro are all worth considering and are a small investment to make considering the scope of the entire engine swap. It's always a good idea to replace the fuel filter as well.

High-performance plumbing, such as these AN fittings and steel-braided hose, can be used instead of inexpensive rubber fuel injection hose. However, be sure to gather the appropriate fittings and adapters, such as this specialized banjo hose end that allows the -6 steel braided hose to connect to the factory fuel filter. (Photo Courtesy Hasport Performance Products)

Cooling System

There are a number of ways to complete the cooling system of any of these chassis. The following have proven to be the most popular and effective.

Radiator

Regardless of what you do, the Civic, CRX, and Integra radiators aren't compatible with any K-series engine swap. Once installed, each upper water neck interferes with the engines' intake manifold. The fix starts with a different radiator, which, in the case of any of these chassis, is based on a shorter, custom unit or one from any 2002–2006 RSX or 2002–2005 Civic Si.

A custom radiator means the original front crossmember and radiator mounts can be retained but custom radiators can be prohibitively expensive. All of this makes the 2002–2006 RSX or 2002–2005 Civic Si radiator a popular choice. Neither fit without modification.

First, the factory crossmember must be discarded and replaced with an aftermarket, tubular piece. Crossmembers, such as those from K-Tuned, typically feature custom,

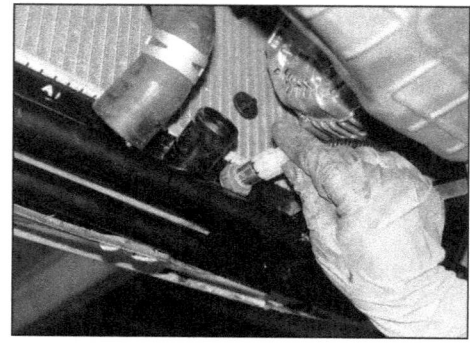

The 2002–2005 Civic Si integrated radiator fan switch provisions mean no aftermarket adapter is needed. Simply thread the original D- or B-series radiator fan switch into place and plug it into the sub-harness' electrical connector. (Photo Courtesy Hasport Performance Products)

adjustable radius rods; this is also good news for Integra chassis that aren't able to use the factory pieces because of limited clearance. Aftermarket crossmembers are also good news for Civic and CRX owners who must otherwise resort to modifying their factory crossmembers for oil pan clearance.

Fitting either the RSX or Civic Si radiator into place with the K-Tuned front crossmember isn't difficult. K-Tuned's included radiator brackets slip over the tubular crossmember

If an aftermarket tubular crossmember has been installed, look to the 2002–2005 Civic Si for a radiator. It features provisions for the radiator fan switch and, because it's from a K-series-native chassis such as the Si, its water necks don't interfere with the engine, which means factory radiator hoses can be used. (Photo Courtesy Hasport Performance Products)

and slide left to right, allowing for ideal radiator placement.

Regardless of which radiator is chosen, allow for even more space by using an intake manifold from either the 2002–2006 RSX Type-S or 2002–2005 Civic Si as well as similarly shaped Type R versions.

Cooling Fan

Cooling fan clearance remains minimal with any of these chassis, which means the factory fan and shroud cannot be used. An aftermarket, 12-inch-diameter fan must be used and, in the case of the Civic and CRX, must be positioned on the opposite side of the radiator. Look to Hayden for inexpensive universal fans or to Spal for high-performance versions that easily outflow the factory cooling fan.

Integra applications can position the fan on either side, although placing it on the engine bay side is typically more effective. The cooling fan pulls air through the radiator and past itself and, because it's on the opposing side, it doesn't pose a restriction. It doesn't matter which side the fan is positioned on, airflow must continue to move in that same direction.

For Civic and CRX applications or for Integra applications where the fan is located on the front of the radiator, the rotation must be reversed. Locate the two fan motor wires and carefully connect them to the battery terminals to verify which direction the fan rotates. Adjust the polarity of the two wires so that, once mounted onto the opposite side of the radiator, the fan may push instead of pull. Be sure that the fan used was designed to push or pull, depending on which side of the radiator it'll be mounted.

Because of fan blade orientation, a fan designed to pull air may not work

1988–1991 CIVIC AND 1990–1993 INTEGRA

A number of different radiator solutions are available, such as this del Sol VTEC version that must be custom mounted to avoid interfering with the intake manifold. Here, a smaller cooling fan has been mounted onto the radiator's opposite side for additional clearance. When mounting the cooling fan on the opposite side, be sure to adjust the polarity of its wires so it pushes air past the radiator, toward the engine. (Photo Courtesy Hasport Performance Products)

The radiator and the cylinder head's upper water neck determine the upper radiator hose choice. Front-mount water necks, such as these that feature straight nipples, are compatible with any 2002–2006 RSX upper radiator hose. In most cases, if the engine features this upper water neck, an RSX radiator hose may be used down below as well.

Here, a 2002–2006 RSX upper radiator hose is being slid onto its corresponding water neck. Because the 2002–2005 Civic Si radiator was used, the hose fits as it would in any K-series-native chassis. (Photo Courtesy Hasport Performance Products)

as effectively when pushing. Cut off the original fan's two-pin connector, preserve at least 4 inches of wire, and solder it to the new fan's exposed wires. Remember to take into account the appropriate polarity. Although the new fan's wires may be soldered directly to the chassis harness' fan connector, using the old connector allows for easy removal later.

Radiator Hoses

Radiator hose choice is based on the engine and the radiator. If a shorter, custom radiator is chosen, hose selection must also be custom. Water neck location and angle can both vary, which means hose selection does, too.

Now is a good time to discuss the two types of cylinder heads in relation to upper radiator hoses. The engine's upper coolant outlet pipe, or water neck, may be oriented in one of two ways: on the front of the cylinder head, as on K20A2, K20Z1, K20A, K20A3, and K24A1 engines, or fitted to the side of the cylinder head, as on every other engine discussed in Chapter 1.

There are also multiple lower water necks, all of which are associated with the same engines as above. K20A2, K20Z1, K20A, K20A3, and K24A1 lower water necks are typically preferred because of how they orient the lower radiator hose. Be sure to consider which lower water neck is being used before purchasing a lower radiator hose.

If one of the RSX or Civic Si radiators is chosen, as well as an engine with a compatible upper and lower water neck, hose choice just got a whole lot easier. Simply use upper and lower hoses from the 2002–2005 Civic Si.

In most other cases, hose selection must be custom.

Cooling Electrical

Later-model Honda engines, such as the K-series, feature coolant temperature sensors (thermo unit) that aren't able to communicate with the instrument cluster as well as radiator

RSX-style radiator hoses from Hybrid Racing are used here with an aftermarket aluminum radiator. Notice the limited clearance between the intake manifold and the thicker radiator. Quality aftermarket engine mounts, such as those from Hasport, are important to avoid excess engine movement, which can lead to all sorts of problems.

CHAPTER 5

fan switches that are integrated into their radiators. Retain both from the original engine and integrate them into the engine swap. The coolant temperature sensor allows the ECU to interpret engine coolant temperature and display everything within the instrument cluster. The radiator fan switch allows the cooling fan to turn on at the appropriate temperature to avoid overheating.

If a 2002–2006 RSX or 2002–2005 Civic Si radiator is used, simply integrate the old engine's radiator fan switch onto the new radiator and complete any wiring when installing the sub-harness. The coolant temperature sensor can be integrated into the system using an inline adapter from Hasport or Hybrid Racing. Another possibility is at the idle air assist valve's original location at the intake manifold. (For more information on the process, see Chapter 4.)

Heater Hoses

The two heater hoses that span from the heater core and its valve assembly at the firewall and connect to the engine must be addressed next. If interior heating will not be retained, or where the exhaust manifold is simply too close (as on Civic or CRX chassis), bypass the inlet and outlet on the engine side.

For Integra chassis, use 5/8-inch (16-mm) cooling hose to connect the heater core outlet and water valve inlet at the firewall to the heater hose inlet and outlet on the engine. A 180-degree hose must be used at the water valve to avoid contact with the exhaust manifold or the water valve inlet can be removed from its bracket and reoriented away from the manifold.

K-series engines feature slightly larger connections compared to

If interior heating will be retained, a section of hose must span from the water valve inlet assembly and heater core outlet at the firewall to the engine. On these chassis, limited engine bay space means the exhaust manifold is positioned close to the firewall. A 180-degree hose (shown) can be used to avoid kinks and direct the heater hoses away from hot exhaust components. (Photo Courtesy Hasport Performance Products)

those of other chassis in this chapter. The 5/8-inch hose must be stretched over the larger nipple or installed in two sections using a 5/8-inch-to-3/4-inch brass reducer. K-Tuned offers its own adapter that simplifies the whole process.

Whichever method is chosen, carefully bend the hoses to avoid kinking and route them away from the exhaust manifold.

Overflow Reservoir

Unlike other K-series engine swaps, the radiator overflow reservoir can remain in its factory location. A section of 5/16-inch tubing must span from the reservoir's nipple to the radiator to complete the cooling system.

A/C and Power Steering

Both A/C and power steering are compatible with any 1990–1993 Integra; however, when it comes to the 1988–1991 Civic and CRX, space is limited. On these chassis, the power steering pump is positioned well above the hoodline, and when eliminated, relocates the alternator to where the A/C compressor once sat. As such, retrofitting either system into the Civic or CRX is not recommended.

For second-generation Integras the situation is better, though, and both can be retrofitted provided the appropriate measures are taken. As with the chassis covered in Chapter 4, the processes vary depending on whether or not A/C and power steering are retained separately, together, or eliminated entirely.

A/C and Power Steering Delete

Space is limited with all of these chassis, which means eliminating the A/C and power steering systems is a popular choice. Removing all of this is slightly more complicated. The K-series drive belt isn't just responsible for rotating the A/C compressor and power steering pump; it also drives the alternator and water pump. All told, the system consists of six pulleys, one of which is paired with the automatic belt tensioner. Once any of these components are eliminated, the belt is no longer compatible. As you'd expect, there are multiple solutions.

Replacing the power steering pump for the 2002–2005 Civic Si engine's idler pulley is the most obvious solution but is only suitable for Integra chassis that have the available hood space. The seventh-generation Civic Si features an electric power steering system, which makes it one of the only K-series engines not to feature a hydraulic power steering pump but instead an idler pulley.

1988–1991 CIVIC AND 1990–1993 INTEGRA

The easiest way to eliminate power steering and retain the factory drive belt orientation is with the 2002–2005 Civic Si idler pulley. The pulley also sits significantly lower than the power steering pump pulley, which means hood clearance can be retained.

When matched with the appropriate seven-rib accessory belt, the combination does away with the power steering pump and the A/C compressor.

K-Tuned offers a similar solution but with adjustability to account for belt discrepancies. Whichever method is chosen, be sure to gather the appropriate idler pulley bracket, bearing cover, and mounting bolts, which can be purchased from Honda.

Eliminating the A/C compressor and power steering pump along with the belt tensioner mechanism entirely is another solution and is suitable for Civic, CRX, and Integra chassis. Here, a shorter belt can be used that spans around the crankshaft pulley, water pump, and alternator. To allow the belt to properly route, a larger-diameter, aftermarket alternator pulley, such as one from AEM (PN 23-7032), designed for the 2002–2005 Civic Si's K20A3 must be used to prevent the belt from rubbing against itself.

To tension the belt, shims must be placed between the alternator and the engine block at its mounting points. Exact belt length varies because of crankshaft pulley options but generally measures approximately 39 inches. This three-pulley method is used frequently because it eliminates the need to clearance the area around the headlight. Keep in mind that because it doesn't include a belt tensioner, generating proper tension and ensuring that it remains consistent can be a challenge.

Hybrid Racing's solution eliminates the need for the K20A3 idler pulley yet offers belt tensioning. Their kit is based on a spring-loaded automatic belt tensioner that replaces the factory piece and is compatible with all K-series engines. The system allows the A/C compressor and power steering pump to be removed and includes the appropriate drive belt. The kit also relocates the alternator to the A/C compressor's original location, which means any trimming near the headlight region can be skipped.

K-Tuned offers an alternative to the 2002–2005 Civic Si idler pulley that eliminates power steering but also relocates the alternator down low where the A/C compressor is normally located. Relocating the alternator means that it is no longer necessary to notch the headlight structure on 1988–1991 Civic and CRX chassis. (Photo Courtesy K-Tuned)

K-Tuned and Karcepts offer similar kits that relocate the alternator. However, they are based on manual tensioners.

Remember that anytime power steering components are removed from a vehicle originally equipped with it, the steering rack should be swapped for a manual version or appropriately looped to prevent debris from entering what was once an otherwise closed system.

Power Steering Delete with A/C

Retaining A/C on the second-generation Integra chassis is an entirely custom procedure; the aftermarket currently does not support this practice. Keeping the A/C on the 1988–1991 Civic or CRX simply isn't recommended because of limited space constraints.

For the Integra, you should start with the same K20A3 idler pulley along with the necessary hardware.

Almost any K-series A/C compressor is mechanically compatible; however, some are preferred over others. Compressors from any 2002–2006 RSX or 2002–2005 Civic Si (top) feature a single-wire thermal protection switch (similar to older Civics and Integras), which means swapping out any electrical connectors isn't necessary. Alternate A/C compressors feature an entirely different three-wire thermal protection switch (bottom). (Photo Courtesy Hasport Performance Products)

The factory K20A3 belt must also be used, which allows the K-series A/C compressor to be installed in stock configuration. For best results, look to the 2002–2006 RSX or 2002–2005 Civic Si for the appropriate A/C compressor.

Fitting the A/C compressor into place isn't easy. The factory crossmember doesn't allow it, which means that it must be notched accordingly or an aftermarket tubular version must be used. The factory condenser and cooling fan may be retained but custom-made lines must be fashioned. Wiring is limited to the compressor's thermal protection switch. Lengthen the one-pin connector's wire from the chassis harness to reach the new compressor's location.

A/C Delete With Power Steering

For Integra chassis only, if power steering is retained without A/C, start with any 2002–2004 RSX power steering pump. Additional clearance may be found by using a smaller-diameter Jackson Racing supercharger pulley (PN 052-154) in place of the original power steering pump pulley to avoid twisting and reorienting the low-pressure return line connection. Belt length may vary significantly depending on crankshaft pulley and power steering pump pulley diameter so measure accordingly.

Once the A/C compressor has been removed, route the new belt following the same path. From there, the Integra's high-pressure feed hose must be modified and merged with one that's compatible with the K-series power steering pump being used. Both lines' rigid, tubular sections must be cut and welded together to form a new piece that's compatible with the Integra's steering rack and the engine's pump. The remainder of the system includes the reservoir and low-pressure lines, which can be fabricated from a combination of the Integra reservoir and bulk hose to allow relocation.

A/C With Power Steering

If A/C and power steering are going to be retained on any second-generation Integra chassis, start with the appropriate power steering pump and crankshaft pulley and use the same combination of Hybrid Racing and factory components outlined above. Belt selection is easy here and is consistent with whatever the donor engine originally calls for. For specifics on hooking up power steering and A/C components, see the previous sections.

Intake and Exhaust Systems

The K-series engine transplant into the 1988–1991 Civic and CRX as well as the 1990–1993 Integra is among the most involved. Former non-issues such as throttle bodies, intake manifolds, and exhaust manifolds must now be taken into consideration because of opposing electrical systems and limited space constraints.

Throttle Body

Unless a customized electrical system is in order, a cable-driven throttle body must be used. (See Chapter 1 for details on what type of throttle body each popular K-series engine features.) Look to the donor engine's intake manifold to determine which throttle body may be used; bolt patterns differ among many of them.

Aftermarket throttle body adapters from Hybrid Racing and Karcepts are also available. These allow

If you'll be seeking emissions-legal status and the evaporative emissions canister is going to be retained, its purge lines must connect to the throttle body or the plastic fitting near the valve cover, depending on the engine.

cable-style throttle bodies to be bolted onto intake manifolds that accept drive-by-wire throttle bodies.

If the engine swap will remain emissions-legal, relocate the charcoal canister onto the chassis, somewhere near the left-side framerail mount using a custom bracket. Connect both canister vacuum ports to the K-series throttle body's nipples or the plastic connector located near the valve cover, depending on the engine.

Intake Piping

Before any intake piping is put into place, the appropriate intake manifold must be bolted on. The 2002–2006 RSX Type-S and 2002–2005 Civic Si's intake manifold is a proven fit for any of these vehicles because of its compact design. The manifold's compact shape lends itself well to the close proximity of the engine and radiator to each other. Similarly, select Type R versions also fit.

An aftermarket intake system, such as a cold-air unit from Hybrid Racing, must be used. It's no surprise that for such a challenging engine swap intake systems are limited. Hybrid Racing's system is only

1988–1991 CIVIC AND 1990–1993 INTEGRA

Engine bay space is limited, especially for the 1988–1991 Civic and CRX. Unless a custom radiator is used that tucks beneath the core support, intake manifold choices are limited. A 2002–2006 RSX Type-S or 2002–2005 Civic Si intake manifold with its shorter, more compact design must be used to allow adequate clearance between it and the intake manifold.

Exhaust manifold choice must also be made carefully, again because of space constraints. An aftermarket exhaust manifold designed specifically for K-series engine swaps, such as one from DC Sports, must be used; however, not every style is compatible. This 4-into-2-into-1 design must be used for appropriate clearance at the chassis and below. (Photo Courtesy Hasport Performance Products)

compatible with Civic and CRX chassis, which means the Integra's must be entirely custom.

Short-ram systems originally designed for the 2002–2006 RSX or 2002–2005 Civic Si have also been shown to work, provided a corresponding intake manifold is used. Whichever is chosen, be sure to install the intake air temperature sensor into the tubing and connect it to the engine wiring harness.

Exhaust Manifold

No factory K-series exhaust manifold is compatible with any of the Civic or Integra chassis in this chapter, which means an aftermarket header must be used. Here, 4-into-1 exhaust manifolds are not compatible; however, most 4-into-2-into-1 headers designed for K-series engine swaps into later-model Civic and Integra chassis are compatible. Be advised that many headers that feature stacked collectors where the four tubes form a box shape under the engine do not fit. Exhaust manifolds, such as PLM's, which are designed specifically for the 1988–1991 Civic and CRX chassis, route underneath the subframe with room to spare.

To take advantage of the header and the larger-displacement more-powerful K-series engine, some sort of high-flowing exhaust system should also be put in place. Be sure to use whichever exhaust system and muffler is compatible with the vehicle and sort out any discrepancies between it and the exhaust manifold using a customized catalytic convertor or test pipe. The appropriate-length tubing and correct flanges are typically all that's needed to adapt them.

Regardless of which exhaust manifold is selected, the exhaust piping following it must be modified to fit. Cut and remove the appropriate amount of tubing so that the K-series exhaust manifold terminates where the remainder of the exhaust piping begins. Be sure to source the appropriate flange for the exhaust piping that matches the exhaust manifold.

ECU Selection

Although the electrical system is often the last to be addressed, the ECU should be chosen early

CHAPTER 5

on. As discussed in Chapter 3, modern Honda ECUs are equipped with immobilizers, which render the vehicle's electronics useless in the event of a theft. This complicates the engine swap process because none of the chassis in this chapter were designed for any of this. There are three common solutions.

One of the simplest solutions is to source a Japanese-spec 2001–2005 Civic Type R or 2001–2006 Integra Type R ECU. Earlier Type R ECUs such as these feature relatively unsophisticated immobilizers that can easily be bypassed. However, they are typically prohibitively expensive and difficult to source. They're also best suited only for 2.0L performance i-VTEC engines such as the K20A2. The main relay must simply be grounded on its own (not through the ECU) to bypass the immobilizer. To do this, cut ECU wire E7 and appropriately ground the wire's main relay side to the chassis.

Both Hybrid Racing and K-Tuned offer immobilizer bypass units that splice directly into the engine wiring harness and disrupt the factory immobilizer. Such bypass units don't work with all ECUs, though; compatible ECUs include those from the 2002–2004 RSX Type-S, 2002–2004 RSX base model, 2002–2005 Civic Si, and 2002–2006 CR-V. Connecting either of these immobilizer bypasses into place is easy and involves splicing four wires into the ECU's A and E connectors.

It's important to know that any of the previously mentioned ECUs can be used with either 5-speed or 6-speed transmissions. However, when using a 5-speed–compatible ECU with a 6-speed gearbox, be sure to address the transmission's reverse-gear lockout using one of the following methods: a hard-wired momentary switch that overrides the reverse gear solenoid or some sort of engine management system such as Hondata's K-Pro, where it can be addressed internally.

Hondata's K-Pro is the third ECU solution, with the exception of stand-alone engine management systems. K-Pro has the ability to disable the ECU's immobilizer and eliminate the secondary oxygen sensor but also does so much more, such as allow for complete fuel, ignition, and cam angle control as well as data logging.

K-Pro also allows any compatible ECU to work with any K-series engine or transmission, despite the type of i-VTEC or number of gears. Compatible ECUs include those from the 2002–2004 RSX base model, 2002–2004 RSX Type-S, 2001–2006 Integra Type R, 2001–2005 Civic Type R, 2002–2006 CR-V, and 2002–2005 Civic Si.

Regardless of the chosen solution, transmission selection must be made carefully when settling on an ECU. Although most K-series transmissions appear the same, they feature two types of vehicle speed sensors. Low-frequency vehicle speed sensors may be found in 2002–2004 RSX, 2002–2005 Civic Si, 2001–2005 Civic Type R, and 2001–2006 Integra Type R transmissions and communicate with the ECU and instrument cluster through a low-frequency signal that's transmitted from the transmission's final-drive gear.

High-frequency vehicle speed sensors may be found in 2005–2006 RSX, 2003–2007 Accord, 2006–2008 Accord Euro R, 2004–2008 TSX, 2006–2011 Civic Si, and 2007–2011 Civic Type R transmissions and communicate exclusively with the ECU, which relays the signal to the instrument cluster through a high-frequency signal transmitted from the transmission's third gear. The transmission, vehicle speed sensor, and ECU along with the engine and chassis wiring harnesses must all be compatible with each other for the ECU and instrument cluster to interpret vehicle speed properly.

Here, a Hondata K-Pro-modified ECU has been connected to its corresponding RSX engine wiring harness and Hasport sub-harness. All three ECU connectors terminate here, along with the 20-pin connector that interfaces between the sub-harness and the engine wiring harness. Also, notice the heavy-gauge wires on the right that lead to the remote-mounted battery in the rear.

1988–1991 CIVIC AND 1990–1993 INTEGRA

Hybrid Racing has the solution for incorrect vehicle speed sensors and instrument clusters with ECUs that aren't able to communicate with them. Its Vehicle Speed Converter allows any high-frequency vehicle speed sensor to be used with just a few simple steps. This is good news if you plan to use, for example, the transmission from a 2006–2011 Civic Si. (Photo Courtesy Hybrid Racing)

Differentiating a left-hand-drive engine wiring harness from a right-hand-drive harness is easy. Notice the distance between the plastic joint (lower center) and the rubber firewall grommet (top center) on this left-hand-drive example. That distance is significantly shorter on right-hand-drive harnesses, making them unable to reach the ECU without extensive modifications.

The obvious solution is to use a low-frequency-type transmission matched with the appropriate 2002–2004 RSX or 2002–2005 Civic Si ECU. With the appropriate engine wiring harness, the process is easy. However, alternate high-frequency-type transmissions may still be used. With the help of K-Pro or a supplemental device, such as K-Tuned's Adjustable Speed Converter or Hybrid Racing's Vehicle Speed Converter, any signal discrepancies can be adjusted.

K-Tuned's converter allows high-frequency speed sensors to communicate with the vehicle's instrument cluster properly. The converter must be wired in place at the engine wiring harness near the ECU. Connections are limited to 12V ignition power, ground, vehicle speed signal input, and vehicle speed signal output.

Once installed, transmissions such as the 2005–2006 RSX, 2003–2007 Accord, 2006–2008 Accord Euro R, 2004–2008 TSX, 2006–2011 Civic Si, and 2007–2011 Civic Type R can be used without any issues.

Wiring

Wiring can begin as soon as the engine and transmission are chosen. Three major areas must be addressed: engine harness, sub-harness, and charge harness.

Engine Wiring Harness

Wiring any of the chassis in this chapter begins with any manual transmission–equipped 2002–2004 RSX, 2002–2005 Civic Si, or 2002–2006 CR-V (automatic versions can be converted) engine wiring harness. Later-model 2005–2006 RSX harnesses may also be used; however, these require extensive modifications to be useful and should be avoided if possible.

The 2002–2004 RSX Type-S harness is typically recommended; it's compatible with either 5-speed or 6-speed transmissions because of its reverse gear lockout connector and offers the most flexibility. Whichever harness is chosen, be sure that it's sourced from a left-hand-drive chassis. Although harnesses from right-hand-drive vehicles may feature all of the appropriate connectors, many of them are located on the opposite side, which means more work.

Finally, any of the above harnesses plug directly into any K-series ECU's A and B connectors, leaving much of the wiring to take place at the harness' 20-pin connector and the ECU's remaining E connector.

Before installing the engine, connect the engine wiring harness. Once the engine is in place, route the harness through the existing wiring harness opening or through the A/C evaporator line's opening if A/C has been removed. Be sure to position a grommet around the harness to protect it against any sharp edges at the firewall regardless of the opening used. With the engine wiring harness inside the cabin, plug the A and B connectors into the ECU.

All that's left is to properly ground the engine wiring harness to the chassis under the hood at least three locations as well as to the engine itself.

Sub-Harness

Every K-series engine swap needs a sub-harness, the intermediary section of wiring between the engine wiring harness, ECU, and chassis. The sub-harness allows everything to work together and is arguably the most challenging part of the entire engine swap. You can make your own but a substantial understanding of Honda electrical systems as well as service manuals for both your chassis and the engine are necessary. Fortunately, plug-and-play versions are available from Hasport, Hybrid Racing, Rywire, and K-Tuned.

CHAPTER 5

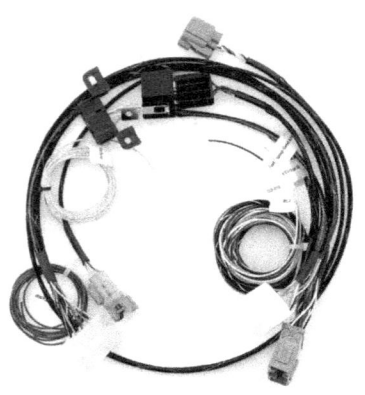

Aftermarket sub-harnesses, such as this one from Hybrid Racing, significantly simplify the wiring process. Each harness features labeled connectors that terminate at the ECU, engine harness, and chassis harness. Instructions are also included for hooking up the few remaining wires that differ slightly depending on the manufacturer. (Photo Courtesy Hybrid Racing)

The sub-harness should include six or seven components, depending on the specific application: an E connector that plugs into the ECU's remaining slot, a 20-pin connector that plugs into the engine wiring harness, two additional connectors that plug into the chassis harness, a data link connector that remains unplugged, and an oxygen sensor connector and relay. Regardless of the aftermarket wiring harness you choose, several wires must be manually spliced into the chassis harness for the fuel pump, check engine light, vehicle speed sensor, and ECU to work.

Follow the individual manufacturer's instructions and be sure to make the necessary splices in the chassis harness where the original ECU plugs connected to the factory computer.

Before moving on, electrical connections for the radiator fan switch and coolant temperature sensor must be addressed. If you're using a 2002–2006 RSX or 2002–2005 Civic Si radiator, the radiator fan switch should have already been threaded into place. For all other radiator applications, it should already be installed via one of the described methods.

Most aftermarket sub-harnesses include provisions for the radiator fan switch and coolant temperature sensor. Simply locate the appropriate wires within the sub-harness and connect them to the existing radiator fan switch plug and coolant temperature sensor plug (which should have been salvaged from the original engine wiring harness).

Charge Harness

Unlike the engine wiring harnesses native to these chassis that integrate charging system wiring within, a separate harness must be made for the K-series. Start with a charge harness from any 2002–2006 RSX. The harness must be modified so that it spans from the positive battery terminal to the starter, alternator, and fuse box. This must be done because the fuse box on K-series-native vehicles is located across the engine bay from any of those covered in this chapter.

Once finished, the modified charge harness should span from the positive battery terminal to the starter, from the positive battery terminal to the fuse box, and from the fuse box to the alternator. The connections that attach to the fuse box must also be swapped for those from the original chassis to ensure that the harness properly adapts to the fuse box.

Suspension and Braking

Even 2.4L K-series engines weigh only roughly 100 pounds more than the D-series that was removed and even less than the Integra's native power plant. Still, any of these chassis' suspensions and brakes are affected by the added weight. The additional weight up front doesn't necessarily affect handling adversely but it can reduce shock travel. Be sure that the shocks are in good working order and, if not, invest in a high-performance set with stiffer dampening characteristics. When it comes to ride height, it's best to proceed cautiously on the high side to avoid conflicts between the oil pan and the pavement.

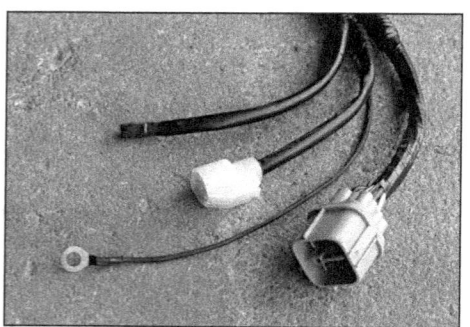

Every Hasport sub-harness features connectors for the radiator fan switch and coolant temperature sensor. Depending on where either has been located, Hasport can even customize the sub-harness to your specific needs. Just let them know ahead of time.

K-series charge harness fuse box connectors (shown) are incompatible with older Civic and Integra chassis. The original Civic or Integra connectors must be reused and grafted onto the donor engine's charge harness.

1988–1991 CIVIC AND 1990–1993 INTEGRA

All of that extra power can put the factory brakes through their paces, especially Civic models that feature drum brakes in the rear. There are many solutions; the most effective is to transfer over the Integra's components both front and rear. For a completely bolt-on solution, source components from any duly-equipped 1990–1991 Civic EX or CRX Si as well as compatible Integras. For even more stopping power, cross-drilled or slotted rotors along with more-aggressive pads and steel-braided brake lines that can withstand the hotter fluid temperatures can even further enhance either of the four-wheel-disc setups previously mentioned.

Rear-wheel-disc-brake conversions are among the easiest ways to increase stopping power on Civic and CRX chassis that were originally equipped with drum brakes in the rear. A number of chassis may be chosen for their components, such as the 1990–1991 Civic EX or CRX Si. Here, five-lug Integra Type R components have also been added.

Company Profile: Hybrid Racing

The story of engine swap parts manufacturer and retailer Hybrid Racing started in 2001, when its co-founder and now CEO, William Davidson, experienced the realities and challenges of performing his own engine swap with little information and less-than-acceptable parts. Following a number of side jobs and B-series engine swaps, Davidson and friends performed what was arguably one of the first K-series engine swaps.

It was 2002 and the K-series was still new; it had yet to be trusted by the Honda community at large but Davidson knew better, rationalizing that if Honda went to the trouble to develop it, the least he could do was have a closer look. That closer look led to a pioneering engine swap and spawned the first company to dedicate itself entirely to making swaps like his a reality for other enthusiasts.

Hybrid Racing was formally founded in 2003 in a small shop financed through years of B-series engine swaps and other odd jobs. Davidson's goal was simple: to change the relationship between shop and customer and deliver innovative and durable products. Davidson and company got to work right away, developing the first K-series engine mount kit for the 1992–1995 Civic as well as the first plug-and-play K-series engine swap wiring harnesses, A/C adapter kits, shifter cables, fuel and clutch line kits, and more. In recent years, Hybrid Racing has continued to lead the way with its swap-specific cold-air intake systems, fabrication-free

Hybrid Racing has long been considered a leader in the K-series engine swap movement. Today, the company offers just about everything you need for a turnkey engine swap. In fact, Hybrid Racing offers swap kits that are designed to do exactly that and include everything from engine mounts to exhaust manifolds to wiring harnesses. (Photo Courtesy Hybrid Racing)

shifter assemblies, and K-series-friendly radiators.

Despite the success and long lineup of K-series wares, Davidson hasn't forgotten what it was like when doing that first engine swap and continues to offer a place where customers can come for "no strings attached" help with what he calls Hybrid Racing's laid-back customers-first attitude. ■

CHAPTER 6

2001–2005 CIVIC

The 2001–2005 Civic brought with it from the factory the first Honda engine bay capable of housing the company's newest twin-cam 4-cylinder engine, the K-series. It was also the first Civic to offer a hybrid version and the first to strip itself of Honda's famed double-wishbone suspension in favor of more cost-effective comfort-minded MacPherson struts. It was the ultimate trade-off in a long line of previously sub-2.0L Civics with power-to-weight ratios that diminished with each model year revision.

The seventh-generation Civic was arguably the first of Honda's entry-level sub-compacts not wholeheartedly welcomed by the performance community. Coupe and sedan models, with their newly refined lines, appealed less to enthusiasts than their predecessors and hatchback models were stripped of their classic, playfully bubble-like shapes that personified earlier generations of three-door Civics. It's no secret that 2001 marked the end of an era when Honda could do no wrong; when it could design, build, and sell Civics to enthusiasts by default. More than a decade later we ought to reconsider Honda's post sub-compact-domination Civic because it just may be more special than we initially thought.

By 2001, Honda's Civic was being sold in more than 140 countries. It became the first Honda to launch simultaneously throughout the world and, frankly, had millions to answer to who didn't care about things like the dynamics of MacPherson struts versus conventional shocks. The new Civic recipe (with select models being built in Swindon, England, and designed in both Japan and North America) was beginning to generate significant interest from the general public. After all, Honda never intended for its award-winning sub-compact to necessarily win the hearts and minds of enthusiasts. Instead, the company went on record and said that the seventh-generation

No other Civic chassis is as welcoming to Honda's K-series engine than the seventh-generation Civic coupe and sedan. That's primarily because its top-of-the-line Si hatchback already features one. However, non-Si chassis are still different enough, which means several issues must be addressed when performing the swap.

Civic would go beyond its traditional role; Honda aimed to elevate it into a class all by itself.

2001–2005 Civic

Before the 160-hp Si 2002 debut, 2001 coupe and sedan models were released. These models boasted the company's most powerful and fuel-efficient D-series engines to date; EX models measured 127 hp and HX trims achieved an impressive 44 mpg. Honda introduced its coupe (EM2) and sedan (ES1, ES2) in EX, LX, VP, DX, and HX (EM2) trims. The more-compact MacPherson strut setup in the front, criticized by some enthusiasts for its shorter range of motion and reduced articulation, afforded more room for the larger-displacement K20A3, which was introduced in the Civic Si a year later. It also offered more room inside, in part thanks to a flatter floor, making the 2001–2005 Civic more spacious than even previous years' Accords. The newly designed double-wishbone rear suspension, which uses the term double-wishbone in the loosest sense, is also more compact, lending itself to even more interior space.

If marketing points such as "more headroom" or "two additional cubic feet of cargo space" bore you, the Si model, released in 2002 and only in hatchback form, would've surely riled you up. Apart from Acura's RSX, the Si was the only North America–bound Honda to be fitted with a 2.0L K-series engine and was the first time North Americans received an Si in hatchback styling since 1995.

Although not as robust as the K20A2, the A3 still featured Honda's VTC system, which improved upon its standardized VTEC technology by continuously manipulating intake camshaft phasing electronically. Combine that with Honda's first-ever dash-mounted shifter that was paired to a close-ratio 5-speed gearbox, standard rear disc brakes, a first-ever electronic power steering system, and a stiffer suspension compared to the rest of the Civic lineup and, on paper, you have the makings of what one would assume to be Honda's best Si to date.

Unfortunately, Honda's failure to produce a 2001 model-year Si stifled its popularity early on. While the company wafted, Subaru was moving to the WRX, Toyota to the Celica GT-S, VW to its GTI, and Ford to its Focus SVT. Honda loyalists waited but many fled for brands that were more readily available. Despite the low production numbers, European-like styling, and performance that (for many) hardly beat the 1999–2000 Si, the seventh-generation Civic (particularly the Si) should continue to hold a special place in the hearts and minds of any dyed-in-the-wool Honda fan.

Chassis Pros and Cons

If any Civic chassis was ever destined for a K-series transplant, it's the 2001–2005. That's mostly because Honda already did all of the work with its Si hatchback, leaving little more to do than take cues from its top-of-the-line Civic and apply them toward the coupe and sedan models.

However, coupe and sedan models aren't exactly like the Si hatchback, and are different enough to require all sorts of modifications when swapping a K-series engine into place. Even after the new engine and transmission have been installed, the fuse box, ABS system, overflow reservoir, battery, and many other components will be located on opposite sides of the engine bay. Most of them cannot be easily relocated, which means some modifications must be made to the 2001–2005 Civic that are not what you'd find underneath the hood of the Si.

Unlike older Civics, 2001- and-newer models feature returnless fuel systems, which are common to all K-series-native vehicles. Shifter cables instead of rod-style shifter mechanisms are also already in place, eliminating much of the work that's required of K-series swaps into older vehicles.

The reason K-series transplants aren't as popular with the 2001–2005 Civic as you'd think has to do with weight. Later-model Civics such as these are among the heaviest in Honda's lineup; they tip the scales as high as 2,700 pounds. For

---

2001–2005 Civic Chassis Codes

2002–2005 Civic Si Hatchback	EP3
2001–2005 Civic DX, EX, HX, LX Coupe	EM2
2004–2005 Civic VP Coupe	EM2
2005 Civic EX and LX Special Edition Coupe	EM2
2001–2005 Civic DX, LX Sedan	ES1
2004–2005 Civic VP Sedan	ES1
2001–2005 Civic EX Sedan	ES2
2005 Civic EX and LX Special Edition Coupe	ES2

example, that makes a 200-hp K20A much less effective than it would be inside a 2,000-pound CRX. The seventh-generation Civic's styling has also proven to be among the least popular among enthusiasts in recent years.

Engine and Transmission

The K-series platform is already native to the seventh-generation Civic chassis in the form of the 2002–2005 Si, which means fitting the same powertrain into any other 2001–2005 Civic trim is as easy as you'd expect.

Just about any K-series engine works but transmission choice is limited to 2002–2006 RSX, 2002–2005 Civic Si, 2001–2005 Civic Type R, 2001–2006 Integra Type R, 2006–2011 Civic Si, and 2007–2011 Civic Type R transmissions because of aftermarket mount compatibility. Be sure to determine the appropriate horsepower requirements, form of i-VTEC, number of gears, and budget before settling on any particular engine or transmission.

Mounts

Regardless of which engine or transmission is chosen, aftermarket engine mount selection remains limited, leaving little to choose from besides urethane hardness and brand. Currently, Hasport is among the few to offer a kit for any of the non-Si chassis covered here. Hasport's ESK3 system is made up of a pair of steel brackets that fasten to the unibody and three urethane-filled aluminum mounts. The company's kit is compatible with all 2.0L and 2.4L K-series engines; however, you must use one of the transmissions mentioned above.

Hasport's engine mount kit designed for the 2001–2005 Civic includes a pair of precision-cut, steel framerail brackets, a rear subframe mount, and a pair of left- and right-side mounts. Non-Si chassis are different enough from the 2002–2005 Civic Si to require custom-made brackets and mounts such as these.

Although the 2002–2005 Civic is similar to the K-series-equipped Si, its engine bay and engine mount provisions are different enough to require custom mounts, such as those from Hasport. Although it may seem logical, the Si factory mounts are not compatible with other Civics. Because of engine position, minor trimming to the hood's underside webbing may be required if power steering is retained. (If the 2002–2005 Civic Si's electric power steering system is used, hood clearance is no longer an issue.)

Car Preparation

A K-series engine swap into any chassis is not for the beginner. In addition to the engine, the drivetrain, fuel system, cooling system, and clutch hydraulics must all be addressed. As with any engine swap, the process begins by removing the original powertrain; you should already be familiar with this job or comfortable taking it on. Refer to your vehicle's service manual for detailed instructions on removing the engine and note the additional points that must be addressed to prepare for the transplant.

Draining the Fluids

Whether or not A/C is retained, its contents must be drained. Be sure to have a professional evacuate the system before continuing. Next, raise the chassis using a jack and jack stands or a lift; drain the transmission fluid, coolant, power steering fluid (if equipped), and engine oil.

Removing the Ancillaries

Remove the intake piping; disconnect and remove the battery along with its tray; and disconnect both cables from the fuse box. From inside the vehicle, access the ECU and unplug the engine wiring harness from it. Underneath the hood, loosen the grommet and pull the harness into the engine bay.

Next, remove the wheels, exhaust piping at the exhaust manifold, catalytic converter, and throttle cable. Disconnect the shifter cables from the transmission and secure them out of the way using zip ties. Disconnect the fuel feed line from the fuel rail as well as the brake booster vacuum hose, and evaporative emissions canister hose. Unbolt the clutch slave cylinder from the transmission. Unbolt the power steering pump from the engine and secure it out of the way using zip ties.

Remove the alternator to access the A/C compressor, unbolt it, and set it aside. Next, remove the radiator, both hoses, and the engine's heater hoses that connect to the chassis. If A/C will be eliminated, remove the system's components now, including the condenser, lines, wiring harness, and cooling fan. When possible, the power steering system should remain intact.

Removing the Axles

Remove the axle's retaining nut from the front knuckle and then the strut's two lower mounting bolts. Once removed, pivot the knuckle assembly outward, allowing the axle's outboard end to be freed from the knuckle. Pry each axle's inboard side free and set them aside. If the inboard joints remain stuck, carefully tap them loose using a ball-peen hammer.

Removing the Mounts

Later-model Civics feature lower subframes that mount directly to the chassis and to the engine. This means that the process for removing the engine is different depending on whether or not the assembly is removed from above using a jack and jack stands or from below with a lift.

If removing the engine assembly from above, disconnect and remove the front engine mount and rear engine bracket. Next, attach the hoist and disconnect the right-side transmission bracket from its mount and the left-side engine bracket from its mount. Ensure that nothing remains connected to the engine or transmission and raise the assembly. Once the engine and transmission have been removed, disconnect the subframe from the chassis and lower control arms and remove it.

If removing the engine assembly from underneath, start by unbolting the subframe from the chassis and lower control arms. From above and with the engine positioned on a cart, disconnect and remove the right-side transmission mount and left-side engine bracket. Be sure that nothing else remains connected and raise the vehicle from the engine assembly.

ABS Considerations

Models equipped with ABS may leave the system intact; however,

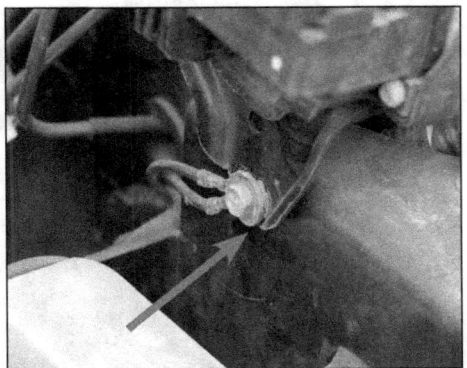

In order for Hasport's left-side framerail bracket to position properly, the ABS pump's lower mounting bracket must be trimmed. Use an angle grinder to cut off the bracket's lower section, just below the 6-1.0-mm bolt that holds it in place. For best results, unbolt the bracket and move it away from the framerail before cutting it. (Photo Courtesy Hasport Performance Products)

the ABS pump's mounting bracket must be slightly modified to allow clearance for the left-side framerail bracket. Simply mock up Hasport's framerail bracket and trim the ABS pump bracket to fit.

Clearance Considerations

Because of the K-series engine's opposite orientation compared to the original engine, the battery must be relocated to the trunk. Be sure to use an appropriate mounting kit and a minimum of 2-gauge wire to span from the fuse box underneath the hood to the battery. The ground wire can connect to any suitable location within the trunk.

If power steering is retained, the original hood prop interferes with the system's pulley. A 2002–2005 Civic Si hood prop may be used but the hood's underside must be moderately clearanced. An alternative is to use aftermarket hood shocks positioned at each side of the hood

Beginning with the 2001 model year, Honda introduced an entirely new subframe that encapsulates the engine and transmission. The original Civic subframe must be removed from the chassis. It is not reused. (Photo Courtesy Hasport Performance Products)

CHAPTER 6

Clearance is minimal between the engine and the core support. As such, intake manifold selection must be made carefully. The 2002–2006 RSX Type-S or 2002–2005 Civic Si intake manifold allows plenty of clearance. Select 2.4L Accord engines with cast-aluminum intake manifolds may also be used. (Photo Courtesy Hasport Performance Products)

Once the original engine and transmission have been removed, along with their brackets and mounts, the Hasport right-side bracket can be mounted onto the framerail. Bolt it in place using the supplied hardware. (Photo Courtesy Hasport Performance Products)

Similar to the right side, Hasport's left-side framerail bracket can be installed next and bolted into place. Hasport's left- and right-side brackets install quickly and require no fabrication or welding apart from the previously cut ABS bracket. (Photo Courtesy Hasport Performance Products)

A subframe from any 2002–2006 RSX or 2002–2005 Civic Si must be used instead of the original Civic piece. If you'll be installing the engine from above, set the subframe aside for now. If you'll be doing so from underneath, mount the engine and transmission onto the subframe now using the rear bracket and mount. (Photo Courtesy Hasport Performance Products)

near the windshield that allow the hood prop to be eliminated entirely.

Applications specific to the 2002–2005 Civic are few so plan on a bit of customization to allow a pair of shocks designed for any older Civic, for example, to fit. Look to Password: JDM and its line of hood shocks.

Right-Side Framerail Bracket

Unbolt the right-side transmission mount from the chassis and set it aside. Next, simply bolt the supplied bracket to the framerail using the included hardware. In some cases, a series of spacers are required to allow the bracket to sit flush.

Left-Side Framerail Bracket

Disconnect and remove the left-side engine mount from the chassis and bolt the Hasport bracket in its place to the framerail using the supplied hardware.

Rear Subframe Mount

If you'll be installing the engine and transmission assembly from above, the rear mount must be

2001–2005 CIVIC

Hasport's billet aluminum rear mount, along with the engine's native rear engine bracket, attaches the engine and transmission assembly to the subframe. Here, the engine and transmission have already been installed into the chassis and the mount and bracket are being tightened. (Photo Courtesy Hasport Performance Products)

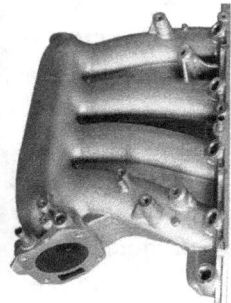 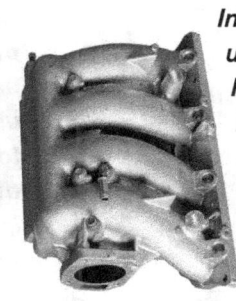

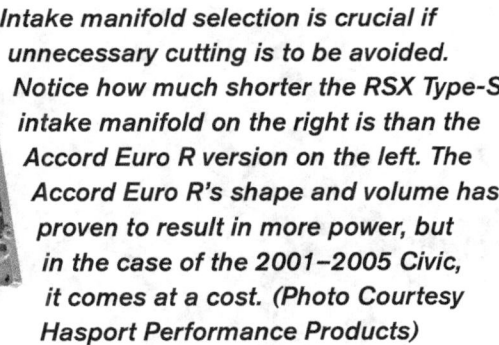

Intake manifold selection is crucial if unnecessary cutting is to be avoided. Notice how much shorter the RSX Type-S intake manifold on the right is than the Accord Euro R version on the left. The Accord Euro R's shape and volume has proven to result in more power, but in the case of the 2001–2005 Civic, it comes at a cost. (Photo Courtesy Hasport Performance Products)

addressed now. First, the subframe must be bolted into place. A 2002–2006 RSX or 2002–2005 Civic Si version must be used, both of which bolt directly to any 2001–2005 Civic chassis. Once in place, attach the Hasport rear mount to the new subframe using the supplied hardware.

If you'll be installing the engine and transmission assembly from below, the subframe and rear mount must be installed later. Use a utility knife and be prepared to trim the Civic's lower splash shield to provide adequate clearance for the subframe.

Engine Preparation

Before moving on, carefully inspect your new engine. Start by making sure that any sensors that may have become damaged during storage or transport have been repaired and plug the appropriate engine wiring harness into place. Tuck the ECU plugs out of the way to make installation easier. If any maintenance is necessary, or if other parts must be swapped out, do it now.

Finally, remove the exhaust manifold as well as any brackets or mounts that may have been sold with the engine and transmission except for the rear engine bracket and timing-chain-side bracket.

2.4L Engine Considerations

Any 2.0L or 2.4L engine may be used but the correct timing-chain-side bracket must be used. If using a 2.4L engine, be sure to source the appropriate bracket from any 2002–2006 CR-V K24A1 engine (Honda PN 11910-PPA-000). Be sure to avoid other 2.4L brackets that are not compatible. Depending on which intake manifold is used, the core support near the radiator may also need to be trimmed. To avoid any cutting, use any 2002–2006 RSX Type-S or 2002–2005 Civic Si intake manifold, for example.

Engine Installation

If using an engine hoist and installing everything from above, the subframe should already be installed underneath. A load leveler, which attaches to the engine hoist and allows the assembly to be lowered into place at an angle, should be used to reduce the risk of damaging the chassis. If a vehicle lift is used and the assembly will be installed from underneath, place the engine and transmission on a cart until it is mounted onto the subframe.

Left-Side Transmission Mount

Lower the engine assembly into place, connect the left-side mount to the transmission, and slip it into the already-installed framerail bracket. Fasten it into place using the

The left-side mount bolts directly to the transmission and to the already-installed framerail bracket. If the engine and transmission are being installed from above, do not install the mount onto the transmission until the assembly is in place. (Photo Courtesy Hasport Performance Products)

CHAPTER 6

Once the left-side transmission mount has been attached, use a floor jack to raise or lower the engine, allowing the right-side Hasport mount to align with the timing-chain-side bracket and already-installed framerail bracket.

A total of three mounts and brackets must align here; slowly and carefully calculated movements of the engine are often needed for all of them to line up. (Photo Courtesy Hasport Performance Products)

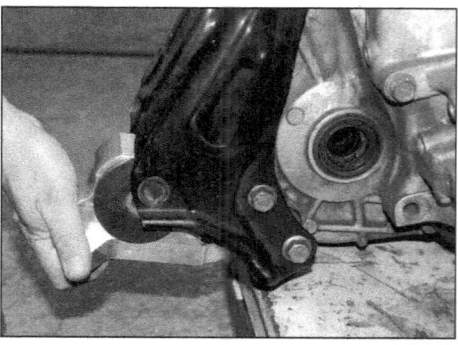

Here, the Hasport engine mount is being positioned inside its rear bracket in preparation for mounting the assembly to the RSX subframe. The 2001–2005 Civic is the only K-series engine swap to make use of any factory brackets or mounts. (Photo Courtesy Hasport Performance Products)

supplied hardware. Don't tighten the hardware completely; this allows the remaining mounts to be positioned more easily.

Right-Side Engine Mount

Position the right-side engine mount onto the existing engine bracket and slip it into the previously installed right-side framerail bracket. Fasten it into place using the supplied hardware, leaving it hand-tight until the rear mount and rear engine bracket have been installed.

Rear Engine Bracket

If the engine and transmission are being installed from above, bolt the K-series engine's original rear engine bracket into place and connect it to the already-installed rear mount. Only brackets compatible with RSX-style transmissions may be used. To simplify the process, the rear engine bracket can be installed before lowering the engine into place.

If installing the engine and transmission from below, start by bolting the rear mount to the subframe. Be sure that the rear engine bracket is in place and raise the subframe into place, bolting it to the chassis and to the rear engine bracket.

Regardless of the method used, finish the process by tightening all engine and transmission mount and bracket hardware to the appropriate specifications.

Axles

Axle selection is among the easiest of all K-series engine swaps; simply source shafts from any 2002–2006 RSX base model or 2002–2005 Civic Si and install them according to the factory service manual. Axles from the 2002–2006 RSX Type-S may also be used; however, because of the Type-S's larger-diameter shafts, the corresponding Type-S knuckle assemblies must also be used, which fortunately easily bolt onto any 2002–2005 Civic.

Aftermarket axles designed for either of these chassis are also compatible. Once the axles have been installed, the lower control arms and struts may be reconnected and the wheels reinstalled. Be sure to use the intermediate shaft from any 2002–2006 RSX, 2002–2005 Civic Si, 2001–2005 Civic Type R, 2001–2006 Integra Type R, 2006–2011 Civic Si, or 2007–2011 Civic Type R transmission.

Throttle Cable

For a factory-like fit, any 2002–2006 RSX throttle cable can be used that connects directly to the Civic's pedal assembly. Older 1992–1995

Axle selection doesn't get much easier than with the 2001–2005 Civic. Presumably because of its close association with the 2001–2005 Civic Si, axles can be sourced from that model or from the 2002–2006 RSX base model (shown).

Civic throttle cables may also be used; however, a special adapter bracket, such as those from K-Tuned, must be used at the throttle body for compatibility.

Clutch Hydraulics

The 2001–2005 Civic features a hydraulic clutch system, as does every K-series-bound chassis; however, the D-series transmission is located on the opposite side of the engine bay. The clutch line that spans from the Civic's clutch master cylinder to the K-series transmission's clutch slave cylinder must be addressed. Any 2002–2006 RSX or 2002–2005 Civic Si clutch line can be used for a factory-like appearance. A custom line made of Teflon-lined steel-braided hose and the appropriate hose ends can also be used.

Brake Booster

Because the K-series intake manifold is positioned at the opposite end of the engine bay, the original brake booster line does not reach. Source the appropriate brake booster line from any 2002–2006 RSX or 2002–2005 Civic Si and connect it to the intake manifold and to the distribution line on the engine, which then connects to the brake booster check valve.

Shifter Assembly

The 2001–2005 Civic is among the few chassis for which the original shifter box may be reused. If for some reason the original shifter box isn't available or the chassis is being converted from an automatic transmission to a manual, the RSX shifter box mentioned in earlier chapters may be

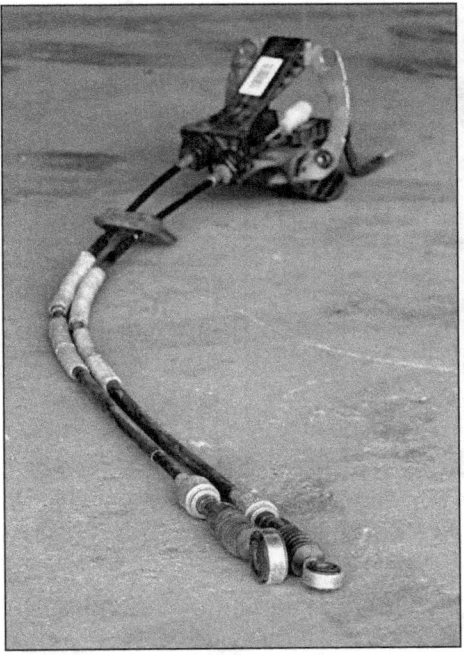

The 2002–2005 Civic Si shifter assembly and cables may seem as if they'd be a direct fit but they aren't. The Civic Si shifter is positioned high on the dash; it's the only Honda to ever feature such a layout. As such, it's completely incompatible with any other seventh-generation Civic without extensive modifications.

used. Although it may seem like an ideal fit, avoid the shifter assembly from the 2002–2005 Civic Si, which is not compatible.

The shifter is positioned on the dashboard, unlike every other Honda, which explains its odd shape and shorter shifter cables. Regardless of the shifter box that is used, 2002–2004 RSX shifter cables must be used. Later-style 2005–2006 RSX shifter cables, which require a bit of modifying to fit, may also be used as may aftermarket cable assemblies from Hybrid Racing or K-Tuned.

The 2006–2011 Civic Si and 2007–2011 Civic Type R transmissions are compatible with these chassis and available engine mounts.

Attaching the shifter cables to the shifter box and the transmission will result in few surprises provided the right components are used. Simply reuse the vehicle's original shifter box and attach any 2002–2004 RSX shifter cables to it and the transmission. (Photo Courtesy Hasport Performance Products)

The 2001–2005 Civic shifter box can be identified by its cable-mounting locations, one of which is oriented on the side, the other on the top. In the case of the seventh-generation Civic, the shifter box need not be removed from the chassis during the swap; simply connect the shifter cables and reinstall any interior components that were removed to access them.

However, the shifter assembly must be swapped with one from any 2003–2007 Accord or 2004–2008 TSX to accommodate either of them. This makes them both unpopular choices for this chassis.

CHAPTER 6

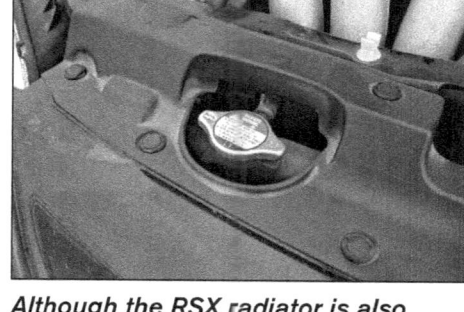

The evaporative emissions line and fuel feed line at the firewall must be reoriented away from where the K-series exhaust manifold will soon reside. Carefully bend them 90 degrees toward the left side of the chassis (right side of frame) so that they're oriented parallel to the steering rack below them. (Photo Courtesy Hasport Performance Products)

Although the RSX radiator is also compatible, only the 2002–2005 Civic Si radiator positions its cap in the same location as every other seventh-generation Civic's. The original plastic radiator cover can even be retained and left unmodified.

Fuel System

Because the seventh-generation Civic already features a returnless fuel system, any modifications are minimal. The flexible fuel feed line that spans from the fuel rail to the rigid fuel line at the firewall must be connected to the fuel rail. Carefully bend the rigid line at the firewall so that it is routed away from the exhaust manifold and connect to the line for a factory-like fit. Bend the other hard line next to it and connect the original evaporative emissions purge hose to it.

Cooling System

As with almost every other aspect of K-series engine swaps into 2001–2005 Civic chassis, the cooling system is relatively straightforward and simply consists of sourcing the right combination of factory components.

Radiator

The radiator must be sourced from any 2002–2005 Civic Si and mounted in the factory location. Because the Si shares a similar chassis with the remainder of the Civic lineup, the radiator can be installed with little trouble. Versions from any 2002–2006 RSX are also compatible; however, the front bumper grill must be trimmed slightly to allow for radiator cap clearance.

Cooling Fan

To retain the factory appearance, source the appropriate Civic Si or RSX cooling fan and mount it to the radiator. To properly clear, the vertical radiator support brace on the chassis must be trimmed. To avoid trimming, a slimmer, universal aftermarket fan may be used; however, it must be appropriately wired into place.

First, cut the electrical connector off the original cooling fan, leaving at least 4 inches of wire exposed. Locate the two wires connected to the fan's motor and carefully connect them to the battery terminals to verify which direction the fan spins once mounted. Adjust the polarity of the two wires so that, once mounted, the fan moves air past the radiator.

Finally, solder the connector onto the new fan's wires, taking into account the appropriate polarity.

If a 2002–2005 Civic Si radiator is used, simply install the corresponding cooling fan along with the shroud. Here, a slimmer, aftermarket fan has been added on the left side for additional clearance and improved performance. You can also see the provision for the radiator fan switch along the bottom of the radiator. (Photo Courtesy Hasport Performance Products)

2001–2005 CIVIC

Radiator Hoses

Before the appropriate radiator hoses can be selected, you have to know which type of upper coolant outlet pipe your engine features: front mount or side mount. You also need to know which lower thermostat housing it has. For applications such as 2.0L RSX engines, which are most common for these chassis, source upper and lower hoses from any 2002–2006 RSX or 2002–2005 Civic Si.

Cooling Electrical

Unlike the D-series engine that's being replaced, the K-series radiator fan switch that triggers the cooling fan is integrated into the Civic Si or RSX radiator you've chosen. Simply thread the D-series engine's radiator fan switch into the radiator's provision and plug the appropriate engine sub-harness connector into it.

Because of incompatibility with the Civic's electronics and instrument cluster, the K-series coolant temperature sensor (not to be confused with the thermo unit that must be changed out on other chassis) must also be replaced with the original D-series sensor and plugged into the K-series engine wiring harness.

Heater Hoses

Two additional hoses must be added to complete the cooling system. The pair of hoses that connect the heater core and its valve assembly to the engine must be connected in order for the heater to function. Use 5/8- and 3/4-inch cooling hose to span from the heater core outlet and water valve inlet on the firewall to the appropriate inlet and outlet on the engine. In some cases, hoses from any 2002–2006 RSX or 2002–2005 Civic Si may also work. Be careful when routing the hoses and position them away from the exhaust manifold.

Overflow Reservoir

Because of the engine's opposite orientation and to allow clearance, the radiator overflow reservoir must be replaced with a 2002–2006 RSX version and relocated someplace near the left-side headlight. A custom bracket can be made and a section of 5/16-inch tubing must span from the reservoir's nipple to the radiator.

A/C and Power Steering

Both A/C and power steering are compatible with every 2001–2005 Civic K-series engine swap and can be retained with little work. A/C may be eliminated for further weight reduction; however, it's recommended that the power steering system remains intact on these chassis.

A/C Delete with Power Steering

The K-series drive belt is responsible for rotating the water pump, alternator, A/C compressor, and power steering pump. Any time one of these elements are eliminated, the entire drive-belt system must be addressed.

The process of eliminating the A/C system begins by removing the A/C compressor. Next, source the appropriate power steering pump or use whichever pump the donor engine is equipped with. Hood clearance is at a minimum here and in some cases the hood prop lever may interfere with the power steering pump pulley, so consider replacing the original pulley with the smaller-diameter Jackson Racing supercharger pulley, which conveniently fits most K-series power steering pumps (PN 052-154).

Unique to the seventh-generation Civic and no other K-series engine swap, the K-series coolant temperature sensor is not compatible with the 2001–2005 Civic electronics. The solution is easy, though. Simply swap the original D-series sensor in its place; it shares the same thread pitch as the K-series sensor.

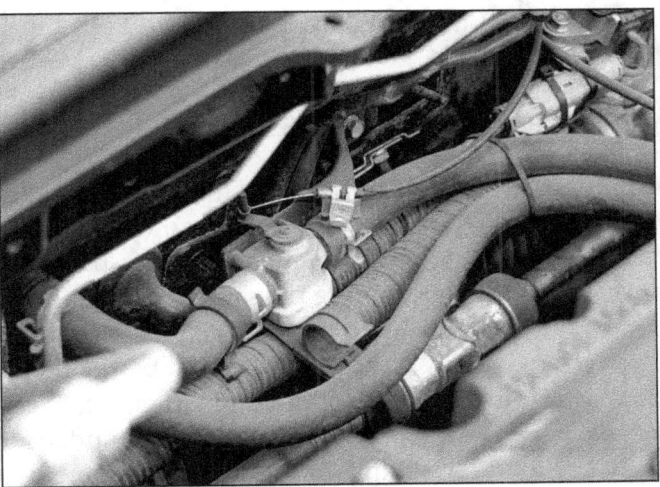

Here, the heater hoses have been tucked and tied away to avoid contact with the exhaust manifold. Heating was retained, which is why the water valve inlet remains in place. Unformed, bulk hose was used also, but notice how bends were made gradually and smoothly to avoid kinking.

HONDA K-SERIES ENGINE SWAPS

Belt length may vary depending on crankshaft pulley and power steering pump pulley diameter so measure carefully before settling on any particular size. The new belt must route around the water pump following the same path once the A/C compressor has been removed but otherwise routes as you'd expect.

With the power steering pump in place, source the high- and low-pressure power steering lines as well as the power steering reservoir from any 2002–2006 RSX and connect them to the pump and steering rack. For a factory-like fit, be sure to order the appropriate brackets and clamps that go with both lines and the reservoir.

You may use the 2002–2005 Civic Si electric power steering system, which means hood clearance issues won't be a problem. You need the accompanying steering rack and

> **A/C and Power Steering Parts**
>
> 2002–2005 Civic Si A/C discharge hose: Honda PN 80315-S5T-E01
> 2002–2005 Civic Si A/C suction hose: Honda PN 80311-S5T-A01
> 2002–2005 Civic Si A/C pipe assembly: Honda PN 80325-S5T-A01
> 2002–2006 RSX power steering feed hose: Honda PN 53713-S6M-A04
> 2002–2006 RSX power steering return hose: Honda PN 53732-S6M-A01
> 2002–2006 RSX power steering fluid reservoir: Honda PN 53701-S6M-003

computer for it to work. This is a more involved process in terms of integrating it into the chassis but adapting the engine for such a system is easy.

Start by fitting any 2002–2005 Civic Si K20A3 idler pulley where the power steering pump would normally be. Belt selection can also vary depending on crankshaft pulley diameter but is always based on a seven-rib design. Plan on an approximate length of 50.5 inches for 2.0L engines and 52 inches for 2.4L engines.

Finally, K-Tuned offers its own solution, similar to the Civic Si pulley but adjustable to accommodate belt-length variations. When using the Civic Si pulley, be sure to source the appropriate idler pulley bracket, bearing cover, and mounting bolts, which can be purchased from Honda and bolted up as if it were meant to be there.

A/C with Power Steering

The process for retaining A/C and power steering isn't difficult. Start with the appropriate power steering pump and crankshaft pulley and use the same combination of factory components. Belt selection is easy and is determined by the donor engine's original requirements. Keep in mind that the hood's underside webbing must also be trimmed to allow clearance for the power steering pump pulley.

A number of parts are needed to complete the A/C system, all of which must be sourced from the 2002–2005 Civic Si: compressor, A/C system discharge hose, suction hose, pipe assembly, and condenser cooling fan. Fortunately the remainder of the Civic's A/C system can be configured to work with all of this and the cooling fan mounts directly to the already-installed Civic Si radiator. Simply fit all of the hoses into place for a factory-like fit. Depending on the engine wiring harness, a simple wiring connector swap may need to be performed at the A/C compressor's thermal protection circuit connector.

The 2002–2005 Civic Si electric power steering system was integrated into this particular swap. The swap is complex and goes beyond the scope of this book; however, it's entirely possible and can be completed using factory components. You need factory service manuals for your vehicle and the 2002–2005 Civic Si as well as the ability to decipher complex electrical schematics.

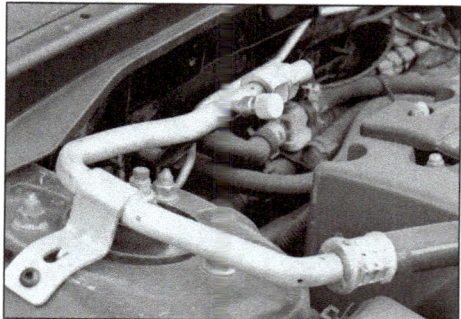

Unlike custom-made A/C lines, the 2002–2005 Civic Si lines feature chassis-specific brackets and mounts that provide a factory-like fit. To complete the conversion, you need the A/C compressor, A/C system discharge hose, suction hose, pipe assembly, and condenser cooling fan.

Intake and Exhaust Systems

Finishing the engine swap with intake and exhaust components is easy, mostly because the 2001–2005 Civic shares so much in common with the 2002–2005 Civic Si, which already features a K-series.

Throttle Body

Be sure that whatever throttle body the donor engine was equipped with is cable driven. Newer K-series engines, which are compatible in almost every other way, feature drive-by-wire electronic throttle bodies that won't be able to communicate with the ECUs that are compatible with the 2001–2005 Civic. However, not every cable-driven throttle body is compatible.

Depending on intake manifold type, only one of two throttle body bolt patterns may be used. Generally, because the K20A2 and K20A3 intake manifold makes for a good fit in terms of chassis clearance, its corresponding throttle body should also be used.

Intake Piping

Look to the 2002–2005 Civic Si for the appropriate short-ram or cold-air intake system. Even factory components may be used; however, a quality cold-air intake system is one of the first and best places to obtain more power.

Note that clearance issues arise at the core support when using some of the longer-runner intake manifolds, such as the 2006–2008 Accord Euro R RBC. Shorter manifolds, such as those found on the 2002–2006 RSX Type-S, ensure proper fitment and avoid further fabrication.

Exhaust Manifold

Similar to the intake system, the 2002–2005 Civic Si exhaust manifold may be used and bolts up without modification. For even better performance, look to the 2002–2006 RSX Type-S exhaust manifold. The exhaust piping underneath the chassis must be shortened to accommodate the longer exhaust manifold. Of course, a number of aftermarket headers can be used as well; simply choose from any that are compatible with the 2002–2005 Civic Si or any 2002–2006 RSX.

ECU Selection

Settle on which ECU to use early on. As with most K-series engine swaps, a number of choices are available but only a few ECUs make good sense. Moreover, because of the 2001–2005 Civic's K-series native electronics and built-in immobilizer system, Honda's anti-theft bypass mechanism doesn't present the sort of problem it does for earlier chassis. However, it must still be addressed.

As with earlier chassis, any Japanese-spec 2001–2005 Civic Type R or 2001–2006 Integra Type R ECU works. More commonly, any 2002–2006 RSX ECU can also be used. Best of all, such computers plug directly into the Civic's wiring harness without modification. For 2.0L economy i-VTEC engines, be sure to use the RSX base model's ECU. For performance i-VTEC engines, you must look to the RSX Type-S computer. Once the engine swap has been completed, if a qualifying ECU is used, the immobilizer bypass must be addressed in order for the ECU to function.

Deliver the car to a qualified Acura dealership and request to have the immobilizer re-keyed. The technician will most likely require you to furnish the appropriate documentation that demonstrates that the engine was purchased legally and hasn't been sourced from a stolen vehicle. Once approved, all the technician must do is recode the ECU to match the security chip in your key.

As with earlier engine swaps, Hondata's K-Pro is the fully programmable alternative that doesn't require addressing the immobilizer system and doesn't require a secondary oxygen sensor. K-Pro is currently compatible with any 2002–2004 RSX base model, 2002–2004 RSX Type-S, 2001–2006 Integra Type R, 2001–2005 Civic Type R, 2002–2006 CR-V, and 2002–2005 Civic Si ECU. Although it isn't required, the immobilizer can be retained when using

Intake piping and filter selection is typically dependent on which intake manifold is used. Here, the Accord's original intake manifold has been retained. RSX intake manifolds, for example, position the throttle body outlet at a more lateral angle, which means an entirely different intake pipe must be used.

K-Pro but still requires a visit to the dealership.

Honda outfitted its K-series transmissions with two vehicle speed sensors, which can complicate the electrical process if the appropriate one isn't chosen. Fortunately, because of engine mount compatibility and shifter assembly limitations, only transmissions featuring the more-compatible low-frequency vehicle speed sensors may be used on the 2001–2005 Civic. Such transmissions can be sourced from any 2002–2004 RSX, 2002–2005 Civic Si, 2001–2005 Civic Type R, and 2001–2006 Integra Type R.

Although all transmissions from the 2005–2006 RSX, 2006–2011 Civic Si, and 2007–2011 Civic Type R are compatible with the 2001–2005 Civic chassis, because of shifter assembly limitations and vehicle speed sensor complications, it's best to avoid them.

Wiring

The wiring process begins with any manual transmission 2002–2004 RSX, 2002–2005 Civic Si, or 2002–2006 CR-V (automatic versions can be converted) engine wiring harness. Later-model 2005–2006 RSX harnesses may also be used but extensive modifications must be made to them. The engine wiring harness must be used along with a pre-wired sub-harness from either Hybrid Racing, Rywire, or K-Tuned.

Aftermarket wiring harnesses such as these serve as intermediaries between the engine wiring harness' 20-pin connector and its corresponding ECU plug.

Any additional wiring remains limited to the primary oxygen sensor. The provided instructions will guide you as you make the sensor's necessary connections: 12V ignition power, 12V constant power, and the oxygen sensor's heater control.

Unlike older chassis for which the charge harness must be modified because of incompatibility with the fuse box, the K-series charge harness is fully compatible, but it just isn't long enough. Once it's lengthened, connect its two connectors to the fuse box terminals as you normally would.

Hasport offers an alternative solution that modifies the provided engine wiring harness for compatibility with the 2001–2005 Civic for a truly factory-appearing engine swap.

Whichever solution is chosen, the two heavy-gauge wires that once attached to the fuse box must be relocated to the other side of the engine bay to reach the Civic's fuse box.

Suspension and Braking

Similar to the relationship between older Civics and Integras, 2002–2006 RSX Type-S and 2002–2005 Civic Si suspension and braking components may be transferred over, yielding better stopping power for the Civic. As a byproduct of the conversion, larger-diameter stronger axles of the RSX Type-S are used. You need a few components from either of these chassis, including the front knuckles, lower control arms, rear trailing arms, shocks, wheel sensors, brake lines, and complete brake assemblies. Finally, be sure to substitute RSX Type-S axles if Type-S knuckles are placed up front instead of anything else you might have been planning to use.

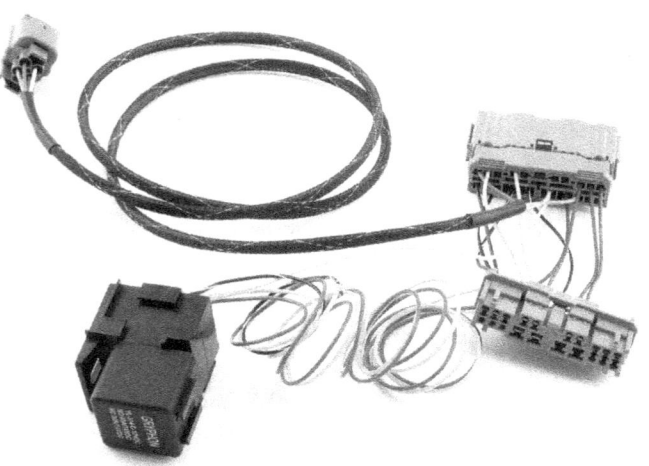

Wiring modifications are limited when it comes to the 2001–2005 Civic. Hybrid Racing's sub-harness is extremely simple and features provisions for connecting to the ECU, engine wiring harness, and oxygen sensor. (Courtesy Hybrid Racing)

K20/K24 Conversion

Another K-series engine swap is every bit as popular as the rest but isn't necessarily specific to any chassis. Some call it the K20 head swap, some call it the K24 block swap, some call it Frankenstein but they're all talking about the same thing: mating one of the higher-flowing performance i-VTEC cylinder heads with a more economically minded but larger-displacement 2.4L engine block. You might call it a poor-man's TSX engine. Right about now you might be thinking that the TSX K24A2 is the best way to achieve 2.4L of performance i-VTEC but with a whole lot less work. It may be but it'll cost you, and its electronic drive-by-wire throttle body, ECU, and engine wiring harness won't do you any good.

If you're starting with a 2.0L performance i-VTEC engine, you first have to choose the appropriate bottom end. Almost any 2.4L economy i-VTEC engine block does fine but the differences are worth mentioning. Look to engines that were more widely produced and are less expensive, such as the 2002–2006 CR-V K24A1.

A number of other 2.4L engine blocks may be used; however, many, such as the K24A4 and K24A8, result in piston-to-valve conflicts if not properly retrofitted with the appropriate pistons.

Later-model K24Z1 or similar engines may also be used; however, because of these newer engines' relocated oil filters, no manual transmission intermediate shaft is compatible without extensive modifications to the engine's oiling system.

Almost any performance i-VTEC cylinder head is acceptable but those from the 2002–2006 RSX Type-S (the K20A2) are among the most widely used.

You need all sorts of parts to make everything happen, some of which you may already have depending on whether or not you have the right top end or the right engine block. Either oil pan works but using the cast-aluminum performance i-VTEC version is preferred. Don't forget its longer mounting bolts.

Next, source the windage tray from the K20A2 along with its oil pump and oil pump drive chain. All of this allows you to remove the 2.4L engine's bulky balance shafts that add drag to the reciprocating assembly.

To retain the factory oil cooler that K20A2 engines have, the 2.4L engine block must be machined to accept the cooling hose adapter. The K20A2's water pump and its housing must also be installed. Any machine shop can do this,

The 2002–2006 CR-V K24A1 is perhaps the most popular engine block candidate for 2.4L engine block conversions. Unlike other economy i-VTEC engines, it shares much of its architecture with the K20A2 and allows for a more reliable and more performance-minded swap.

although the process can be skipped if oil temperature isn't a concern or an alternative aftermarket cooler that sandwiches between the oil filter and the engine block is used instead.

Be sure to use the taller-deck engine's timing chain, timing chain guide, and timing chain cover after the larger-bore 2.4L head gasket and either engine's head studs have been installed with the new top end.

Either crankshaft pulley can be used; however, 2.0L versions are smaller and are generally preferred.

Finish things off with the 2.4L engine's longer oil dipstick and a series of spacers to support the intake manifold against its mounting bracket that are now spaced about 3/4 inch away from one another, the exact difference of the taller engine block. The engine wiring harness connector for the crankshaft position sensor also needs to be swapped for one from any 2.4L engine wiring harness.

The whole conversion is slightly more complex than similar B-series-based LS-VTEC conversions but is every bit as factory-derived as you'd expect. ■

CHAPTER 7

1990–1997 ACCORD AND 1992–1996 PRELUDE

Honda's family of Accords and Preludes has never been embraced by the performance community in the same way that Civics and Integras have. Entry cost as well as curb weight and aftermarket support are partially to blame. However, with the prevalence of K-series engine swaps and their direct compatibility with fourth- and fifth-generation Accords as well as fourth-generation Preludes, it would be a mistake to discount any of these chassis.

1990–1993 Accord

If any Honda was never meant to live a life of high performance, it is the Accord. It was designed and built with sophistication, comfort, and style being paramount, not speed or agility. Few competitors have garnered the decades' worth of respect the Accord has. It may not appeal directly to performance-minded Honda fans but for just about everybody else, its reliability, strong resale value, and emphasis on safety tick nearly every other box. If you look close enough, a layer of performance can be found within every Accord. For example, an independent, double-wishbone suspension is present on every 1990–1993 model as are available rear disc brakes and some of the most powerful 4-cylinder engines of their time.

Honda's 1990–1993 Accord is available in three configurations (coupe, sedan, and wagon) in trim levels ranging from the entry-level DX to the fully loaded EX. However, regardless of the body style or trim level, every fourth-generation Accord's engine bay is the same and only three engines were made available to the chassis. All of them feature a non-VTEC architecture and an SOHC layout.

K-series engine swaps into Prelude and Accord chassis aren't nearly as prevalent as they are among Civics and Integras, but they're still worth considering. Interestingly enough, the engine swap process for any of these chassis is much the same as it is for the 1992–1995 Civic and 1994–2001 Integra.

124   HONDA K-SERIES ENGINE SWAPS

1990–1997 ACCORD AND 1992–1996 PRELUDE

For years, the 1990–1993 Accord played host to H-series engine swaps. It's a relatively simple, bolt-in process for Accords of this era and results in an instant, emissions-legal, power bump. However, despite the merits of the H22A, it doesn't come close to the capability of the K-series engines, especially larger-displacement 2.4L versions.

1990–1993 Accord Chassis Codes

1990–1993 Accord DX, EX, LX, SE Coupe	CB7
1990–1993 Accord DX, EX, LX Sedan	CB7
1991–1993 Accord SE Sedan	CB7
1993 Accord LX Anniversary Edition Sedan	CB7
1991–1993 Accord EX, LX Wagon	CB9

The 1990–1993 Accord has long been the recipient of the more-powerful twin-cam H22A engine.

Similar to B-series engine swaps into fifth-generation Civics, the H-series has typically been the donor engine of choice for Accord fans. That's primarily because of the relationship the Accord shares with the Prelude, where, similar to Civics and Integras, a number of engine bay similarities can be found, making the engine swap process an obvious and easy one.

Chassis Pros and Cons

According to 1990s' standards, the fourth-generation Accord is a heavy car. Today, though, at around 2,900 pounds, it's no heavier than Honda's current Civic Si. With room underneath the hood and easy compatibility with even the taller-deck 2.4L engines, the 1990–1993 Accord makes as good a K-series engine swap candidate as any.

Perhaps the most significant shortcoming to the fourth-generation Accord chassis in terms of a K-series engine swap is engine bay configuration. Here, basic fabrication and welding must be performed before any engine swap can take place. There are also limitations on the number of K-series transmissions that may be used because of the limited number of aftermarket engine mount kits available. Still, as with Civic and Integra chassis of the same era, retrofitting a K-series engine and transmission into place is entirely doable.

1994–1997 Accord

Honda introduced the first-ever VTEC F-series engine along with the fifth-generation Accord, which featured an entirely revised body and chassis. Available only in EX and SE trims, the F22B1 was Honda's most-powerful SOHC 4-cylinder engine, measuring 145 hp. Less-expensive DX, LX, and VP models featured the less-powerful F22B2 engine. Both engines remain native to the three available chassis: coupe, sedan, and wagon. Finally, and for the first time ever, Honda also made available a V-6 Accord, available in LX and EX trims. The 90-degree,

1994–1997 Accord Chassis Codes

1994–1997 Accord EX, LX Coupe	CD7
1994 Accord DX Coupe	CD7
1997 Accord SE Coupe	CD7
1994–1997 Accord DX, EX, LX Sedan	CD5
1996–1997 Accord VP Sedan	CD5
1996 Accord DX Anniversary Edition Sedan	CD5
1997 Accord SE Sedan	CD5
1995–1997 Accord EX V-6, LX V-6 Sedan	CE6
1994–1997 Accord EX, LX Wagon	CE1

six-cylinder engine remained unique to the Accord before being superseded by the company's long line of 60-degree engines that came later.

Chassis Pros and Cons

Little can be said of the 1990–1993 models that doesn't apply to fifth-generation Accords in terms of K-series engine swaps. The newer chassis is just as heavy yet just as willing to accept almost any K-series engine. Fabrication and welding is also required and the same transmission limitations apply but, once the appropriate engine mounts and shifter components are sourced, that's of little concern. Be sure to look to 4-cylinder models when considering K-series-compatible chassis. Six-cylinder models feature entirely different configurations under the hood, which means that some engine mount kits are incompatible. The Accord's C-series V-6 is also an exceptional engine for its time; swapping it for a smaller-displacement K-series might not prove to be as beneficial as with 4-cylinder models.

1992–1996 Prelude

The 1992–1996 Preludes (particularly Si VTEC models) have a lot going for them. Available only in two-door configuration, every trim features standard rear disc brakes, front and rear anti-roll bars, ABS, and an impressive double-wishbone suspension up front. The Prelude is heavy, just like the Accord, weighing nearly 3,000 pounds. Even the Si VTEC model's impressive 190-hp H22A1 engine has never been enough to make up for it.

Fourth-generation Preludes are available in four trims, ranging from the entry-level SOHC F-series-equipped S to the top-of-the-line H22A1-powered Si VTEC. Mid-range Si models feature the larger-displacement H23A1 engine that boasts an entirely different non-VTEC cylinder head.

1992–1996 Prelude Chassis Codes

1992–1996 Prelude S	BA8
1993–1996 Prelude Si VTEC	BB1
1992–1996 Prelude Si	BB2
1995 Prelude Si Special Edition	BB2
1992–1994 Prelude Si 4WS	BB2

Chassis Pros and Cons

In terms of weight, the Prelude has the same disadvantage as the Accord. However, the chassis' stiffer unibody and sport-minded suspension almost make up for it. Like the Accord, fabrication and welding are prerequisite to fitting the K-series assembly into place and the number of transmissions that are compatible is limited.

Engine and Transmission

Hasport is the source when it comes to mounts for any of these chassis. As with the company's other engine mount kits, its Accord- and Prelude-specific mounts are compatible with any K-series engine. However, only 2003–2007 Accord, 2006–2008 Accord Euro R, and 2004–2008 TSX transmissions may be used.

Refer to Chapter 1 to select which engine and transmission is right for you. Carefully consider horsepower, torque, the type of i-VTEC, budget, and displacement. When selecting a transmission, determine whether five or six gears are desirable and whether or not it's sourced from a foreign or North American chassis.

Accord-style transmissions, such as those from the 2003–2007 Accord, 2006–2008 Accord Euro R, and 2004–2008 TSX, can be identified by their rear-mount orientation. Here, the two bolt holes that are present on every RSX-style transmission are missing. Instead, Accord-style transmissions are mounted by means of the two bolt holes positioned to the right of the differential that are also used to fasten the transmission to the engine block.

Mounts

Hasport offers individual kits for all three chassis in this chapter and the transplant process is similar for all of them. The CBK1 kit is for the 1990–1993 Accord, the CDK1 kit is for the 1994–1997 Accord, and the BBK1 kit is for the 1992–1996

Hasport's engine mount kits for Accord and Prelude chassis include a right-side framerail bracket that must be welded to the chassis, a left-side transmission bracket, a rear transmission bracket, and mounts that correspond to each bracket.

1990–1997 ACCORD AND 1992–1996 PRELUDE

Prelude. All three kits are compatible only with the transmissions mentioned earlier and allow for optimal clearance for 2.0L or 2.4L engines, even with power steering and A/C retained.

Car Preparation

The K-series engine swap into any of these chassis is a complex process. If you aren't familiar with the process of removing and replacing a typical engine, seek help or contact a qualified professional. The factory service manual is helpful; however, there are several key points that aren't necessarily addressed during a standard engine removal that apply exclusively to K-series engine conversions.

Draining the Fluids

Whether or not A/C is retained, its refrigerant must be drained. Contact a qualified professional to evacuate the system before beginning the engine removal process. Next, raise the car using jack stands or a lift and drain the transmission fluid, power steering fluid, engine oil, and coolant from the radiator.

Removing the Ancillaries

Disconnect and remove the battery and battery tray. Next, disconnect the engine wiring harness from its connectors near the shock tower and the underhood fuse box; remove the positive battery cable completely. Remove the wheels, exhaust A-pipe, catalytic converter, fuel feed and return lines, as well as the throttle cable. Disconnect the shifter cables from the transmission.

The radiator should also be removed along with the cooling fan and both radiator hoses to allow for additional clearance. Remove both

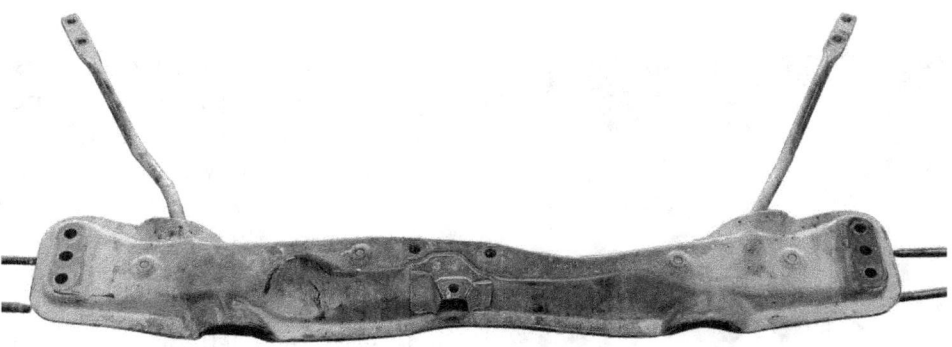

Along with the original engine and transmission, the crossmember and its radius rods must also be removed. All of this can be reinstalled once the K-series powertrain is in place, but the center support beam that travels longitudinally below the chassis must be permanently removed. (Photo Courtesy Hasport Performance Products)

heater hoses exiting the heater core at the firewall as well as the brake booster vacuum hose. Disconnect the hydraulic clutch line from the clutch slave cylinder.

If A/C will be eliminated, remove the system's lines, condenser, wiring harness, and cooling fan. The front crossmember, along with its radius rods and center support beam, must also be removed. The center support beam will not be reinstalled.

Removing the Axles

Remove the axle retaining-nut located on the center of the knuckle's outboard side using a pneumatic air ratchet or large breaker bar. Disconnect and remove the shock's lower fork from its lower control arm and set it aside; remove the lower ball joint retaining nut.

Next, disconnect the ball joint using a ball joint separator or with a dead-blow hammer, carefully strike the side of the lower control arm near the ball joint. Once loose, swing the knuckle upward, outward, and away from the axle's outboard side. Pry the axle's inboard side free from the transmission or intermediate shaft (depending on the side) and remove the axle.

A ball joint separator must be used to disconnect the ball joint from its lower control arm. Alternatively, a dead-blow hammer can be used to strike the lower control arm, between the ball joint and the shock fork. Loosen the ball joint retaining nut and strike the side of the arm to dislodge the joint from its seat. Be careful not to strike the ball joint or its retaining nut.

Removing the Mounts

Disconnect the rear engine bracket from its mount so that the engine and transmission are held in place only by the left- and right-side mounts. (The front engine mount should have been disconnected when removing the crossmember). Disconnect the remaining two mounts and remove the assembly from the chassis. Once removed, unbolt the rear mount from the subframe and the front mount from the

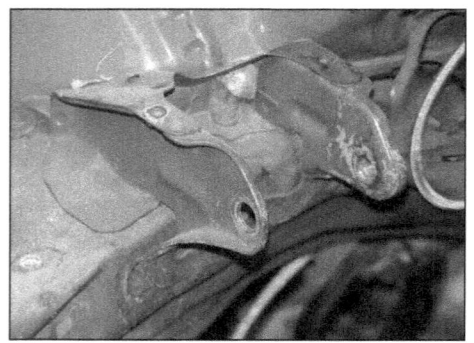

Similar to older Civic and Integra chassis, the right-side framerail bracket must be removed. Follow the same process as with other chassis: Drill out the spot welds, pry the bracket free, and grind any stray metal away to leave a smooth, clean surface. (Photo Courtesy Hasport Performance Products)

already-removed crossmember. All of the original mounts and brackets should now be removed from the chassis.

Right-Side Framerail Bracket: The right-side bracket located on the chassis of every 1990–1997 Accord and 1992–1996 Prelude must be removed. Plan on a fair amount of fabrication to do this.

Mark each of the bracket's existing spot welds with a center punch and drill them out with a 1/8-inch pilot drill bit followed by a 3/8-inch drill bit or spot-weld-removing drill bit. Once properly drilled, remove the bracket using a pry bar or air chisel. Once removed, clean any stray metal or jagged edges left by the drilling process using an angle grinder.

Position the Hasport right-side framerail bracket in the same location and use one of the battery tray's bolts located on the top of the framerail to align it into the available bolt hole.

Next, weld the bracket to the framerail. Hasport recommends waiting to weld the bracket into place until optimal engine placement has been confirmed.

Important: Do not rely on the already-installed battery tray bolt to support the bracket. This is only used to locate the bracket and can be removed once it is welded into position. For best results, fill the original spot-weld holes with body filler. Then prime and paint the framerail and bracket to match the engine bay.

Here, the right-side framerail bracket is being temporarily mounted into place, using the original battery tray's bolt holes and hardware as a guide. In some cases, depending on chassis wear, the bracket may have to be moved forward or backward for ideal engine placement. (Photo Courtesy Hasport Performance Products)

Left-Side Framerail Bracket: Fortunately, the left-side framerail bracket doesn't need to be modified. Hasport's engine mount is designed for easy compatibility with it.

Rear Subframe Mount: Bolt Hasport's supplied rear mount to the subframe using the included hardware and torque it to the appropriate specifications.

Hasport's right-side framerail bracket must be welded to the chassis. First, though, the bracket must be temporarily bolted to the framerail using the original battery tray's bolt holes; however, don't rely on them for any sort of support beyond test fitting. On older chassis, install the engine and transmission into the engine bay with the unwelded framerail bracket connected to its corresponding mount. Decide its exact location without temporarily bolting it down, and then tack weld it into place. Remove the engine and transmission to finalize welding. This will allow additional movement for the bracket on older chassis. (Photo Courtesy Hasport Performance Products)

The rear mount should be bolted to the subframe first. It's best to leave all mounts and brackets slightly loose until each has been installed. (Photo Courtesy Hasport Performance Products)

1990–1997 ACCORD AND 1992–1996 PRELUDE

Engine Preparation

Before installing the engine and transmission, be sure that everything is in good working order. It isn't uncommon for a throttle position sensor or miscellaneous electrical connectors to break during transport or while in storage. Depending on which engine you've chosen, its wiring harness may need to be removed and replaced with the appropriate one. Doing this before the engine has been installed makes things a whole lot easier.

Next, remove all engine and transmission mounting brackets; exclude the bracket located on the engine's timing chain side. Now is also the ideal time to swap intake manifolds, throttle bodies, clutches, or to perform any pre-swap maintenance.

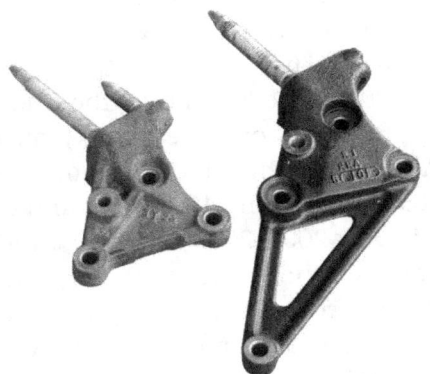

Larger-displacement 2.4L engines require an entirely different timing-chain-side bracket that ultimately attaches to the right-side engine mount. Look to the 2002–2006 CR-V K24A1 for the appropriate bracket. Although all 2.0L brackets (left) are the same and may be interchanged, not all 2.4L brackets are similar to one another. For example, the bracket found on most Accord engines (right) is not compatible with aftermarket engine mount kits.

2.4L Engine Considerations

Few chassis offer as much room for the taller-deck 2.4L engines than any of the Accords or Preludes covered here. When using a 2.4L engine, be sure to replace the timing-chain-side engine bracket for one from the CR-V K24A1 engine (Honda PN 11910-PPA-000). The revised bracket takes into account the deck height variances between the two engines, allowing for a factory-like fit.

Engine Installation

If installing the assembly from above, lower the engine and transmission into the engine bay now. An optional load leveler should be used with an engine hoist that allows the angle of the engine and transmission to be adjusted while lowering the assembly into place. This reduces the risk of damage and simplifies the process. If installing the engine and transmission from below, lower the car onto the engine and transmission assembly.

The difference between 2.4L and 2.0L timing-chain-side engine brackets is subtle. Notice the equidistant spacing between the three 10-mm bolt holes on the 2.4L bracket (left) and the close spacing of the right-side bolt holes of the 2.0L bracket (right). (Photo Courtesy Hasport Performance Products)

Left-Side Transmission Bracket and Mount

Position Hasport's left-side bracket on top of the transmission and fasten it using the supplied hardware. (The original mounting studs should have already been removed.) Next, with the engine and transmission already lowered into place, slip the corresponding left-side mount into the car's framerail bracket using the original bolt and then onto the previously installed transmission bracket using the supplied hardware. Wait to tighten any nuts or bolts until all mounts have been installed.

Right-Side Engine Mount

Position the right-side engine mount into the already-installed framerail bracket and slide it onto the engine bracket's studs. Gently rock the engine and transmission assembly back and forth to line up the mounting holes or use a floor jack to adjust the installation height. Use the supplied hardware to fasten the mount into place but don't tighten it down completely.

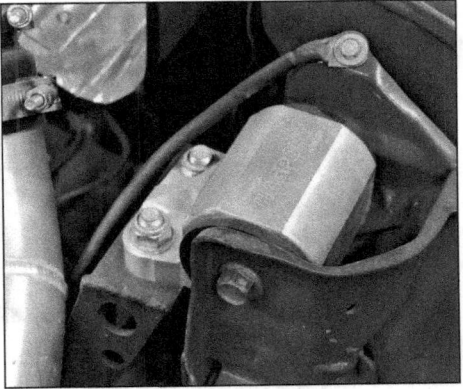

Once the engine and transmission are in place, the Hasport transmission bracket can be bolted along with the left-side engine mount. Again, all hardware should not be fully tightened until each mount and bracket is in position.

Here, the engine is being test-fitted to position the right-side framerail bracket properly before welding it into place. It's a lot of extra work but is often necessary with older chassis that may not be as straight as they once were. (Photo Courtesy Hasport Performance Products)

Rear Engine Bracket

Because of the rear engine bracket's complexity, it's best to bolt it onto the engine before lowering the engine and transmission into place. Once in place, lower the assembly into the engine bay and slide the engine and transmission toward the rear, allowing the rear engine bracket to slip over the already-installed rear mount before connecting either of the two side mounts. Use the supplied hardware and fasten the mount to the bracket.

Finally, release the engine hoist or raise the vehicle so that the mounts are fully supporting the engine and transmission. Tighten all engine mount, transmission mount, and bracket hardware to the appropriate specifications provided by Hasport.

Axles

Axle choices are few with each of these chassis. Hasport's engine swap-specific axles are designed to work with any compatible K-series engine and transmission provided the appropriate 2002–2006 RSX, 2002–2005 Civic Si, 2001–2005 Civic Type R, 2001–2006 Integra Type R, 2006–2011 Civic Si, or 2007–2011 Civic Type R intermediate shaft from any manual transmission-equipped engine is used. Simply reinstall the axles into the knuckles just as the original ones were removed for a factory-like fit.

The Hasport rear bracket can be slipped into place last. The engine and transmission assembly may need to be gently rocked back in forth for each bolt hole to line up. Bolt the bracket onto the transmission before connecting it to the rear mount. (Photo Courtesy Hasport Performance Products)

Custom axles must be used for these chassis. Hasport axles such as these were designed specifically for such conversions and are stronger than any factory components that you may be able to piece together.

Aftermarket throttle cable brackets, such as this one from K-Tuned, allow throttle cables that are most compatible with Accord and Prelude chassis to hook up with most cable-actuated K-series throttle bodies. Without it, the appropriate amount of tension wouldn't be possible between the cable's end and its mounting nut. (Photo Courtesy K-Tuned)

Throttle Cable

A number of Civic or Integra throttle cables are compatible with each of these K-series engine transplants. The 1996–2000 Civic's throttle cable is among the shortest, making for a neat appearance. Alternative throttle cables may be sourced from the 1994–2001 Integra GS-R or 2002–2005 Civic Si, which are also short and connect at the firewall for a factory-like fit on all of these chassis provided they were originally equipped with manual transmissions.

If throttle bodies will be used, be sure to source the appropriate adapter bracket since the throttle cable wasn't originally designed for the K-series. Aftermarket cable assemblies are available from Karcepts and K-Tuned.

Clutch Hydraulics

Every 1990–1997 Accord or 1992–1996 Prelude clutch master cylinder

1990–1997 ACCORD AND 1992–1996 PRELUDE

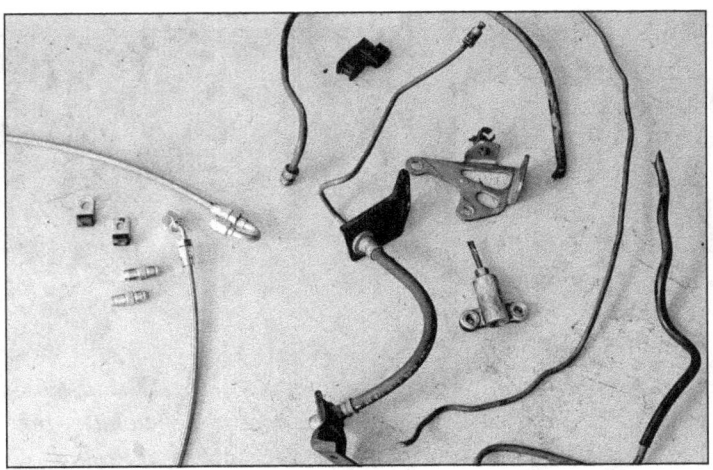

All sorts of ways are possible to connect the chassis' original clutch master cylinder to the K-series transmission's clutch slave cylinder. A combination of factory components can be used or a custom-made steel-braided hose with a series of metric-to-AN adapters will work.

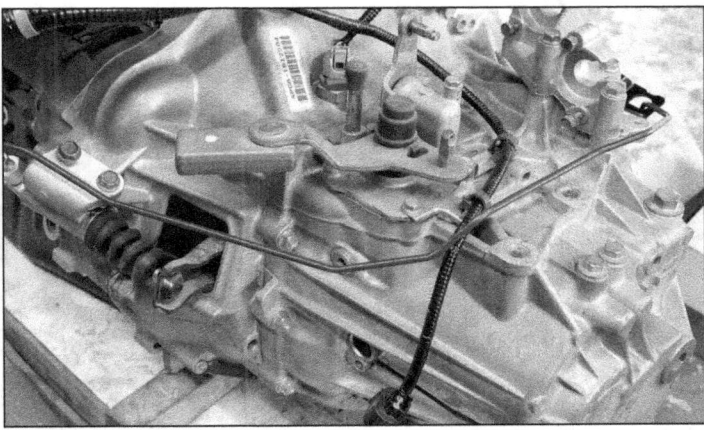

A factory hydraulic clutch line has been adapted to span from the K-series transmission's clutch slave cylinder and, ultimately, to the clutch master cylinder. Somewhere, though, a section of flexible hose must be added to allow for engine movement. (Photo Courtesy Hasport Performance Products)

is compatible with every K-series transmission's clutch slave cylinder; however, modifications must be made to adapt them. Because the K-series transmission sits on the opposite side of the engine bay, an extended flexible clutch line must be added that spans from the clutch line damper mounted on the chassis to the clutch slave cylinder. A custom line made of Teflon-lined steel-braided hose along with the appropriate hose ends can also be used.

Special inverted-flare metric adapters can be used to properly seal against the clutch line damper and slave cylinder; they allow for the new line to properly hook up. Be sure to pressure test the line before installing it and use at least one mounting clamp to attach it to the engine or transmission someplace mid-line to avoid flexing once the clutch is disengaged.

Once finished, bleed the hydraulic clutch system to ensure proper operation, following the procedure outlined in any Honda service manual.

If equipped, the engine's original brake booster hose that connects to its rigid distribution line can be retained. Simply use a section of bulk hose to transition from the other end of the distribution line to the Accord or Prelude brake booster check valve.

Brake Booster

Once the engine is in place, the intake manifold sits near the front of the vehicle. Replace the original brake booster line, which is significantly too short, with any 2002–2006 RSX brake booster hose. Be sure to route the hose away from any moving parts and connect it to the engine's distribution line or to the vehicle's original check valve (located at the firewall) if using a section of surplus hose.

Shifter Assembly

Every 1990–1997 Accord and 1992–1996 Prelude features a cable-style shifter mechanism; however, they're different enough from those used by every K-series transmission to require replacement.

As with any K-series engine swap, success lies in choosing the appropriate shifter components; mismatched pieces that appear to work together may seem like a good idea but will prove to be a costly mistake that

HONDA K-SERIES ENGINE SWAPS

CHAPTER 7

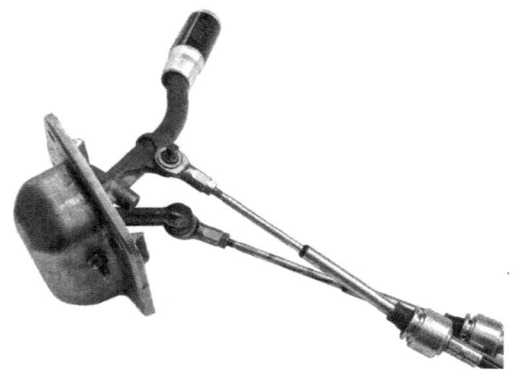

Although the Accord or Prelude (shown) cable-style shifter mechanism may seem compatible with K-series transmissions, it isn't. The transmissions' shifter mechanisms operate in entirely different ways, which means only K-series-compatible shifter boxes and shifter cables may be used.

renders any transmission useless. Fortunately, because only transmissions from the 2003–2007 Accord, 2006–2008 Accord Euro R, and 2004–2008 TSX are compatible with Hasport's engine mount kit, sorting through compatible shifter components is far less confusing than with other chassis.

RSX-style transmissions are identified by their rear mounting holes. Notice the two bolt holes to the left of the differential. Accord-style transmissions don't feature these, and instead attach to Hasport's rear transmission bracket using the two bolt holes on the right, which are integrated onto all K-series manual transmissions.

Shifter Box

The shifter box mounts in the original shifter location and connects to the transmission by a series of cables. (Chapter 4 outlines many of the differences between the various shifter boxes, shifter cables, and transmissions as well as their compatibility with one another.) Because only the previously mentioned Accord and TSX gearboxes may be used, shifter box choice is limited to one from any 2003–2007 Accord or 2004–2008 TSX. Whichever is used, the shifter box must also be matched with its appropriate cables.

Mounting the shifter box here isn't as challenging as it is with other non-native K-series chassis, primarily because every 1990–1997 Accord and 1992–1996 Prelude already features something similar. Start by removing the center console and positioning the K-series shifter box in the chassis' original location.

Next, use a felt-tip pen to mark the chassis below each of the shifter box's four mounting holes. Drill the

RSX-style (left) and Accord-style (right) shifter boxes are quite different from each other and can only be used with their respective transmissions. The difference lies in the fulcrum points of each shifter box's shift lever. When one moves forward, a cable is pulled; when the other moves forward, a cable is pushed.

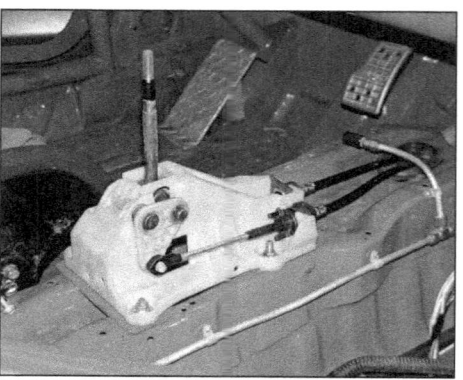

Mounting the Accord-style shifter box into any of these Accord or Prelude chassis isn't difficult. Simply place it on top of the unmodified exhaust tunnel, drill the appropriate mounting holes, and bolt it into place using a series of nuts, bolts, and washers. The shifter cables may even pass through the original opening in the exhaust tunnel. (Photo Courtesy Hasport Performance Products)

appropriate holes in the chassis and secure the shifter box in place with a series of nuts and bolts. Use washers as spacers to allow the shifter box to sit flat.

You need a helper to hold onto either the nut or bolt (depending on which side they're on), to keep the hardware from spinning while tightening.

Shifter Cables

Because shifter box selection is limited to those from the 2003–2007 Accord and 2004–2008 TSX, look to the same two chassis for shifter cables. Hybrid Racing offers its own line of aftermarket cables that are compatible.

Because every Accord and Prelude in this chapter already features a cable-style shifter mechanism, simply route the K-series shifter cables through the same passage toward the K-series transmission. Attach the

HONDA K-SERIES ENGINE SWAPS

1990–1997 ACCORD AND 1992–1996 PRELUDE

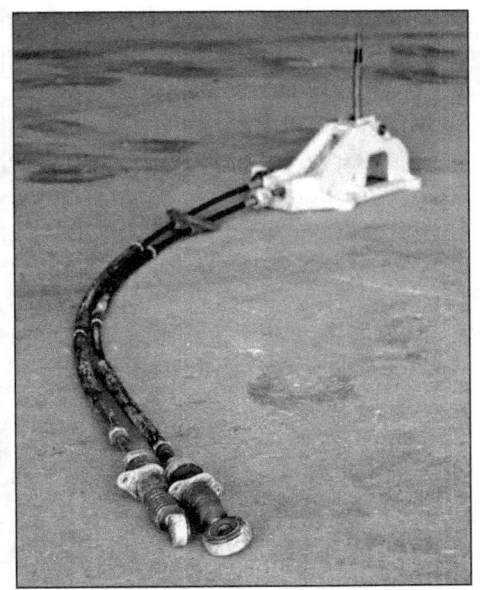

Be sure to source the appropriate shifter cables that are compatible with your shifter box. Here, a 2003–2007 Accord shifter box is matched to its corresponding cables. Shifter boxes and cables from the 2004–2008 TSX are also compatible; however, Accord versions have proven to be the least expensive.

shifter cables to the transmission, locating each end in their respective brackets before attaching their rod ends to their respective levers.

Use a hammer to tap the retaining clips into place and be sure to use the appropriate washers and cotter pins to ensure that nothing comes loose. Once fastened into place, test the shifter for proper engagement.

Fuel System

All Hondas and Acuras native to K-series engines feature returnless fuel systems where a single feed line travels from the fuel tank to the engine. Their fuel pressure regulators are also mounted inside of their gas tanks. Every Accord and Prelude covered in these pages features a more-conventional return-style fuel system, which can be retained but requires some modifications.

Fuel Rail and Fuel Pressure Regulator

An aftermarket bypass-type fuel pressure regulator suitable for fuel injection applications matched with either the factory fuel rail or an aftermarket version featuring inlet and outlet ports is the only thing needed to retain each of these chassis' return-style fuel systems.

Stock Fuel Rail, Aftermarket Fuel Pressure Regulator: For the most cost-effective method, look to whatever fuel rail the donor engine already has. Unlike the original fuel rail on any of these Accord or Prelude chassis, K-series fuel rails feature only a single inlet port. A bypass-type fuel pressure regulator with a minimum of two inlet ports and a single outlet port must be used to allow unused fuel to make its way back to the tank.

Before any of that can happen, though, the factory fuel rail must be adapted to the system. First, cut away the plastic connector at the fuel rail barb and slip a section of 5/16-inch fuel injection hose over it.

To slip a section of fuel injection hose over the factory fuel rail's feed line, its polyethylene fuel line must be removed and the plastic quick-disconnect fitting cut away. Here, the remaining section of the plastic fitting is about to be pulled away.

Connect it to one of the fuel pressure regulator's upper ports using the appropriate fittings once finished. Generally, these consist of -6 or -8 female O-ring-sealed AN ports, depending on the fuel pressure regulator. Once the size has been determined, source the appropriate male-to-male union and thread it into the regulator's inlet port along with the matching AN female-to-male-barb adapter. Slip the fuel injection line over the barb next and fasten it using fuel injection hose clamps.

The other upper inlet port must connect to the chassis' original fuel feed line that spans from the fuel filter. Carefully cut the line away from its banjo connection, exposing its barb, and slip a section of fuel injection hose over it. Next, connect it to the remaining inlet port at the fuel pressure regulator using the same series of fittings mentioned earlier.

The original fuel feed line can also be cut in half, and a 5/16-inch male-to-male barb can be used to join the two lines together. A variety of methods can be used.

Finally, a return line must also connect the fuel pressure regulator's lower exit port to the fuel return hard

Always use fuel injection hose clamps when securing rubber-based fuel lines. Worm-gear hose clamps can damage the hose when they're tightened, resulting in a potential fuel leak.

An aftermarket fuel pressure regulator must be integrated with every K-series engine swap into any non-native chassis. There are two reasons for this: First, K-series engines don't feature fuel pressure regulators; the system is regulated from within the fuel tank on native K-series chassis. Second, the fuel pressure regulator serves as a bypass tee that allows fuel to travel toward the fuel rail but to also return to the fuel tank.

An aftermarket fuel rail such as this allows a feed line and a return line to span to and from itself. The layout is similar to 1990–1997 Accord and 1992–1996 Prelude original configurations.

line located near the firewall. A similar male-to-male AN union and AN female-to-male-barb adapter must be used along with 1/4-inch fuel injection hose and the appropriate clamps. Simply slip the new hose over the existing hard line, fastening it with fuel injection hose clamps.

Aftermarket Fuel Rail, Aftermarket Fuel Pressure Regulator: Retaining the factory fuel rail is certainly the least expensive route; however, bypassing the inlet stream through the fuel pressure regulator before entering the fuel rail isn't always acceptable for applications that demand more fuel. An aftermarket fuel rail with inlet and outlet ports is the answer.

Simply connect a feed line from the fuel filter to the fuel rail's inlet port using the same method mentioned earlier and an AN-to-barb adapter to connect it to the fuel rail's inlet port. On the opposite end, the fuel rail can be mounted directly to the fuel rail or externally, using the same AN-to-barb adapters and fuel injection hose. Regardless of where the fuel pressure regulator is mounted, connect its lower return port to the factory fuel line using 1/4-inch fuel injection hose and the appropriate hose clamps.

Anytime the fuel injectors are removed from the fuel rail, care must be taken to avoid damaging their O-rings. Apply a small amount of liq-

This fuel pressure regulator from Hybrid Racing features multiple inlet ports and a single outlet port below for delivering unused fuel back to the fuel tank. Static fuel pressure may also be adjusted by tightening or loosening the setscrew on top that controls the regulator's internal diaphragm.

uid hand soap to lubricate the O-rings before reinstalling them. A twisting motion should also be applied when pulling or pushing the fuel injectors into place. All of this helps reduce the risk of damage and allow the fuel injectors to easily slip into place.

Finally, be sure to leave the fuel pressure regulator's vacuum reference port open; K-series engines do not require this feature.

Specialty Fittings and Lines

Anodized-aluminum AN fittings and steel-braided hose may be used to complete the fuel system in lieu of modifying any existing rubber hoses. Hybrid Racing, Karcepts, and K-Tuned each offer hose-and-fitting kits that can simplify all of this. Kits include all necessary -6 AN fittings and hose along with a specialized adapter that allows the factory fuel filter to be retained.

Fuel Pump

If horsepower demands remain close to what any K-series yields in stock form, the remainder of the fuel system can be left alone. However, once significant modifications are made, consider upgrading the fuel injectors, fuel filter, and fuel pump. High-mileage or significantly older Accords and Preludes may benefit from a fuel pump upgrade. Aftermarket in-tank fuel pumps from AEM, DeatschWerks, and Walbro are worth considering and are a small investment to make considering the scope of the entire engine swap.

Cooling System

You have at least two ways to address the cooling system on any of the chassis in this chapter. The difference lies in radiator selection, which can either lead to additional fabrication or additional electrical work.

Radiator

The most obvious radiator choice is the Accord or Prelude original radiator. Unlike the Civic's or Integra's, this inlet doesn't interfere with the intake manifold, which means it can remain in its original location with its original cooling fan and condenser fan.

Unfortunately, retaining the factory radiator introduces two problems. Both its upper and lower hoses must be entirely custom and the K-series engine's coolant temperature sensor and radiator fan switch must be introduced into the system elsewhere, which means additional components are necessary.

Another option is to use the 2002–2005 Civic Si radiator, which doesn't directly mount into place but eliminates any hose and sensor complications. The radiator support brackets located on the chassis must be drilled out, cut off, and welded back onto the core support to align with the Si radiator's lower mounting posts. (This is similar to how the right-side framerail bracket was removed.) New top brackets to prevent the radiator from moving away from its lower mounts must also be fabricated.

Best of all, the Si radiator is even compatible with the Accord's and Prelude's cooling fan and condenser fan.

Cooling Fan

If either the Accord or Prelude radiator is retained, simply reuse the original cooling fan and, if A/C remains intact, the condenser fan also.

When using the 2002–2005 Civic Si radiator, a few simple modifications must be made. First, remove the original fan assembly from its shroud and mount it in a 2002–2005 Civic Si fan shroud. Next, position it on the opposite end of the radiator, compared to the Accord or Prelude. The Accord or Prelude condenser fan can then be mounted next to it.

Radiator Hoses

If the Accord or Prelude original radiator is retained, hose choice is entirely custom. To help source the appropriate hoses, use a section of thick wire to outline the desired hose shape once the engine and radiator are in place. You can look for a match of the pre-bent section of wire at any auto parts warehouse. Don't forget to consider the hose's internal diameter.

When using a K-series-native radiator, such as the 2002–2005 Civic Si's, it's important to know which upper coolant pipe the engine features before settling on any radiator hoses. All K20A2, K20Z1, K20A, K20A3, and K24A1 engines share a similar design that integrates the water neck onto the front of the cylinder head. Every other engine

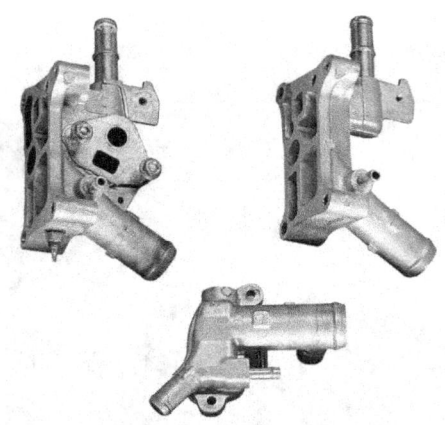

A number of different upper coolant pipes can be found, but there are really only two styles of upper radiator hoses. Front-mount water necks (bottom) can typically be found on K20A2, K20Z1, K20A, K20A3, and K24A1 engines; most other K-series engines feature side-mount versions (top). (Photo Courtesy Hasport Performance Products)

Frequently, a custom radiator hose must be made. Here, the Prelude's original radiator was retained, which almost always results in no K-series radiator hoses being compatible. A combination of two hoses was used, spliced together for a relatively smooth transition. The good news, though, is that the original radiator can be retained. (Photo Courtesy Hasport Performance Products)

With the appropriate radiator, such as this custom aluminum radiator, a K-series-compatible upper radiator hose may be used. Custom radiator applications for K-series-swapped Accords and Preludes are few, though, which means manufacturing your own custom radiator hoses is often the most likely option.

There are just as many different lower thermostat housings as there are upper coolant pipes. Be sure to appropriately match your thermostat housing with the right lower radiator hose.

K-Tuned has the solution that takes the guesswork out of lower radiator hose selection. Its adjustable lower water neck is compatible with any K-series lower radiator hose because it can rotate to accommodate just about any orientation. The housing also features provisions for the radiator fan switch and two additional threaded ports. (Photo Courtesy K-Tuned)

covered in Chapter 1 features a water neck that's fitted onto the side of the cylinder head.

For applications similar to the K24A1, for example, hoses can be sourced from any 2002–2006 RSX or 2002–2005 Civic Si. Look to the 2004–2008 TSX for other configurations.

The lower thermostat housing with its integrated water neck must also be considered before selecting the lower radiator hose. As with the upper coolant pipe, multiple versions can be classified by the same engine. In most cases, the K20A2, K20Z1, K20A, K20A3, and K24A1 thermostat housing is ideal.

Cooling Electrical

As previously mentioned, every K-series engine integrates its radiator fan switch directly into the radiator. This presents a problem if the original Accord or Prelude radiator is retained. Without it, the cooling fan doesn't work. The coolant temperature sensor (thermo unit) is also partially incompatible and can't communicate with any of these chassis' instrument clusters. The solution is to integrate the original F- or H-series coolant temperature sensor so that the instrument cluster's temperature gauge functions correctly.

Start by removing the original F- or H-series coolant temperature sensor and radiator fan switch or locate suitable replacements if necessary. In some cases, you may also

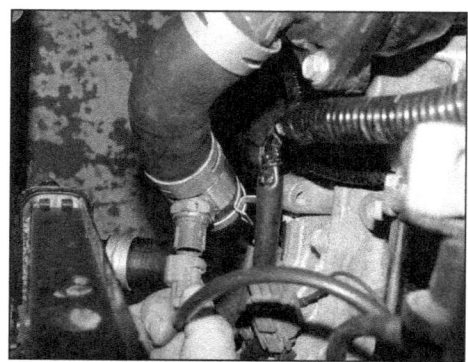

An inline hose adapter, such as this one from Hasport, splices between the lower radiator hose, which allows the radiator fan switch to thread into place. It's the simple alternative to Accord and Prelude radiators that don't feature provisions for the switches that every K-series-native chassis have.

need to retain both of the electrical connectors that plug into each sensor; cut them off the original wiring harness, leaving at least 4 inches of wire intact so that they may later be reintegrated into the system.

Hasport and Hybrid Racing offer hose inserts that have threaded provisions for the coolant temperature sensor and the radiator fan switch that can be placed in-line within the lower radiator hose. To work effectively, the adapter must be grounded to the engine or transmission using the supplied grounding posts. Although such adapters position the coolant temperature sensor along the lower radiator hose, if possible, the sensor should be mounted higher in the system for greater accuracy.

Hybrid Racing and K-Tuned offer special adapter fittings designed to replace the unused idle air assist valve located on the intake manifold and that feature provisions for the coolant temperature sensor. The adapter threads into the coolant port that is located on the intake manifold; this allows provisions for the

1990–1997 ACCORD AND 1992–1996 PRELUDE

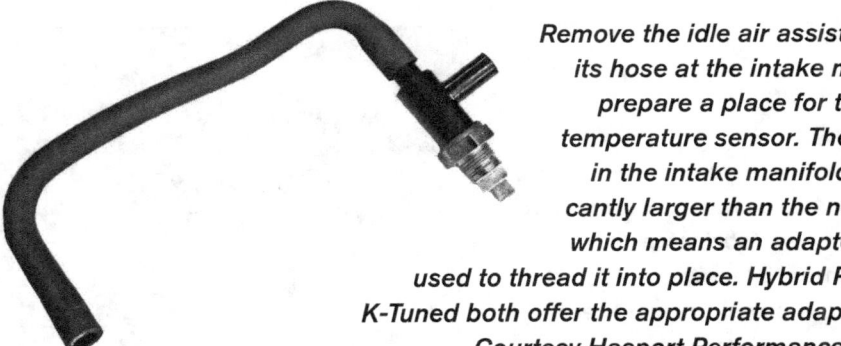

Remove the idle air assist valve and its hose at the intake manifold to prepare a place for the coolant temperature sensor. The provision in the intake manifold is significantly larger than the new sensor, which means an adapter must be used to thread it into place. Hybrid Racing and K-Tuned both offer the appropriate adapter. (Photo Courtesy Hasport Performance Products)

coolant temperature sensor. When using such an adapter, simply plug the now-unused coolant temperature sensor port in the lower adapter because it won't be used.

Most engine management systems, such as Hondata's K-Pro, can activate the cooling fan through the ECU. This means the radiator fan switch doesn't need to be installed. Instead it's triggered by the engine coolant temperature sensor, which is already integrated into the engine wiring harness, communicates directly with the ECU, and can be programmed to activate at any temperature. Still, as previously outlined, the cooling fan should be activated by the radiator fan switch, which allows K-Pro's feature to only be used as an emergency backup.

Heater Hoses

The two heater hoses that exit from the heater core and its valve assembly at the firewall must be addressed next. If the heater won't be retained, simply bypass the inlet and outlet ports on the engine. In cases where the heater will be retained, use 5/8-inch (16-mm) cooling hose to connect the outlet and water valve inlet at the firewall to the corresponding inlet and outlet on the engine. A section of 180-degree hose should be used to connect to the water valve to avoid contact with the exhaust manifold. The water valve inlet can also be removed from its bracket and positioned inline, allowing it to point away from the exhaust manifold.

Connect the heater hoses that span from the water valve inlet and heater core outlet at the firewall to the engine's 16- and 19-mm coolant pipes. Be sure to route the hoses away from the exhaust manifold.

Remember that all K-series engines feature slightly larger ports than on the Accord or Prelude. Carefully stretch the hose over the engine's larger 19-mm fitting or install it in two sections, using a 5/8-inch-to-3/4-inch brass reducer. (K-Tuned offers its own reducer with a hard-anodized black finish.) When routing the hoses, be sure to avoid kinking and position them away from hot exhaust components.

Overflow Reservoir

To finish the cooling system, the radiator overflow reservoir must be relocated near the right-side headlight. A custom bracket can be made to mount it and a section of 5/16-inch hose can be used to span from the reservoir's nipple to the radiator.

A/C and Power Steering

Both A/C and power steering are compatible with every 1990–1997 Accord or 1992–1996 Prelude K-series engine swap and can be retained with little work. A/C may also be eliminated for further weight reduction; however, retaining the power steering system is recommended because all of these chassis were equipped with such steering racks to begin with, and converting a native power steering rack to a manual one often yields undesirable results.

A/C Delete with Power Steering

Unlike with older B- or H-series engines, the K-series drive belt is critical to engine life. It's responsible for rotating the water pump, alternator, A/C compressor, and power steering pump. However, it only works as Honda intended when all of those accessories are present. Eliminating

When retaining power steering, look to the 2002–2004 RSX for a power steering pump. Its lower-profile design and slightly smaller pulley maximize hood clearance.

HONDA K-SERIES ENGINE SWAPS   137

CHAPTER 7

Here, a custom, high-pressure power steering feed line was fabricated that's compatible with the Prelude at the power steering rack and the K-series at the power steering pump.

If the evaporative emissions canister is retained, connect its hoses to this plastic fitting near the valve cover on duly equipped engines. In other cases, the hoses may span directly to the throttle body, depending on the engine.

just one of them, such as the A/C compressor, means the entire drive belt system must be addressed.

To properly eliminate A/C, start by removing the A/C compressor from the engine block and be sure that the desired power steering pump is fastened to the engine. Depending on the crankshaft pulley, belt length may vary so be sure to measure correctly before ordering. Once sourced, route the belt following the same path around the water pump pulley to account for the eliminated A/C compressor.

With the power steering pump in place, custom high-pressure and low-pressure lines must be made to allow integration into the Accord or Prelude chassis and the power steering reservoir must be moved somewhere near the right-side headlight. (For more information on how to configure power steering, see Chapter 4.)

A/C with Power Steering

Retaining A/C and power steering is easy. Begin with the power steering pump, crankshaft pulley, and drive belt that the engine is equipped with. A number of parts are needed to complete the A/C system, though. For example, the A/C lines must be entirely customized because no kits are currently available. Additionally, the crossmember must be modified or replaced with an aftermarket, tubular piece to allow clearance for the A/C compressor. A lot of customization is involved here, which makes eliminating the A/C altogether frequently a popular choice. (To retain A/C, see Chapter 4 for detailed instructions.)

Intake and Exhaust Systems

K-series engine transplants present their own concerns compared to the older H-series engine swaps that were common to these chassis. Here, throttle body and exhaust manifold choice must be considered carefully. With older engine swaps the only concern was whether or not they were compatible with the engine. Now, compatibility with a specific chassis is also a concern.

Throttle Body

Some later-model K-series engines are equipped with drive-by-wire electronic throttle bodies, all of which are not directly compatible with any of these chassis. Before beginning the engine swap process, be sure that the appropriate cable-actuated throttle body has been sourced and fastened to the engine. Bolt patterns differ among various K-series intake manifolds as does throttle body compatibility so be sure to consider all of that before settling on the appropriate one.

Aftermarket throttle body adapters are available from Hybrid Racing and Karcepts that allow cable-style throttle bodies to be bolted onto intake manifolds that typically only accept drive-by-wire ones.

In cases where the evaporative emissions canister will be retained, connect the canister's lines to the throttle body's nipples or the plastic connector located near the valve cover, depending on the engine.

Intake Piping

After the engine assembly has been installed, the intake system can be fitted into place. Be sure to select an intake that's compatible with the intake manifold and not necessarily the engine. For example, a short-ram intake system designed for the 2004–2008 TSX should be used if the K24A2's native intake manifold is in place.

Regardless of which intake manifold or intake system is used, be sure to install the intake air temperature sensor into the tubing and connect it to the engine wiring harness.

138   HONDA K-SERIES ENGINE SWAPS

1990–1997 ACCORD AND 1992–1996 PRELUDE

Exhaust Manifold

No factory K-series exhaust manifold is compatible with any of these chassis. Surprisingly, though, the solution lies with aftermarket headers designed for K-series engine swaps into any of the chassis covered in Chapter 4, such as the 1992–1995 Civic. Hybrid Racing, K-Tuned, DC Sports, and PLM offer engine swap headers in various configurations. These bolt directly to any K-series engine, clearing the Accord or Prelude subframes and other components.

Once in place, the header conveniently bolts directly up to most exhaust systems, provided the catalytic converter is eliminated. Of course, removing the catalytic converter isn't always an option and is almost always illegal. The header must remain intact and, instead, the exhaust piping shortened to allow space for the catalytic converter to fit. A shorter aftermarket version can be used if space is limited.

ECU Selection

In terms of ECU selection and wiring, the 1990–1997 Accord and 1992–1996 Prelude are more like fifth- and sixth-generation Civics and second-generation Integras than any other models. As with engine swaps into any of those chassis, the ECU should be chosen early on. Modern Honda ECUs feature built-in immobilizers that render the vehicle's electronics useless until properly matched with the appropriate transponder key and receiver. All of this can present all sorts of problems on vehicles like any of those in this chapter that weren't built with such equipment. There are three common solutions.

As it turns out, the easiest solution is to source a Japanese-spec 2001–2005 Civic Type R or 2001–2006 Integra Type R ECU. K-series ECUs such as these feature immobilizers that can be easily bypassed but can be expensive and difficult to source. Moreover, unless they're modified, they are typically only suitable for 2.0L performance i-VTEC engines like the K20A2. To bypass the immobilizer, simply ground the main relay to the chassis instead of to the ECU. Cut ECU wire E7 and appropriately ground the wire's main relay side to a suitable ground.

An alternative solution is a Hybrid Racing or K-Tuned immobilizer bypass unit. A simple circuit board enclosed in a small plastic case is spliced directly into the engine wiring harness, disabling the immobilizer. Compatible ECUs include those from the 2002–2004 RSX Type-S for performance i-VTEC engines, 2002–2004 RSX base model for economy i-VTEC engines using the dual-stage intake manifold, 2002–2005 Civic Si for economy i-VTEC engines not using the dual-stage intake manifold, and 2002–2006 CR-V for 2.4L economy i-VTEC engines. (Note that 2005–2006 RSX ECUs are not compatible.)

The CR-V ECU also shares its pinouts with the RSX, which can simplify wiring harness selection. Disabling the immobilizer is easy and involves tapping four wires into the ECU's A and E connectors, which are outlined in the provided instructions.

It's also important to know that any of the above ECUs can be used

The same K-series engine swap exhaust manifolds that are used on 1992–1995 Civic chassis may be used here. This DC Sports 4-into-2-into-1 exhaust manifold fits with room to spare and features the appropriate bung for the oxygen sensor.

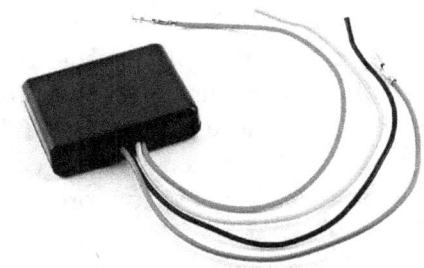

Until recently, few ways existed to get around Honda's built-in immobilizer, internal to all K-series ECUs. Hybrid Racing's simple circuit board connects to the ECU's A and E connectors with four wires, completely eliminating the immobilizer; it allows all sorts of K-series ECUs to be used without any expensive modifications. (Courtesy Hybrid Racing)

on either 5- or 6-speed gearboxes; however, when using an ECU from a 5-speed vehicle with a 6-speed transmission, the reverse-gear lockout must be hard-wired into place using a momentary switch or addressed using an engine management system, such as Hondata's K-Pro.

Hondata's K-Pro is likely the most widely used ECU solution. K-Pro disables the ECU immobilizer, eliminates the secondary oxygen sensor, and offers several other features, such as fuel and ignition tunability as well as cam angle control, data-logging, and pre-installed base maps.

ECUs that feature K-Pro can also be configured to work with any K-series engine or transmission and the appropriate outputs are provided for reverse-gear lockout functionality with 5-speed ECUs. A properly functioning K-series ECU must be provided to Hondata to have it converted. Currently compatible ECUs can be sourced from the following manual-transmission chassis: 2002–2004 RSX base model, 2002–2004 RSX Type-S, 2001–2006 Integra Type R, 2001–2005 Civic Type R, 2002–2006 CR-V, and 2002–2005 Civic Si.

Normally, transmission selection must also be considered when settling on an ECU because Honda offers two types of vehicle speed sensors, each of which are designed to work only with specific ECUs. However, every transmission that's compatible with Hasport's engine mount kit (those from the 2003–2007 Accord, 2006–2008 Accord Euro R, and 2004–2008 TSX) features a high-frequency-type sensor, which means compatibility lies with addressing the ECU.

If K-Pro is used, all of this is a non-issue, because the appropriate conversion can be made by using Hondata's software.

A supplemental device such as K-Tuned's Adjustable Speed Converter can also be used. K-Tuned's converter allows the high-frequency speed sensor signal to appropriately communicate with the Accord or Prelude instrument cluster and ECU. The converter must be wired into the engine wiring harness near the ECU. Wiring connections aren't complicated and are limited to 12V ignition power, ground, vehicle speed signal input, and vehicle speed signal output.

To learn more about Honda's two vehicle speed sensors and their compatibility issues, see page 76 in Chapter 4.

Wiring

Now that the engine, transmission, and ECU have been chosen, wiring can begin. K-series engine swap wiring has three major components: engine harness, sub-harness, and charge harness.

Engine Harness

Unlike H-series engine swaps into any of the chassis with which the original Accord or Prelude engine wiring harness is retained and modified, here, it must be removed and replaced with the appropriate K-series version. Any manual transmission 2002–2004 RSX, 2002–2005 Civic Si, or 2002–2006 CR-V (automatic versions can be converted) has the appropriate engine wiring harness. To reduce any unnecessary labor, avoid 2005–2006 RSX harnesses as well as those from any right-hand-drive chassis. Each of the preferred harnesses plugs directly into any K-series ECU's A and B connectors, which means that any necessary wiring takes place at the harness' 20-pin connector and the ECU's E connector.

Connect the engine wiring harness to the engine before installing the assembly and route the remaining plugs into the car's interior through the existing wiring harness opening located on the firewall's right side. Once the plugs are passed through, retrieve them from inside the cabin and plug each of them into the ECU.

Finally, be sure that the engine is grounded to the chassis in at least three locations and that the engine wiring harness is grounded to the engine.

Sub-Harness

Every non-native K-series chassis, such as those in this chapter, requires some sort of intermediary wiring

As with every other non-native K-series engine swap, a sub-harness is needed between the K-series engine wiring harness, ECU, and chassis wiring harness. Few solutions are available for Accord or Prelude chassis, but Hybrid Racing's universal sub-harness is the next best thing. The installation process can be slightly more complex because it isn't specific to any particular chassis, but all of the appropriate connectors are included, which makes the process a whole lot easier than starting from scratch. (Courtesy Hybrid Racing)

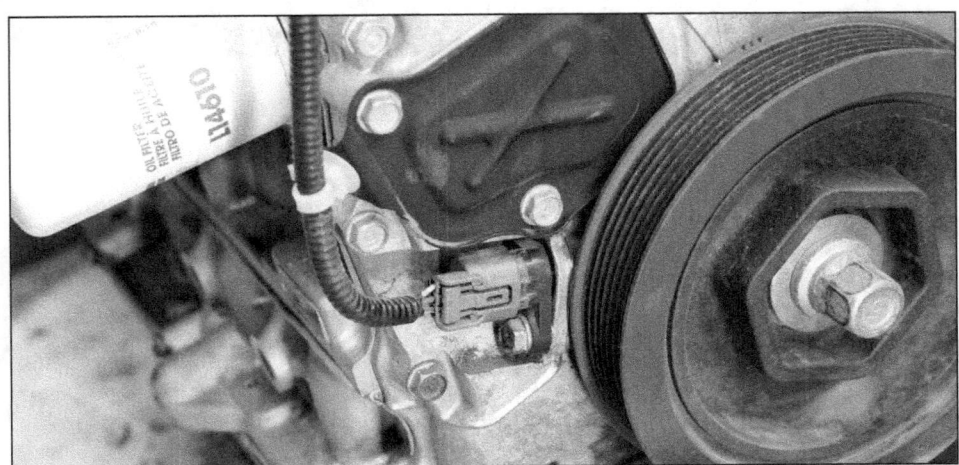

Smaller-displacement 2.0L engines feature crank angle sensors that are different from the 2.4L engines' sensors. If you're using an RSX engine wiring harness on a 2.4L engine, you have to swap connectors for the appropriate one. Simply de-pin the connector or cut it off with several inches of wire remaining and solder the new one into place.

The K-series charge harness must be modified to reach the battery as well as for compatibility with the Accord or Prelude fuse box. The harness' centrally located battery terminal must be removed and repositioned; it should be similar to the original charge harness found on the chassis.

harness to link the K-series engine wiring harness, ECU, and chassis. You can make your own sub-harness, purchase a universal sub-harness from Hybrid Racing, or look to Hasport or Rywire for a plug-and-play version that's designed specifically for each of these chassis.

The sub-harness is made up of six components: the E connector that plugs into the ECU's remaining slot, a connector that plugs into the engine wiring harness' open 20-pin connector, a connector that plugs into the chassis wiring harness, an oxygen sensor connector, an oxygen sensor relay, and either a data link connector for monitoring error codes or another chassis wiring harness connector, depending on the vehicle.

For more details on sub-harnesses and what's all entailed in configuring them to any of these chassis, see page 78 in Chapter 4.

Charge Harness

A charge harness directs power from the positive battery terminal to the alternator, starter, fuse box, and engine wiring harness. K-series-equipped vehicles feature fuse boxes that are located near the front bumper, unlike Accords or Preludes. This means the harness must be lengthened to reach the necessary components, such as the fuse box, which is located near the firewall. A combination of the Accord or Prelude original charge harness and the K-series engine's charge harness must be used.

A proper charge harness should span from the positive battery terminal to the starter, from the positive battery terminal to the fuse box, and from the fuse box to the alternator. When modifying the charge harness, be sure to transfer the original fuse box connectors from the original harness to the new harness; the Accord and Prelude fuse box connections are entirely different than K-series-compatible ones.

Finally, exclusive to a K-series swap into any of these chassis, if ABS is retained, the battery must be relocated. A smaller battery may remain in the original location; however, a custom bracket may have to be fabricated to properly secure it.

Suspension and Braking

In most cases, the new K-series engine and transmission are lighter than those being removed. This means that vehicle dynamics will only change for the better. Even so, any time horsepower or the potential for overall vehicle speed is significantly increased, stopping capabilities should also be increased. Be sure that disc brakes have been fitted to the rear. You should also acquire upgraded cross-drilled or slotted rotors along with more aggressive pads and steel-braided brake lines that can withstand hotter fluid temperatures from harder braking.

Appendix

Diagnostic Trouble Code Reference

MIL	DTC	Source
0	P0606	Engine Control Module (ECM) processor malfunction
3	P0107	Manifold Absolute Pressure (MAP) sensor circuit low voltage
3	P0108	Manifold Absolute Pressure (MAP) sensor circuit high voltage
4	P0335	Crankshaft Position (CKP) sensor no signal
4	P0339	Crankshaft Position (CKP) sensor circuit intermittent interruption
5	P1129	Manifold Absolute Pressure (MAP) sensor circuit lower than expected
5	P1128	Manifold Absolute Pressure (MAP) sensor circuit higher than expected
6	P0117	Engine Coolant Temperature (ECT) sensor circuit low voltage
6	P0118	Engine Coolant Temperature (ECT) sensor circuit high voltage
7	P0122	Throttle Position (TP) sensor A circuit low voltage
7	P0123	Throttle Position (TP) sensor A circuit high voltage
7	P0222	Throttle Position (TP) sensor B circuit low voltage
7	P0223	Throttle Position (TP) sensor B circuit high voltage
7	P2135	Throttle Position (TP) sensor A/B incorrect voltage correlation
8	P0365	Camshaft Position (CMP) sensor B no signal
8	P0369	Camshaft Position (CMP) sensor B intermittent interruption
10	P0112	Intake Air Temperature (IAT) sensor circuit low voltage
10	P0113	Intake Air Temperature (IAT) sensor circuit high voltage
13	P2227	Barometric Pressure (BARO) circuit range/performance problem
13	P2228	Barometric Pressure (BARO) sensor circuit low voltage
13	P2229	Barometric Pressure (BARO) sensor circuit high voltage
14	P0506	Idle control system RPM lower than expected
14	P0507	Idle control system RPM higher than expected
20	P1297	Electric Load Detector (ELD) circuit low voltage
20	P1298	Electric Load Detector (ELD) circuit high voltage
21	P2648	VTEC solenoid valve circuit low voltage
21	P2649	VTEC solenoid valve circuit high voltage
22	P2646	VTEC oil pressure switch circuit low voltage
22	P2647	VTEC oil pressure switch circuit high voltage
23	P0325	Knock sensor circuit malfunction
30	U0107	Lost communication with Throttle Actuator control modulator
34	P0563	Engine Control Module (ECM) power source circuit unexpected voltage
37	P2122	Accelerator Pedal Position (APP) sensor A circuit low voltage
37	P2123	Accelerator Pedal Position (APP) sensor A circuit high voltage
37	P2127	Accelerator Pedal Position (APP) sensor B circuit low voltage
37	P2128	Accelerator Pedal Position (APP) sensor B circuit high voltage
37	P2138	Accelerator Pedal Position (APP) sensor A/B incorrect voltage correlation
40	P1683	Throttle valve default position spring performance problem
40	P1684	Throttle valve return spring performance problem
40	P2101	Throttle Actuator system malfunction
40	P2108	Throttle Actuator control module problem
40	P2118	Throttle Actuator current range performance problem
40	P2176	Throttle Actuator control system idle position not learned
40	P2552	Throttle Actuator control module relay malfunction
41	P0134	Primary Air/Fuel (A/F) Ratio sensor heater system malfunction
41	P0135	Primary Air/Fuel (A/F) Ratio sensor heater circuit malfunction
45	P0171	Fuel supply system too lean
45	P0172	Fuel supply system too rich
48	P1157	Primary Air/Fuel (A/F) Ratio sensor line high voltage
48	P2195	Primary Air/Fuel (A/F) Ratio sensor signal stuck lean
48	P2238	Primary Air/Fuel (A/F) Ratio sensor positive line low voltage
48	P2252	Primary Air/Fuel (A/F) Ratio sensor negative line low voltage
56	P0010	Variable Valve Timing Control (VTC) oil control solenoid valve malfunction
56	P0011	Variable Valve Timing Control (VTC) system malfunction
57	P0340	Camshaft Position (CMP) sensor A no signal
57	P0341	Camshaft Position (CMP) sensor and Crankshaft Position (CKP) sensor incorrect phase detected
57	P0344	Camshaft Position (CMP) sensor A intermittent interruption
61	P0133	Primary Air/Fuel (A/F) Ratio sensor response malfunction

APPENDIX

MIL	DTC	Source
61	P2A00	Primary Air/Fuel (A/F) Ratio sensor range/performance problem
63	P0137	Secondary Heated Oxygen (HO2) sensor circuit low voltage
63	P0138	Secondary Heated Oxygen (HO2) sensor circuit high voltage
63	P0139	Secondary Heated Oxygen (HO2) sensor slow response
65	P0141	Secondary Heated Oxygen (HO2) sensor heater circuit malfunction
67	P0420	Catalyst system efficiency below threshold
71	P0301	Number-one cylinder misfire
72	P0302	Number-two cylinder misfire
73	P0303	Number-three cylinder misfire
74	P0303	Number-four cylinder misfire
86	P0116	Engine Coolant Temperature (ECT) sensor range/performance problem
86	P0125	Engine Coolant Temperature (ECT) sensor slow response malfunction
87	P0128	Cooling system malfunction
90	P0442	Evaporative Emission (EVAP) system small leak detected
90	P0456	Evaporative Emission (EVAP) system very small leak detected
90	P0457	Evaporative Emission (EVAP) system leak detected or fuel cap loose/missing
90	P0497	Evaporative Emission (EVAP) system low purge flow
91	P0451	Evaporative Emission (EVAP) control system Fuel Tank Pressure (FTP) sensor range/performance problem
92	P0452	Evaporative Emission (EVAP) control system Fuel Tank Pressure (FTP) sensor circuit low voltage
91	P0453	Evaporative Emission (EVAP) control system Fuel Tank Pressure (FTP) sensor circuit high voltage
91	P1454	Fuel Tank Pressure (FTP) sensor range/performance problem
92	P0443	Evaporative Emission (EVAP) control system canister purge valve circuit malfunction
92	P0496	Evaporative Emission (EVAP) system high purge flow
109	P2279	Intake air system leak detected
117	P0498	Evaporative Emission (EVAP) system vent shut valve circuit low voltage
117	P0499	Evaporative Emission (EVAP) system vent shut valve circuit high voltage
117	P2422	Evaporative Emission (EVAP) canister vent shut valve stuck closed
122	P0720	Countershaft speed sensor circuit malfunction
131	P0603	Engine Control Module (ECM) internal control module Keep Alive Memory (KAM) error
135	P0685	Engine Control Module (ECM) circuit malfunction

Post-Swap Checklist

Once the engine, transmission, and their ancillaries have been installed and the electrical system has been completed, it's time to start the engine and test-drive the vehicle. Before doing so, a number of precautions should be taken to ensure against any damage to the engine or injury to yourself.

Before starting the engine, be sure to check these:

- Engine oil level
- Engine coolant level
- Transmission fluid level
- Power steering fluid level (if equipped)
- Fuel system connections
- Cooling system and heater hose connections
- Drive belt tension
- Throttle cable tension
- All electrical connections and grounds

When initially starting the engine, disconnect all four ignition coils, turn the key, and engage the starter for approximately five seconds, allowing oil to distribute throughout the engine without being subjected to combustion. This process reduces the excessive wear often associated with initially starting an engine that hasn't operated for a significant amount of time.

As the engine approaches its operating temperature, be sure to:

- Check for oil, coolant, or other fluid leaks.
- Observe for erratic idling and possible brake booster or vacuum connection leaks.
- Confirm that the thermostat opens and that the engine cooling fan switches on.

Before test-driving the vehicle, ensure that:

- All wheels have been properly tightened.
- All engine and transmission mounts have been properly tightened.
- Both axle retaining nuts and all suspension and subframe hardware have been properly tightened.
- The clutch pedal operates properly and its system is free of leaks.
- The shifter engages properly into all forward gears and reverse.

While driving, ensure that:

- The exhaust does not emit excessive smoke.
- The malfunction indicator lamp does not light up.
- Engine coolant temperature does not excessively rise.
- Engine oil pressure remains sufficient.
- The vehicle is free of any unusual sounds when accelerating, braking, or turning.

APPENDIX

Swap Difficulty

Model	Transmission	Fabrication	Electrical Difficulty Rating[†]	Clearance Considerations
1992–1995 Civic	All	Cutting, drilling	Advanced	ABS, power steering
1993–1997 del Sol	All	Cutting, drilling	Advanced	ABS, power steering
1996–2000 Civic	All	None	Advanced	ABS, power steering
1994–2001 Integra	All	Cutting, drilling	Advanced	ABS, power steering
1988–1991 Civic	RSX-style only *	Cutting, drilling, welding	Advanced	Power steering, hood
1988–1991 CRX	RSX-style only *	Cutting, drilling, welding	Advanced	Power steering, hood
1990–1993 Integra	RSX-style only *	Cutting, drilling, welding	Advanced	ABS, power steering
2001–2005 Civic	RSX-style only *	Minor cutting	Intermediate	ABS, power steering
1990–1993 Accord	Accord-style only **	Cutting, drilling, welding	Advanced	None
1994–1997 Accord	Accord-style only **	Cutting, drilling, welding	Advanced	None
1992–1996 Prelude	Accord-style only **	Cutting, drilling, welding	Advanced	None

* RSX-style transmissions include 2002–2006 RSX, 2002–2005 Civic Si, 2001–2005 Civic Type R, 2001–2006 Integra Type R, 2006–2011 Civic Si, and 2007–2011 Civic Type R
** Accord-style transmissions include 2003–2007 Accord, 2006–2008 Accord Euro R, and 2004–2008 TSX
[†] Electrical difficulty rating assumes premanufactured sub-harness will be used. Self-made harnesses significantly increase difficulty rating.

Source Guide

Hasport Performance Products
2849 S. 44th St.
Phoenix, AZ 85040
602-470-0065
hasport.com

Hybrid Racing
12231 Industriplex Blvd., Ste. B
Baton Rouge, LA 70809
225-932-9588
hybrid-racing.com

K-Tuned
33 Peelar Rd., Unit 4
Concord, Ontario, Canada L4K 2M9
877-958-8633
k-tuned.com

Laskey Racing
2860 E. Gretta Ln., Unit H
Anaheim, CA 92806
714-688-0222
laskeyracing.com

Makspeed Motorworks
42346 Rio Nedo Dr., Ste. G
Temecula, CA 92590
951-200-5133
mak-speed.com

Sportcar Motion
2766 S. Santa Fe Ave.
San Marcos, CA 92069
760-597-0414
sportcarmotion.com

Whitfield Manufacturing
8465 Loma Pl.
Upland, CA 91768
909-608-7123
whitfieldmfg.com

www.ingramcontent.com/pod-product-compliance
Lightning Source LLC
Chambersburg PA
CBHW081451070526
44586CB00019B/2303